C0-AVZ-333

Understanding
Business
Systems
in Developing Countries

Understanding Business Systems in Developing Countries

Edited by
Gurli Jakobsen
Jens Erik Torp

Sage Publications
New Delhi • Thousand Oaks • London

Copyright © Gurli Jakobsen and Jens Erik Torp, 2001

All rights reserved. No part of this book may be reproduced or utilized in any form or by any means, electronic or mechanical, including photo-copying, recording or by any information storage or retrieval system, without permission in writing from the publisher.

First published in 2001 by

Sage Publications India Pvt Ltd
M–32 Market, Greater Kailash, Part 1
New Delhi 110 048

Sage Publications Inc		**Sage Publications Ltd**
2455 Teller Road		6 Bonhill Street
Thousand Oaks, California 91320		London EC2A 4PU

Published by Tejeshwar Singh for Sage Publications India Pvt Ltd, typeset by Siva Math Setters, Chennai in 10.5/12.5 Baskerville and printed at Chaman Enterprises, Delhi.

Library of Congress Cataloging-in-Publication Data
Understanding business systems in developing countries/edited by Gurli Jakobsen, Jens Erik Torp.
    p. cm.   (cloth)   (pbk.)
Based on papers from an international workshop on Business in the South, Copenhagen Business School, Jan. 1997.
Includes bibliographical references and index.
   1. Industrial management—Developing countries—Congresses.
   2. Corporate culture—Developing countries—Congresses. 3. Business enterprises—Developing countries—Congresses. 4. Competition, International—Developing countries—Congresses. 5. Interorgani-zational relations—Developing countries—Congresses. I. Jakobsen, Gurli. II. Torp, Jens Erik.
   HD70.D44 U53   338.09172′4—dc21   2000   00-030743

ISBN: 0–7619–9435–1 (US-Hb)   81–7036–905–3 (India-Hb)
              0–7619–9436–X (US-Pb)   81–7036–906–1 (India-Pb)

Sage Production Team: Parul Nayyar, Goldy Bhatnagar and
                          Santosh Rawat

Contents

Preface

Third world companies have often been described as having their competitive strength in low labour costs. Recently, however, throughout the third world, local companies are looking for ways to upgrade their existing products and wherever possible include higher value-added products as well as marketing and design functions, the latter often representing the highest value-added activities within global value chains. The contributions to this volume show how the embeddedness of firms in the larger societal context of nations impacts on their ability and particular ways of adjusting to the present forms of international competition. It becomes clear that researchers studying business in developing countries should locate the firm in the societal context in which it is rooted and from there link it to the international context. Areas covered by the contributors include studies of business systems and firm behaviour in Malaysia, South Korea, India, Indonesia and Ghana. These essays and discussions of the variations of business systems indicate how different business systems relate to the international context, and hence under which circumstances trajectories similar to the upgrading approach are relevant and under what circumstances such a standardized approach is modified by the national context.

Acknowledgements

The idea of making this book came from the international workshop on 'Business Systems in the South' held in Skodsburg in January 1997. It was organized by the Copenhagen Business School and had a cross-disciplinary approach. It brought together 29 international scholars of development studies and became the forum of very interesting and inspiring discussions. We want to thank the participants for their contributions towards a common understanding of the area of 'business in development' as a research focus in development studies. During 1997, we took part in the development of a research platform with the participation of Jehn Kuada, Henrik Schaumburg-Müller, Olav Jull Sørensen and Peter Wad. This led to a 'Pilot Project on Business in Development' and has been an important inspiration for the introduction to this book. We want to specially mention Peter Wad for his share in making the concepts of this research field more clear. We also want to thank Kell Jarner for his careful and competent technical adaptation of the manuscripts.

Gurli Jakobson and Jens Erik Torp

January 2000

Business in Development: An Introduction

Gurli Jakobsen and Jens Erik Torp

Business in Development

Private companies in developing countries have come to play a more prominent role as economic actors, following the greater say given to market forces by most third world governments in the 1980s. Concurrently, the role of the state has increasingly been geared towards the provision of an enabling environment conducive for private sector development and competitiveness, while previous forms of direct state intervention in the economic decisions of private sector companies have been on the decline.

In the case of many developing countries, selected aspects of this process of change are by now well documented. This is particularly true of the economic and social impact of structural adjustment and economic liberalization. Whereas the International Monetary Fund (IMF) and the World Bank (WB) have often been criticized for a standard design in their approach to structural adjustment and liberalization in developing countries, ironically enough many of the studies examining the impact of such programmes can also be said to follow a standard design either by focusing on possible alternatives to the suggested macro-economic policies or by examining the social impact of WB and IMF programmes on areas like the distribution of income and access to public services.

Irrespective of the valuable insights documented in such studies, it is nevertheless apparent that the changes which have taken place during the last 15 years in the macro-economic setting and in the role of the various economic actors have led to new types of societal dynamics, which are either overlooked or still not fully understood in most of the literature. In sum, the role of local companies as socially embedded and acting economic organizations (Granovetter 1985) continue to be a somewhat overlooked and under-researched area, while the changing role of the state has stimulated more discussion, albeit related more to its overall regulatory functions than to its changing role with regard to private companies. This is not a satisfactory situation since the radical changes in the role of private companies must be better understood in order to fully grasp the dynamics of the economic drivers in the present conjuncture within developing countries. In other words, in the wake of structural adjustment and liberalization a number of new and important questions should be raised with regard to the role of local companies, which may very well lead towards a rethinking of the existing notions of relations between private companies, the state and society.

When trying to respond to this quest it may be a useful point of departure to re-examine the perception of private companies in existing development theory. Within development theory the dynamics of the private sector have traditionally been linked to the role of the state in favouring the development and growth of productive capacity within a given sector. The focus has typically been on the lack of enterprise development, and how it can be overcome through programmes initiated and sponsored by the state. Sure enough standard textbooks on economic development will include chapters on entrepreneurship and small business development as well as on the role of transnational companies. However, they will often end up on the one hand deploring the lack of organic growth by local companies (the so-called missing middle debate) while on the other hand also pointing towards how (larger) transnational companies often limit the productive potential of (smaller) local companies. In our opinion, therefore, the economic potential of the local firm and its ability to coordinate economic activities has not been a perspective given high priority within the dominant development paradigms and theories, so far.

In all fairness, interesting enterprise studies are found in the literature on third world development and a number of them have been available for some time. They can, however, often be understood as part of an effort to examine the role of companies in developing countries inspired by the neoclassical paradigm and will therefore normally be based on universal assumptions about firm profit-maximizing or optimizing interests and behaviour. As a consequence, often they have little to offer when the search is to understand the changing setting and new roles which private local companies took up in the aftermath of structural adjustment and liberalization.

In parts of the literature of the 1990s, we do however see a renewed interest in getting the focus centred on the role of the local company in developing countries. Some of the recent and promising attempts in this regard are found within the literature on business systems (Whitley 1987, 1992a, 1992b, 1996b; Whitley and Kristensen 1996), industrial districts (Humphrey 1995; Nadvi and Schmitz 1994; Schmitz and Musyck 1994), production chains (Kogut 1991; Gereffi 1994, 1996a; Whitley 1996a), new economic sociology (Granovetter and Swedberg 1992; Swedberg 1997) and new economic geography (Blakeley 1994; Storper and Scott 1992). This renewed interest in the local firm as an economic actor has raised other pertinent questions about the role of the firm in the development process, such as how the firms interact with other companies as well as with other institutions and whether they represent the state apparatus or parts of civil society. This set of literature is clearly gaining from insights coming from business economics as well as from development theory and shares the common concern of placing the company as an economic actor within a development perspective. Without neglecting the differences within the said literature, we find that the above-mentioned areas of literature, i.e., business systems, industrial districts, production chains, new economic sociology and new economic geography are contributing to a new understanding of the local firm as a socially embedded and acting economic organization in the present international context, and, therefore, we find it relevant to discuss them under the uniform heading of literature on 'business in development'.

In other words, when turning from the mainstream literature on development theory towards this new literature on business in development, we see it as no coincidence that the more prominent role of the local company in developing countries has led to a renewed interest in the company as an economic actor interrelating with other companies, institutions and levels of society.

The increase in this type of literature has had an important side effect, that of a renewed interest within development research for challenging the assumptions about the universal nature of the firm and for investigating the diversity and complexity of enterprise organizations, their business cultures and management strategies, as well as policies and practices of firms in developing countries. Within this vein of investigation and with the specific objective of further exploring the connectivity between business economics and development studies, a number of the participants in this new debate were brought together at an international workshop on 'Business Systems in the South', which was organized by the Department of Intercultural Communication and Management at the Copenhagen Business School in January 1997. The workshop demonstrated that a perspective which combines companies seen as economic actors, with an understanding of the companies as socially embedded entities, is a very powerful and promising analytical approach. Moreover the papers presented at the workshop gave evidence of business in development as being a relevant research area in its own right. The workshop also demonstrated that the area is in need of further conceptual clarification, and that research on industrial reorganization, industrial districts and business systems provides important pivots for further explorations.

Theoretical Approaches Highlighted in the Book

The theoretical field for the study of business development in 'the South'[1] is broad in scope, and, as already suggested,

[1] The terms 'developing countries' and 'the South' are used interchangeably in this book.

different theoretical frameworks can be chosen. However, we find that in terms of this volume it is of special theoretical interest to critically review the business systems approach. This shall be done partly by seeing it in relation to the insights offered by other approaches which understand local companies as socially embedded and acting economic organizations, and partly in relation to insights from the tradition of international business economics. The reason for this focus here is in part a pragmatic one. The business systems approach has been developed over the last 10 years and is based on the practical and empirical experience of a number of East Asian countries. It therefore offers a well-documented approach, which can be related to particular institutional forms and economic dynamics of other developing countries in Asia and Africa. A second reason for this choice is to be able to reflect and mirror the business system approach with insights from international business economics, and thus attempt to overcome the somewhat static nature of the business systems approach. It emphasizes the national (or regional) stability of existing institutional relations through a confrontation with insights coming from studies of the changing context and forms of doing international business.

The key theoretical approach to be highlighted in this book is the concept of a 'business system' as elaborated by Richard Whitley and associates. Whitley defines business systems as 'particular arrangements of hierarchy-market relations which become institutionalized and relatively successful in particular contexts' (Whitley 1992b:10). 'They develop and change in relation to dominant social institutions, especially those important during processes of industrialization. The coherence and stability of these institutions ... determine the extent to which business systems are distinctive and integrated and nationally differentiated' (Whitley 1992a:13). The business systems approach studies the economic division of roles in a particular legislatively and/or culturally defined region (often the nation-state). Basically the approach assumes that there are some features of the way economic actors are organized that are characteristic and particular to a given country and/or region and are the result of historically derived structures. Rather than study the general features of economic actors across countries, it thus proposes to study 'how "firms" are constituted as discrete economic actors in different market contexts'. 'Economic actor' is understood in a more general sense than strictly an enterprise. The focus is on the 'sort of organization that authoritatively selects and controls economic activities', i.e., it may thus comprehend more than one enterprise and organization, and be more or less formally constituted, the distinguishing feature being that they are administrative structures with decision-making power regarding economic activities which add value to human and material resources through the collective organization of work. Variations in the organization and policies of financial institutions are seen as possible explanations of some of the differences found between these economic actors across business systems. As pointed out by Whitley in his contribution (Chapter 1) 'firms are certainly a key component of such systems, but only one aspect of them. Indeed, it is an important feature of this framework that the nature of the firm as ownership based units of control varies between business systems and is to be explained rather than assumed.'

The main components of a business system are: the nature of the firm, the market relations, and the authoritative coordination and control system. While these three components appear rather consistently in Whitley's writings, the defining content varies somewhat depending on the particular system under study. Whitley's business system approach has been developed on the basis of analysis of economic behaviour in societies which until the recent financial crisis were brought to the fore, internationally and in the research community, for their striking economic success. In spite of the uniqueness of each business system it is possible to distinguish various types of organizing the roles of economic actors. Whitley demonstrates how the approach enables us to differentiate between at least three different business systems in East Asia: the Japanese *kaisha* system, the Korean *chaebol* system and the Chinese family business system. Later the approach has been applied to the development of European societies and has produced interesting insights into the dynamics and diversity of economic behaviour in developed capitalist economies. It stands out as one of the key findings, that not so clearly differentiated and particularistic systems are found among European enterprising systems compared to Whitley's findings in East Asia. Nevertheless the approach appears promising for the analysis of important aspects of European economic development, e.g., the dynamics of transnational acquisitions in a local–global perspective (Kristensen 1994; Whitley and Kristensen 1996; Torp 1997). It is only with Whitley's contribution to this book that the concept has, for the first time, been applied more extensively to the analysis of the transformation and development of business systems in developing economies. In his comparative analysis of emerging business systems in the South, Whitley emphasizes the specific and different role of the state and its nuanced forms of relations with private companies.

However, the business systems approach is not the only theoretical approach being discussed and examined in this book. Another interesting perspective on industrial, enterprise and work reorganization highlighted in the discussions throughout the book has been developed by researchers at the Institute of Development Studies in Sussex within the research programme on the productive enterprise and its context (Nadvi and Schmitz 1994). One focus has been on the transfer and adoption of Japanese-oriented techniques of management and work organization, labelled 'Easternization' by Kaplinsky (1994). Another approach has focused on the concepts of industrial districts and business networks of small- and medium-sized firms. This approach is rooted in research on the experiences from the Emilia-Romagna region in Italy, Baden-Württemberg in Germany and West Jutland in Denmark among others (Schmitz and Musyck 1994). The dynamic interplay between these two aspects: the intra-firm restructuring and inter-firm relationships in developing countries has been explored systematically in several studies (Humphrey 1995).

A third approach is the old research focus on transnational companies (TNCs) within international business economics as well as in development studies. It has been revived in the wake of the expansion of TNCs and their foreign direct investment in the South. This renewed interest as well as the expansion of third world TNCs (e.g., Korean) into the European and

American countries have enhanced the discussion on TNCs' contribution to the development process within a more global perspective than before.

The TNC leverage and impact on the formation or transformation of viable domestic enterprise systems have become important themes in the discussions within international business economics. Recent years have witnessed former well-known approaches—like Michael Porter's and Bruce Kogut's general and more abstract utilisation of the value chain (Kogut 1985; Porter 1980)—being developed into more precise observations about the present forms of TNC–local company cooperation, in which an analytical distinction is often made between buyer-driven and producer-driven global commodity chains (Gereffi 1994, 1996b; Whitley 1996a).

This book aims at presenting, contrasting and elaborating on these approaches to the study of contemporary business transformations and developments in the South, in order to re-examine critically the business systems approach as an appropriate theoretical framework which can further the understanding of the dynamics and trajectories of the private sector of developing countries in the 1990s.

Overview

In order to address the concerns indicated, the book comprises seven studies which take up key assumptions and conclusions in the business systems approach and discuss their relevance for the developing countries not forming part of the group of newly industrialized countries (NICs). Through this the aim is also to get a clearer understanding of what are the questions that can be dealt with, i.e., the potential and limitation of this particular approach. This is being done partly by means of general analysis and partly through country-specific critical reviews of the applicability of the business systems approach. The book offers new insights in the following areas:

1. A theoretical reflection on the applicability of the business systems approach for the understanding of developing capitalisms in the South.

2. A study of new ways of how to do business in India as firms adapt to more competitive markets.
3. A comparison of the inter-firm linkages in the Indonesian *jamu* industry and the characteristics of the Chinese family business system.
4. A critical assessment of the business systems approach based on a case study of the transformation of the Malaysian auto industry.
5. A discussion of the organization of technology management as one essential characteristic of the Korean business system.
6. A study of entrepreneurship focusing on the social capital of entrepreneurs in Ghana and their institutional context in the internationalization of Ghanaian firms.
7. An analysis of the theoretical contributions of business system, industrial district and commodity chain approaches to the understanding of the internationally working enterprise as presented within the tradition of business economics.

Moreover, the studies have been selected in order to provide a sample of empirical cases which vary along more specific dimensions of business dynamics in developing countries:

• Different scales of enterprise activities: entrepreneurial activities, small/medium-size firms, large firms and business groups.
• Different industries: automotive, machine tools, agro-processing, garment and metal products.
• Different characteristics and dynamics of internationalization: from domestic companies' attempt to penetrate the TNC-controlled auto industry in alliance with TNCs (Malaysia and South Korea), to defensive adaptations towards rising competition from foreign companies in the domestic market (India and Indonesia).
• Different national and institutional contexts: low-income countries (Ghana), middle-income countries (Indonesia, India and Malaysia) and South Korea, which has recently entered the high-income bracket.

The business systems approach has been developed in relation to NIC economies, and has been characterized by a clear historical perspective. Therefore, the book attempts to throw light on the usefulness of the business systems approach for other developing countries including middle- and low-income countries. Likewise, an attempt is made to examine the relevance of the business systems approach in a development context. In other words, what is being discussed is which policy recommendations follow from a concern for the strengthening of nationally based enterprises. The book mainly provides examples from other Asian countries, although a single African country, i.e., Ghana, is included as a complementary example.

The book opens with a chapter by Richard Whitley. Clarifying what is the purpose and nature of the comparative business systems framework, he underlines its intention to 'describe significant differences in the market economies and explain them in terms of variations in the nature of dominant societal institutions', the research questions being guided by 'HOW and WHY particular differences in prevalent modes of economic co-ordination have become established and continue to be reproduced'. His reflections on the distinctive nature of developing economies highlight two differences. As mentioned earlier, Whitley emphasizes the need for a more nuanced view of the role of the state in the emerging market economy than has been done in the more developed market economies. He also proposes a set of dimensions to be looked at. The other crucial distinguishing factor to be accounted for in studying emerging business systems in the South, is the economic role of international aid institutions in these countries. Whitley raises the question: how significant are domestic institutions and agencies in managing the flow of funds and other resources, and to what extent do they act as coordinating organizations integrating such flows with domestic resources for long-term economic development goals? He formulates three hypotheses on the possible development of types of business systems in societies which are in transition from a strong state-dominated economic system to an emergent market system.

Chapter Two presents an analysis of the case of Indian business conditions applying business systems thinking. As expressed by the author, Mark Holmström,

in an ideal-type market economy, firms are hierarchies, relations between firms are competitive. This reflects a universal contrast: one morality inside the group, another outside. But since colonial times, India's market economy depended heavily on the state, and many firms were controlled by powerful hierarchies ('industrial lineage firms', managing agencies). Nehru introduced a strict planning regime ('Licence-Permit Raj') to achieve self-reliant development and protect vulnerable groups, with moderate success. State employees, business enjoying state patronage, 'organized sector' workers, and low castes had some protection from insecurity and competition. How was this half-planned economy co-ordinated, how were hierarchical authority relations within the private and public sectors organized, and how have they changed with liberalization? New ways of doing business emerge as firms adapt to more competitive markets: Less security; more Subcontracting; some networking between interdependent 'flexibility-specialized' firms. Lines between public and private, 'organized' and 'unorganized sectors' become blurred. But the impact of liberalization has been modest so far.

Through his analysis, Holmström presents a theoretical dilemma that is valid for several of the lesser developed countries which have combined a strong state planning of national economic life with a capitalist market economy, and gone through the liberalization of economic restructuring of the last 10 years—the case of 'half-planned economies'.

Where the previous two authors employ a macro-level approach in their chapters, the following four chapters are all empirical studies and of particular industrial sectors in four different countries. Their analyses concentrate on particular aspects of the business systems approach, as is adequate to the particular situations. The chapter of Rademaker and van Valkengoed results from a study which has experienced with a direct empirical application of the conceptual framework of Whitley's approach to business systems analysis, while the other authors discuss, expand and complement with other concepts and approaches to the understanding of business systems analysis and business dynamics. Martijn Rademaker and Jos van Valkengoed focus in Chapter Three on the applicability and relevance of the market organization concept with respect to the analysis of single industries. The concept is concerned with the way in which inter-firm relations are shaped by nationally distinctive social institutions. The nature of six key social institutions in Indonesia are outlined, and, on the basis of an empirical investigation among large- and medium-sized *jamu* firms, the characteristics of inter-firm relations in the Indonesian *jamu* industry are described. The mode of market organization in this industry appears to correspond remarkably well with the expected influences of the key social institutions that were derived from previous business systems studies of other authors. The *jamu* firms are strongly self-reliant and resemble the 'centrifugal' business system type. Notably the social institutions 'the basis of trust' and the state can be considered to have an important impact on the mode of market organization characteristics in the industry.

Chapter Four by Peter Wad examines the transformation of the Malaysian auto industry through the dynamics of international and national forces in the creation and maintenance of a nationally based industry. The chapter discusses the applicability of the business systems approach to understanding these processes of transformation in the auto industry. While finding the approach useful as far as institutional analysis at the national level is concerned, the author applies a broader and more dynamic sector approach for the analysis of business in development. Through his analysis, Wad questions whether a new business system is evolving in the sector or whether this process is part of the formation of a national business system. Sector and national business systems are in the making, positioned within a multi-ethnic and state-led development context and a global industry, which is dominated by Western and Japanese transnational companies. Hence, Wad finds that the outcome in terms of sector/cluster business systems is uncertain. The explanatory logic to be identified is composed of the internal business rationality of a cluster, its institutional context and the international linkages.

Chapter Five deals with another rapidly changing business reality, the Korean electronics industry. Dieter Ernst focuses on the organization of technology management as one essential characteristic of the Korean business system. Ernst sees the business systems approach, firm organization and strategies, as shaped by peculiar sets of institutions which are unlikely to converge and he points out that nothing is predetermined about the impact of globalization. He contrasts the assumption of evolutionary economics: that the speed of change in economic institutions and firm organization has accelerated, with business systems findings which say that 'such changes are relatively slow' (Whitley 1991:23–24). Key features of the Korean way of building technology capabilities have been shaped by a broad congruence of interests between the government and the leading *chaebol*, which has lead to a close interaction between both actors. This system has come under increasing pressure since the late 1980s. Exposed to increasingly complex requirements of global competition, there is a search for new approaches that would enable Korea to upgrade its national system of innovation.

The business system approach has not yet been applied to an African context. However, in Chapter Six Olav Jull Sørensen and John Kuada examine the impact of different national contexts on international business relations based on an African case study. It is a theme which is yet very little explored in studies of business systems, but which is of great relevance in the context of lesser developed countries. The argument of the article is developed on the basis of empirical material from Ghana. It centres on the study of the institutional context for internationalization of Ghanaian firms. The foundational concepts of this essay are 'interaction' and 'perception'. It discusses how participants in business systems construct the perceptions they carry of themselves as well as the units with which they interact, and how these perceptions influence their behaviour. The authors advocate that individual and shared perceptions established through daily interactions are among the critical factors that shape the dynamics of business systems and the economic growth capabilities that they generate. Ghana being another case of a semi-planned economy becoming liberalized, this research also gives evidence of how extremely difficult it is to repair the damage and restore mutual confidence in government–business relations when they have been characterized by mutual suspicion and discontent over several decades. The authors thus advocate an explicit inclusion of and study of the interactive dynamics of government–business relations when studying business system development. By taking the perspective of the interaction between businesses from different types of business systems as occurs when export–import cooperation is established between firms in a developing country (in this case Ghana) and a developed country (in this case Denmark) their proposal is to study these relationships as potentials for changed basic relationship of the actors in question within the particular business systems.

Henrik Schaumburg-Müller also focuses on the effect of internationalization and globalization on national business systems. This last chapter of the book is mainly theoretical. Schaumburg-Müller explores how analytical concepts and tools from international business can be combined with the embeddedness approach to the understanding of business organization. The aim is to bridge the gap between theories of business behaviour based on the embeddedness approach and international competitive dynamics. The analysis is mainly theoretical although it reflects on empirical contributions from studies of industrial districts when discussing the interaction between the local and the international market. Pointing out how globalization has affected national financial institutions and integrated them into the global financial market, Schaumburg-Müller reflects on when these changes produced through international relations and actors result in more fundamental changes in a business system at the national level, or when foreign actors or institutions contribute to the formation of a business system without being part of the social context of the country. He does not forward definite answers to this question but presents interesting research perspectives and questions. With the hope of having succeeded through these chapters to give a nuanced presentation of the importance of this focus for the understanding of present economic changes for business in developing countries, we also hope that the reading will invite further research within this field of business in development.

It goes without saying that the contributions of this book do not aspire to be a fully-fledged theoretical constitution of the area labelled business in development based on a complete review and integration of contributions from business systems approach, industrial districts approach, production chains approach, new economic sociology, and new economic geography. The contributions of this book should rather be seen as a presentation and critical review of the business systems approach being one of the pertinent contributions within the area, leaving a full construction of business in development as a theoretical area and approach for further works. Hence, in this particular book the business systems approach is presented and critically assessed from theoretical as well as from empirically based arguments which draw on insights from other theoretical approaches as well as from country studies on the application of the business systems approach. Acknowledging that the business systems approach primarily addresses problem areas of business in the newly industrialised countries of East Asia and to some extent the Eastern European industrial and Western European post-industrial societies, and that it has been empirically documented and elaborated accordingly, we argue that a combination of a deductive (theoretical based) and inductive (empirical based) approach in the selection of articles for this book is pertinent and appropriate. This allows us to confront existing East Asian and European-based theories with the empirical realities of business dynamics in developing countries, as well as with the local interpretations by businessmen/women and stakeholders in these countries. Thus, various insights into existing business systems are available, but they must be looked at critically in order to assess their potential for understanding business and business dynamics in developing countries. Within this perspective it is the ambition of this book to contribute to a deeper understanding of business systems in developing countries.

1

Developing Capitalisms: The Comparative Analysis of Emerging Business Systems in the South

Richard Whitley

The chapters in this book focus on the development of market economies in industrializing countries in Africa and Asia. Although many of these countries have pursued similar state-led industrialization policies over the past four or five decades, there have been significant differences in the organization and role of the state across these economies that have, together with other factors, led to contrasting kinds of market arrangements emerging. To understand these differences, and the processes generating distinct patterns of economic coordination and control, most of the authors have used parts of the comparative business systems framework.

This framework was originally developed to describe and explain the major differences in economic organization between the economies of Japan, South Korea (henceforth Korea), Taiwan and Hong Kong in the period after the Second World War (Whitley 1992a). It attempted to highlight the critical ways in which the nature of firms, their competition and collaboration in markets, and the ways in which they organized work, varied, and to account for these variations in terms of pre-industrial institutions and processes of industrialization.

Subsequently, this framework has been extended to the comparative analysis of economic coordination and control systems in Western Europe, and to the study of emerging capitalist economies in Eastern Europe (Whitley 1992b, 1999; Whitley and Kristensen 1996, 1997). Most of the economies considered in these analyses have successfully industrialized, albeit recently in some cases, and have established relatively stable institutional contexts for the market-based coordination and control of economic activities.

In these respects, most economies of the South are different, and the comparative business systems framework has to be modified to be useful in understanding them. Just as the analysis of the former state socialist societies of Eastern Europe has required some development of the approach to deal with the highly fluid and contested nature of their emergent types of capitalism, so too the particular circumstances of industrializing economies need to be taken into account when applying this framework to their analysis. This brief chapter considers the key features of these economies that require consideration in any comparative study of their development and how they affect the sorts of analysis that could be conducted. Before this, however, a number of issues about the purpose and nature of the comparative business systems framework need to be addressed in the light of the chapters included in this book. In conclusion, I make a few suggestions about how an extended version of the framework could be applied to the economies discussed here, using the material presented by the contributors as well as from other accounts.

The Comparative Business Systems Framework

The comments and criticisms of this framework by some of the contributors to this book raise a number of issues that require some discussion before considering the specific characteristics of industrializing countries. First of all, it is important to clarify what the framework is intended to do, and, equally importantly, what it does not claim to do. Its central purpose is to describe significant differences in the organization of market economies and explain them in terms of variation in the nature of dominant societal institutions. As Chandler (1990), Lazonick (1991) and many others have shown, there have been substantial differences in the nature of industrial capitalist economies in the twentieth century, and the rise of the East Asian economies after the Second World War has forcibly emphasized the continuing divergence of economic systems, together with their roots in institutional differences. The recent upheaval in Asian financial markets and the long recession in Japan do not indicate any convergence to a single efficient form of capitalism or a globalized economy (Hollingsworth and Boyer 1997). Given this historical and contemporary divergence of market economies, it is important to understand how and why particular differences in the prevalent modes of economic coordination have become established and continue to be reproduced. This is what the comparative business systems framework sets out to do.

This approach does not seek to explain industrial dynamics or to focus on short-term changes in firm behaviour, as Dieter Ernst apparently says it should in his contribution to this book. Nor, it should be noted, does this framework imply that each nation-state necessarily generates its own, unique and coherent business system. Indeed, the emphasis on the interdependence of economic organization and institutional contexts, coupled with significant similarities in some major institutional features across market economies, imply that a number of business system characteristics are likely to be shared between, say, Anglo-Saxon societies. Furthermore, the contested nature of many social arrangements and continuing conflicts over priorities and the centrality of particular sectors, expertise and organizations in most capitalist economies, ensure that both dominant institutions and economic coordination and control systems remain open to development (Whitley 1997, 1999).

The key differences between market economies that are emphasized by the comparative business systems framework concern the degree and mode of economic coordination. As Lazonick (1991) and Lazonick and West (1998), among many others, have emphasized, a major feature of the past 200 years of industrial capitalism has been the replacement of mercantile capitalist trading systems by more systematically integrated and authoritatively structured coordination of economic activities. In Chandler's (1977) terms, this can be seen as a move from the 'invisible' hand of market coordination to the 'visible' hand of managerial coordination. However, this development is not, with all due respect to Chandler, simply the story of large managerial hierarchies replacing spot-market transactions between small firms. Rather, it reflects the general increase in organized economic coordination at the expense of disorganized, ad hoc and singular spot-market transactions. Industrial capitalism in general has developed more organizationally integrated means of coordinating economic processes, both within and between the units of financial control conventionally called 'firms'. This does imply that models of market economies premised upon the universality of spot-market transactions are even less helpful in understanding types of capitalism in the late twentieth century than they were at the start of the nineteenth century.

This organizational integration of economic activities varies in both degree and prevalent mode between market economies. For example, the post-Second World War Japanese economy is commonly regarded as being more highly coordinated than the United States economy (Westney 1996; Whitley 1999). Particularly important differences arise from the role of unified ownership entities, or firms, on the one hand, and non-ownership alliances and networks, on the other hand. As many studies of Asian and European economies have shown, inter-firm alliances, agreements and federations constitute significant coordination mechanisms that may, on occasion, prove more economically important than the behaviour of individual firms (see, for example, Daems 1983; Orru et al. 1997; Shiba and Shimotami 1997). These networks may, furthermore, be based predominantly on personal links and obligations between owners and managers, as in many Asian societies, or be more organizational and impersonal.

In general, then, there are important differences between market economies in terms of: (a) the overall level of organizational integration of economic activities; (b) the extent to which such integration is achieved through ownership-based hierarchies; or (c) through alliances and networks between ownership-based units; and (d) whether coalitions and agreements between firms are predominantly personal or organizational. This last feature is typically related to prevalent patterns of owner control, in that personal, direct control of businesses by owners tends to be linked to personal connections between them.

Comparing economies in terms of the degree of ownership-based coordination and the extent of non-ownership or alliance-based organizational integration of economic activities generates four ideal types of business systems.

Fragmented business systems resemble the relatively disorganized industrial districts, of the type defined by Marshall, in being dominated by small firms that specialize in a narrow range of economic activities and engage in adversarial relations with each other. Inputs and outputs are traded on large, liquid spot markets in such economies.

Coordinated industrial districts are also dominated by small, specialized and owner-controlled firms, but exhibit greater levels of inter-firm collaboration and cooperation. Often stimulated by local government agencies, as discussed by Mark Holmström in this book, but also encouraged by some types of trade unions, educational facilities and banks, such collaboration ensures considerable coordination of economic activities through cooperative marketing and distribution arrangements, joint training initiatives, technology improvements and sharing, collective guarantees for investment funds and many other forms of cooperation (Friedman 1988; Kristensen 1996a, 1997; Lazerson 1988).

Compartmentalized business systems are dominated by large firms that typically operate at arms' length from each other. Exemplified by many sectors in Anglo-Saxon economies, these business systems have high levels of ownership coordination through large managerial hierarchies that typically control many stages of production chains and often are quite diversified across industries. They do not, however, develop close and long-term alliances with suppliers or customers or usually collaborate with competitors on a stable basis.

A sub-type of this business system is the state-organized one. This kind of economy is dominated by very large firms that are highly vertically and horizontally integrated but display adversarial and zero-sum competitive relationships with other firms. Typically, growing rapidly with substantial state support—often through highly subsidized credit—these firms remain owner controlled, with the founding family in clearly dominant positions. Exemplified by the Korean *chaebols*, such conglomerates integrate widely diverse activities through strong central control (Fields 1995; Janelli and Yim 1993; Whitley 1992a).

Collaborative business systems combine large firms that are often quite vertically integrated with considerable cooperation between them. This cooperation typically extends over training programmes, trade union negotiations and political lobbying activities, and may extend to production and profit-pooling federations and price-fixing cartels. In many of the more corporatist societies of continental Europe, this cooperation between firms is encouraged by centralized arrangements for policy development.

A sub-type of this form of economic organization is the highly coordinated business system. This exhibits more extensive alliances and networks within production chains and across sectoral boundaries. Business groups here, coordinate a wide range of activities that are not integrated into unified ownership hierarchies, as in post-Second World War Japan's 'alliance capitalism' (Gerlach 1992). Large firms also integrate the bulk of their workforce into the organization through long-term employment commitments, and thus treat labour costs as fixed in the short to medium term.

This contrast between ownership and alliance forms of economic coordination and control, highlights the importance of distinguishing between business systems as forms of economic organization from firms as units of financial control. Analyzing business systems—in the South or anywhere else—involves considering the overall level and mode of organizational integration of economic activities in an economy. Firms are certainly a key component of such systems, but only one aspect. Indeed, it is an important feature of this framework that the nature of firms as ownership-based units of control varies between business systems and is to be explained rather than assumed. Some contributions to this book appear to conflate these two levels of analysis and thereby ignore an important set of differences between business systems. As many studies of industrializing countries have emphasized, the non-ownership alliances and obligations are often especially important in structuring markets in such economies (Orru et al. 1997).

The Distinctive Nature of Developing Economies

Bearing these points about the comparative business systems framework in mind, I now turn to a discussion of the important differences between many developing economies and the more established ones of East Asia and Europe. One of the most significant is that they are in the midst of institution-alizing market economies, and so, many of the key institutional arrangements for governing them remain unclear and weak. As the economies of Eastern Europe demonstrated in the early 1990s, and other former state socialist societies continue to show today, this fluidity and the openness of central institutions generate high levels of uncertainty for economic actors and inhibit strategic actions and commitments (Bunce and Csanadi 1993; Csanadi 1997). Where the institutional framework governing the competitive game is unclear and subject to rapid change, opportunism is encouraged and the rational evaluation of alternatives based on the predictable interests and actions of other participants is difficult, if not impossible, to achieve.

This is exacerbated by the related fluidity and fragmentation of collective actors in many developing countries. Where traditional loyalties and social groupings are breaking down, and new ones are still being developed, the organization of interest groups around identifiable and relatively stable concerns is weak and changeable. This lack of strong collective intermediaries mobilizing commitments for the pursuit of segmental economic interests is often reinforced by central state agencies in authoritarian regimes. It can, however, also inhibit the development of any collective commitments beyond the immediate family or kinship group and thus limit the establishment of complex organizations beyond purely personal fiefdoms, as seems to have happened in Ghana.

This combination of emerging institutions and weak social groupings in many developing economies often means that the only significant collective agency beyond the family is the state, and this is frequently fragmented and factionalized. While some industrializing economies, such as Korea and Taiwan, have manifested quite 'strong' states in terms of their autonomy from private interest groups and capacity to implement long-term economic development policies since 1961 (Fields 1995), many others appear much more dominated by personally controlled factions and/or particular ethnic groups seeking to extract rents through the state machinery. Where civil society is also weakly established, as it is in most of these societies, this combination results in highly short-term opportunistic behaviour aimed at maximizing personal gain with little development of collective loyalties or organized cooperation and integration of economic activities. Fragmented business systems are thus endemic in many developing economies.

As the economies discussed in this book exemplify, however, the degree to which key societal institutions and agencies such as the state, private property rights and the legal system are firmly established and follow predictable procedures and priorities can vary considerably between developing societies. Such variation does have significant consequences for the sorts of economic actors that develop, and how they compete and cooperate. In particular, as the analyzes of Ghana, India, Indonesia and Malaysia presented here show, the structure and policies of the state have major effects on developing market economies since it is often the only collective actor beyond the family capable of mobilizing resources and activities for large-scale economic projects. Furthermore, the state has been seen by many political élites in these countries as the central agency of economic transformation, often to the exclusion or subordination of private capital. It is, therefore, the critical agency in most developing societies and has dominated the emergent market economy.

In this respect, these economies resemble most of the former state socialist societies of Eastern Europe where the state, albeit weakened and fragmented, remained the only collective agency capable of managing the transformation to liberal democracy and a market economy. The typical dominance by the state of the financial system and control over labour supply and organization means that state policies and practices in these areas are often more important features of the business environment than their formal characteristics. As in the case of East European societies, these points suggest that the comparative analysis of business systems needs to take into account more features of state structures and policies when studying developing economies, than when focusing on Western Europe and Japan.

In particular, the extent of state autonomy and risk-sharing with private interests is insufficient to deal with the variety of state-business relationships found in developing economies. Assuming a basic commitment to rely on private enterprises for capital accumulation, five additional aspects need to be considered. First, the integration and cohesion of bureaucratic and political élites affects the so-called strength of the state. Second, the competence, cohesion and commitment of the bureaucracy to economic development affects the capacity of the state to implement decisions. Third, the extent of state control over, and regulation of, private capital and enterprises, whether through direct controls or the credit system, and related; fourth, the state's ability and willingness to sanction failure and reward enterprise success in a predictable and even-handed manner, are major features that affect private enterprise behaviour and success. Finally, the extent to which state élites prefer to extract economic rents for personal and/or political gain at the expense of longer-term economic development goals, with or without private-sector allies, is a critical factor in the success of developmental policies.

As the examples of Indonesia, Korea and Malaysia demonstrate, these aspects of state policies differ significantly between countries and also over time. Broadly speaking, the more predatory, fragmented and unpredictable the state is, the less likely an economy is to develop either large, integrated firms coordinating production chains, or substantial, long-term alliances. As the example of Ghana shows, fragmented business systems seem much more likely to develop. In Korea, on the other hand, there is a relatively competent and well-paid bureaucracy pursuing long-term economic development goals under the direction of strong executives. Thus, over a number of decades, Korea has been able to generate large vertically integrated and horizontally diversified firms through extensive control, rewarding success and punishing failure. Such state-organised business systems, however, typically discourage horizontal alliances and coalitions, because the state cannot tolerate collectivity it does not control.

Another important feature of many developing economies is their dependence on international agencies and companies. As many of the contributors to this book emphasize, the role of agencies such as the World Bank and various state aid departments in economic development, together with the increasing importance of foreign direct investment by multinational companies from industrialized countries, have meant that many developing economies are quite 'internationalized' in the sense that much industrial activity and trade is coordinated by foreign organizations. As a result, the institutionalization of coherent and cohesive, distinctively national business systems seems unlikely in many of these societies.

As I have indicated, there is no particular reason to expect every nation-state—even those with established and stable institutional arrangements—to develop distinctive and integrated systems of economic coordination and control. This depends on the extent to which the prevalent political, financial, labour and cultural systems within each national territory have mutually reinforcing features and are, as a totality, different from those in other states. Furthermore, foreign capital and technology have been important influences in most industrialization processes, including those of the distinctive economies of Japan, Korea and Taiwan. In these respects, the countries of the South are not greatly different from many in Asia and Europe.

What is more important to the nature of business systems than the flow of capital and technology from outside is the way these external resources are transferred and which organizations control them. In particular, how significant are domestic institutions and agencies, especially the state, in managing the flow of funds and other resources, and to what extent do they act as coordinating organizations integrating such flows with domestic resources for long-term economic development goals? In East Asian countries, the considerable amount of capital and technology-transfer that occurred after the Second World War was controlled by state agencies pursuing developmental goals (Fields 1995; Wade 1990; Woo 1991). In Japan, strong and distinctive domestic institutions ensured that such importation was implemented by domestic firms and groups, and thus modified to suit their needs and objectives. As a result, the effects of foreign imports on the nature and operation of the domestic economy were indirect and limited.

The economies discussed in this book have mostly been more open to foreign direct investment by multinational companies, and many of their domestic institutions have been less established and stable than those in post-Second World War Japan. Furthermore, not all state élites have been as concerned with long-term economic development as some groups in East Asia. However, the impact of foreign agencies and companies on the developing structure of their business systems has varied considerably and has scarcely been overwhelming in most cases. Whatever the outcome of recent liberalization policies in India, for example, the effects of the 'licence raj' on the organization of the economy remain significant and it seems unlikely that foreign direct investment will dominate it in the near future, if ever. Similarly, the considerable flows of foreign direct investment into Malaysia over the past few decades have scarcely turned that economy into a clone of the Japanese, Taiwanese or United States economies, or significantly altered the direction and implementation of Mahathir's new economic policy. The current financial crisis in many of these countries seems unlikely to encourage state élites to deregulate their markets further or to give up their coordinating roles, despite the wishes of many western agencies.

These points highlight the differences between developing economies with regard to the impact of internationalization. They also reflect the capacity and priorities of the state in managing capital and technology inflows as well as the overall strength and cohesion of domestic institutions and organizations. They also result from variation in the nature of foreign investments and where they come from. Portfolio investment tends to be liquid and disruptive in its effects—as the financial crisis in Asia demonstrates—but often has little long-term consequences for domestic economic structures and relationships. This is especially so when it is concentrated in financial institutions and property, as it has been in many East Asian economies. Direct investment, on the other hand, involves greater commitment and may help to structure firm type and behaviour through, for example, the supply chain and labour management practices. However, the impact of inward foreign direct investment varies according to its relative size and provenance.

The effects of investment by multinational companies on developing economies will be more marked when it constitutes a substantial proportion of total investment, particularly in leading sectors. However, this typically comes from a variety of different kinds of business systems so that the impact of any one set of multinational companies from distinctive home economies is limited. Although a developing economy may be dominated by multinational companies from, say, Anglo-Saxon or Japanese business systems, this is certainly not common after the end of colonialism. In most of the period after the Second World War, inward foreign direct investment to developing economies has come from multinational companies in the United States, United Kingdom, continental Europe and Japan, together with Korea and Taiwan more recently. While, then, this investment may limit the establishment of a distinctive and cohesive national business system, it is unlikely to turn Indonesia or Malaysia into a clone of the Anglo-Saxon or Japanese business systems. Rather, developing economies will evolve into various amalgams of contrasting forms of economic organization depending on the particular mix of inward foreign direct investment, the strength of various sectors and the nature of domestic institutions. In the light of these points, I will now briefly consider the economies discussed by the contributors to this book.

Developing Business Systems: Ghana, India, Indonesia, Malaysia and Korea

Though the five countries analyzed in this book differ considerably in their economic structures and institutional arrangements, they do share a number of characteristics. First of all, they implemented state-led industrialization policies after the end of the colonial period, albeit in very different ways and in different circumstances. Thus, any comparative analysis of their business systems has to consider the organization and behaviour of their states over the past several decades as central phenomena. Second, they have tended to have weak intermediary institutions for mobilizing loyalties beyond kinship groupings, especially for dealing with and influencing the state. India might be an exception to this point, but Mark Holmström suggests that such loyalties were, and are, highly particularistic and usually personally based. Third, trust in formal institutions and reliance on formal procedures for managing exchange relationships and disputes seemed rather low in these societies, partly because of colonial legacies. Fourth, authority and subordination relationships are overwhelmingly personal and typically based on ideologies of paternalism in which leaders justify their domination through claiming their superior knowledge of, and commitment to, the interests of the people led (Beetham 1991).

This combination of characteristics has had significant consequences for the sorts of economic systems that have developed in the post-colonial period in these countries. State dominance of the economy and weak intermediary associations have inhibited the development of horizontal alliances and stable, long-term business groups of the kind evident in post-Second World War Japan. Coupled with the highly personal nature of trust relations, this combination has meant that most economic coordination outside the state sector has taken place within ownership-based organizations controlled by owning families. Where the state has discouraged private concentrations of wealth and control over economic activities, as in Ghana for much of the post-colonial period, this has meant that the level of economic organization in the market economy is generally low. Not surprisingly, the legacy of this opposition to private enterprise-led economic development continues to inhibit the growth of privately controlled organizations. State dependence, low trust and paternalist authority relations additionally lead to highly centralized authority patterns within firms and low levels of employee discretion. Since most of these states have not developed strong public training systems, skill levels are typically poorly developed thus further discouraging the delegation of work control.

These points do not preclude partnerships and mutual obligations developing, but rather emphasize their typically particularistic and personal nature. Collaboration and joint involvement in new opportunities between family-controlled businesses are not uncommon in many of these economies, but they are usually based on personal knowledge and trust in the patriarchs involved, and restricted to specific projects. The unpredictable and often adversarial business environment limits the extent and scope of such partnerships, especially where the state is antagonistic towards privately controlled alliances. Similarly, trust of employees in such societies typically depends on personal ties of obligation, which encourages the formation of cliques and clientelist factions within large organizations.

The major differences between these countries that affect the kinds of market economies that became, and are becoming, established in them stem from the nature of their state-led development. Principally, this concerns the organization of the state during the post-colonial period and the policies it has followed. As indicated earlier, one of the key features of developing economies is the cohesion and autonomy of the state, particularly the ability of the bureaucracy to pursue long-term economic development goals without having to accommodate special interest groups seeking short-term rents. This requires the establishment of a highly educated and reasonably well-paid state bureaucracy that is strongly supported by a policy élite focused on development goals. Where the support is weak and/or the state executive is unwilling to rely on the bureaucracy for implementing developmental policies consistently, the state is likely to become more vulnerable to short-term pressures and clientelist practices. This seems to have been the case in Ghana and Indonesia for much of the post-colonial period and has become more so in Malaysia with the development of what Gomez (1998) has termed 'political business'.

In terms of the policies developed and implemented by the state, one obvious difference between these five economies concerns the extent to which state élites have been willing to delegate control of key sectors and activities to privately controlled enterprises. In Ghana, this has been rather limited until recently and quite limited in India, whereas in Korea, Indonesia and Malaysia it has been considerable, albeit with considerable state guidance and control over the developmental process. As a result, the growth of privately owned and controlled enterprise has been faster and has produced larger private ownership-based coordination of economic activities in Korea, Indonesia and Malaysia.

Other important differences in economic policy concern the state's commitment to economic development in contrast to personal or group enrichment, and the stability and predictability of its priorities, decisions and willingness to discipline private enterprises in the pursuit of developmental goals. Although all these countries have manifested some reciprocity between state favours and the private funding of political factions and parties, the degree to which state élites colluded with private businesses in extracting rents from the economy for joint enrichment clearly differed between them, as well as over time. The greatest perhaps in Ghana and Indonesia, this collusion seems to have been less in India and Malaysia, and largely limited to election campaigns in Korea (Cumings 1997; Koo 1993; Woo 1991).

Consistency and predictability in policy development and implementation have also varied considerably, together with the state's capacity and willingness to share investment risks—typically through subsidized credit—with enterprises, and to police subsequent behaviour. It is especially this last feature that differentiates Korea from many other industrializing economies in the second half of the twentieth century. Although state support for individual enterprises, owning families and whole sectors—such as exporting ones—has been quite common in these economies, the ability and willingness of the state élites to sanction their later performance have been less evident. The Korean developmentalist state has demonstrated both high levels of support for firms pursuing particular policies and a commitment to reward successful ones while punishing failures (Moon 1994; Woo 1991). This encouraged considerable organizational learning and very high growth rates among successful enterprises (Kim 1997). In other countries where rewards were tied to reciprocal favours and the performance in international markets was not so critical to state support, firm development has been slower and more limited (Bowie 1994; Jesudason 1989; MacIntyre 1994).

The consequences of the differences in state structures and policies across these five economies can be summarized as follows. Weak states that pursue inconsistent development policies and/or discourage large-scale private enterprises are unlikely to establish market economies dominated by vertically integrated firms that are competitive in export markets. Rather, insofar as entrepreneurs do develop and thrive in this environment, they will either do so in alliance with particular state élites for short periods or remain small in size and highly flexible to minimize both political and market risks. Capital-intensive sectors are typically controlled by the state in such economies, and private sector coordination of economic activities is quite restricted.

Stronger, more autonomous states that rely more on the private sector for economic development will encourage large, privately controlled firms to develop under state tutelage. Where, however, reciprocal favours for particular individuals and groups are expected in return for state support, and this support is more personal and particular than systemic and driven by policy, such firms will be encouraged to concentrate more on securing political commitments than on developing organizational capabilities in competitive markets. Uncertainty over state policies will limit personally funded capital investments and encourage diversification across a range of activities. Horizontal integration through family ownership is thus typically higher than backward vertical integration in these kinds of situations, unless the state underwrites the bulk of the investment.

Finally, strong autonomous states that pursue developmentalist policies through private sector enterprises and can discipline them effectively on the basis of performance, encourage the growth of large firms. This is because they typically provide cheap credit to fund such growth without the family owners ceding control (Janelli and Yim 1993), and coordinate the acquisition of foreign technologies and access to markets, at the same time as high business dependence on the state leads to the pursuit of growth goals to manage political risks and to meet continuously evolving policy demands. The leading Korean conglomerates are thus highly vertically and horizontally integrated and are highly centralized and still controlled by the owning family (Fields 1995; Ziele 1996).

In conclusion, although there are some important differences between many of the developing economies of the South and the more industrialized ones, the general business systems framework for analyzing variation in economic organization seems quite applicable to them. As I have just suggested, it helps to describe and explain some of the important contrasts between developing economies in addition to showing how they vary from the more established variants of industrial capitalism. It is, however, important to bear in mind the purpose of this kind of analysis and to be clear about the level of analysis being adopted. By distinguishing between the overall degree and mode of economic organization and the nature of firms as ownership-based units of financial control and employment, this framework enables an explanation of how and why different kinds of firms come to dominate different business systems. Finally, as in the analysis of the transforming economies of Eastern Europe, the study of developing business systems led to the extension and elaboration of the business systems framework to deal with different kinds of economic processes and phenomena. The basic logic of accounting for significant variation in how economic activities are coordinated and controlled across market economies in terms of differences in institutionalized rules of the game and dominant agencies, however, remains.

2

Business Systems in India

Mark Holmström

How can India meet the challenge of global markets in a way that will increase employment, incomes and welfare for the mass of its people? Can it repeat the success of the East Asian tigers? What are the opportunities and constraints of the present ways of doing business? We need to understand the economy in order to improve it, to achieve such goals as prosperity, greater social and sexual equality, and freedom. These ends are matters of moral and political choice: the study of business systems may suggest the means. Whitley describes business systems as,

> rather general patterns of economic organization which deal with the three basic questions that arise in any market economy: how are activities to be coordinated, how are markets to be organized and how are economic activities within authority hierarchies to be structured and controlled? (Whitley 1992b:271).

These problems arise not just in a market economy but in any economy. The Soviet command economy, which was not designed on market principles, solved some of its problems by means of an unofficial market system of barter or illegal payments between directors of state enterprises, favours given and received, fixers collecting their percentage of deals and bypassing the bureaucracy. In our terms, this is systematic corruption, but also a market that made the unworkable command economy work after a fashion, as a system of competing bounded hierarchies instead of the single hierarchy of the command economy.

This is relevant to India, because although India never tried to abolish markets as the Soviet Union did, in the thirty-odd years after Independence, Indian governments tried to subordinate both the private sector and the large public sector to a planning regime that severely constrained market forces: the 'licence-permit raj'. The state looked after its own: public sector employees; businesses that benefited in one way or another from state patronage or help; the workers covered by labour laws, and; social groups that won special protection.[1] So the questions as they apply to India are rather: how was such a half-planned economy coordinated, how were hierarchical authority relations within the private and public sectors organized, and how have they changed in the long gradual running down of the licence-permit raj?

Solidarity Inside, Competition Outside: A Universal Contrast

In an ideal-type market economy, the corporate decision-making units are firms. Relations inside each firm are governed by hierarchy, authority, loyalty and trust; relations between firms by competition, limited only by law and commercial morality—a system brought to perfection by Weber's Calvinists. Reality is always more complex: there is competition and conflict within firms, and relations of trust, cooperation or collusion between firms. However, the contrast between *inside* and *outside*, where different patterns of behaviour are expected, is a good starting point for the discussion of how real economies work, and the chances of making them work better to achieve our social and economic goals.

---

[1] I use 'state' in the commonly understood sense, to mean the government, especially the central government. However, India, like the United States, is a federation of states: when I refer specifically to these, I write '(regional) state'.

This reflects a universal contrast in all societies. One morality applies within the group, another outside. Jane Jacobs (1992) says that human societies have evolved two distinct moral systems, 'guardian' and 'commercial', each appropriate to a different kind of organization. The two must be kept separate: it is dangerous to mix them. Simon Caulkin sums up her argument:

> The 'guardian' syndrome arises from foraging and protecting territory and governs the behaviour of governments, bureaucracies, political parties, armed forces, police, religions and the justice system. Being about the effective use of power, it stresses loyalty, tradition, hierarchy, honour, vengeance, exclusivity and the distribution of largesse. It shuns trading. On the other hand, the 'commercial' syndrome, emerging from the needs of trade, depends on honesty, voluntary agreements, easy collaboration with strangers, the panoply of enterprise and industriousness, and shuns force (Caulkin 1994:8).

A business system, by definition, is about trade; yet relations *within* the firm—at least the firm organized on Weberian bureaucratic lines, or on Taylorist lines—have some features of the guardian morality: hierarchy and loyalty within and competition outside (see for example, Japanese companies). The contrast between the guardian state and the private firm is not so sharp.

Karl Polanyi (1957, 1959) distinguishes sharply between three modes of exchange: reciprocity, redistribution and market exchange.

> Market exchange is the exchange of goods at prices based on supply and demand. Redistribution is the movement of goods up to an administrative center and their reallotment downward to consumers. Reciprocity is the exchange of goods that takes place neither through markets nor through administrative hierarchies (Keesing 1985:205).

Where these writers see a sharp contrast between different moralities, Marshall Sahlins (1972)—building on social anthropological theories of exchange that go back to Mauss' *The Gift*

(1954, originally 1925)—sees a continuum. Redistribution or pooling is also a kind of reciprocity. Most social relations, including those called 'economic', can be placed along a 'spectrum of reciprocities', ranging from 'generalized reciprocity, the solidary extreme' (Malinowski's 'pure gift'), through 'balanced reciprocity, the midpoint' (direct exchange), to 'negative reciprocity ... the attempt to get something for nothing with impunity'(Sahlins 1972:193–95). Each type of society— hunter-gatherers, peasants, etc.—has its own typical ways of drawing lines between the spheres of social relations where different rules apply: in-groups and out-groups. There are conventionally defined situations in which convention defines the situations where 'economic' rules of exchange apply: here it is legitimate to trade, to maximize utility, to act as 'economic man'.

In a capitalist society, relations within the firm are theoretically governed by pooling or redistribution, a hierarchically organized type of generalized reciprocity. Market relations between firms range from short-term balanced reciprocity to negative reciprocity, depending on how ruthless the competition is. However, in real business systems the lines are not so neatly drawn. A web of social relations—cooperation, trust and conflict—cuts across the boundaries of firms.

Reconstructing Traditional Business Systems in India

This contrast, between hierarchy inside and competition outside, has been worked out in distinctive ways in Indian civilization. We have to look at the past to understand the present reality, but we should avoid the temptation to exaggerate the continuity and unity of Indian culture, or to see everything since colonialism and modern industry as new. The past, as Indians and foreigners perceive it, is often an idealized 'traditional' past: the joint family to which people look back, or the self-sufficient village community beloved of Gandhian and other intellectuals. It is a mistake to oppose the 'traditional' to the 'modern' (equated too easily with colonial or post-colonial India).

Remembering that tradition is an amalgam of real history and nostalgia, traditional business systems in India can be reconstructed, especially but not only among the Hindu majority. Most people were, and still are, peasants. Their dominant business system was the so-called *jajmāni* system: the exchange of goods and services between families belonging to interdependent castes, each carrying out its customary duties—high or low—in return for customary rewards of food and other perquisites from the dominant-caste peasants and landowners. In principle—and this principle was deeply rooted in popular ideology—there was little or no competition, as long as everyone kept to the traditional occupation of his or her caste, sanctified by religious duty. Members of each caste (barbers, washermen, carpenters, etc.) divided up the available work according to custom. In principle, and to some extent in practice, everyone had security as long as they carried out their caste duties to a minimum required standard. Wiser (1936), who introduced the term 'jajmāni system', saw it as an all-embracing system that gave some protection even to the poorest. Gandhi wanted to revive this non-competitive order which, he believed, had been corrupted; but Meillassoux (1973:99) saw it only as 'a relationship of clientship affecting a relatively weak part of the population', a thin disguise for exploitation.

Although the system was found in its most complete form in villages, many of its features existed in the traditional Indian city. The *jajmāni* system is almost dead, but the ideal and nostalgia linger on.

The *jajmāni* system had one enormous loophole, through which market forces and technical innovation could pass. Some castes (such as leather workers, barbers and priests) held genuine monopolies. Other castes were traditionally farmers or traders, but they had no monopoly: in practice, agriculture and trade were more or less open to all who had the means to engage in them (Pocock 1962), although the lowest castes, being poor, had few chances to acquire the means. Each caste, subcaste or sub-subcaste might exploit a niche in the economy—a new product or service—while doing its best to keep out competitors from other castes.

In theory, there was no way to translate economic success into higher caste status. In practice, successful castes or splinter subcastes staked their claim by 'sanskritization', copying high caste customs such as vegetarianism, and could gain tacit recognition as 'originally' members of a higher caste if they were rich and strong enough to persuade their neighbours. This process of sanskritization—mobility within the caste system—has been well documented and appears to have gone on for centuries (Silverberg 1968). Only the highest and lowest castes, Brahmans and 'Untouchables', remained almost closed. Muslims and other non-Hindus fitted roughly into the system and were divided into their own caste-like groups.

The *jajmāni* system was not a command economy and did not abolish the market, but it was an attempt to subordinate the market to the overarching principles of hierarchy and interdependence. The pursuit of profit was a legitimate aim for the castes of traders and cultivators, just as the pursuit of power and wealth (*artha* in Sanskrit) was the proper aim of the Kshatriya or warrior castes. The eternal dharma had to be reconciled with the reality of markets, competition, technical and population change, and political accidents.

The merchants and artisans of the cities had, and have, their own work ethic, justifying ruthless competition in the market, and sometimes sharp practice, while setting limits to it in the name of commercial morality and the solidarity of families, castes and guilds.

Peasants, merchants, artisans, priests and nobles all had some idea—partly based in reality—of a sphere of social life fenced off from competition and the market, an area where hierarchical relations of authority, loyalty and trust were considered proper; and areas where naked competition, the unbridled pursuit of wealth and power, was legitimate and approved. Above all, the joint or extended family was seen as an area of ideal cooperation, a haven against conflict. In practice, families were split by personal tensions, struggles over property and conflict between brothers and in-laws: a traditional excuse for the break-up of joint families was that women's quarrels turned brothers against each other. At the village level, endemic factionalism everywhere set subcaste against subcaste, family against family.

The Colonial and Post-colonial State and Business Systems

Security and hierarchy within the group, competition outside: this is how the lines were drawn in colonial and earlier times. Contemporary India draws the lines in different places, but we need to go back to these institutions in the 'traditional' society—as it was, and as people now believe it was—to find the roots of the business systems that exist now. These lie in what Whitley (1992b:269) calls background social institutions, deep-rooted cultural patterns 'covering trust relations, collective loyalties to non-kin, individualism and authority relations'. The other kind of institutions which shape business systems are 'proximate social institutions', which 'concern the availability of, and conditions governing access to, financial and labour resources, together within the overall system of property rights and political control ... The political, financial and labour systems' (Whitley 1992b:269).

This distinction between 'cultural' background institutions and proximate ones is difficult to maintain in India, because of the pervasive influence of the state on relations between and within firms: the colonial state and the post-colonial state, the reforms that got underway in the 1990s and are still incomplete. It is hard to distinguish traditional ideas about authority, trust and hierarchy from those that grew up under the shadow of colonial law and administration, and then the democratic-bureaucratic government of independent India.

Nineteenth-century British rulers such as James Mill and Macaulay set out to do in India what they could not do in Britain itself: to design a new system of law and administration on utilitarian principles, 'with power devolved downwards to assignable individuals through a disciplined chain of command' (Stokes 1959:148), for the common benefit—they believed—of Indians and British alike.[2] The élite Indian Civil Service, nicknamed the 'twice-born' after the highest castes, was staffed almost entirely by the British until well into the twentieth century. Under its protective wing, a new Indian middle class grew up, filling the lower ranks of the bureaucracy and the learned professions, especially law (Misra 1961). Most came from the highest castes, and their careers depended largely on the goodwill of British officials; except for some independent-minded, sometimes heroic mavericks in the Indian ranks. The British-led army, of course, was equally hierarchical and its influence almost as pervasive. These hierarchical structures fitted in very well with the ideological model of a hierarchical, non-competitive society that ideally gave security to everyone who conscientiously performed the duties of his or her station.

The British did not invent this whole mixture of bureaucracy, despotism and petty legalism that marks most working relationships in formal settings, but they embodied them in precise and lasting structures and gave them a powerful impetus, after which these systems of relations seemed to become self-sustaining, feeding on their own practice and ideology (Heuzé 1992:13, my translation).

The new system of commercial law was largely designed to favour British companies, which needed an intermediate class of Indian managers and foremen to mediate between them and the labourers they employed; but a vigorous Indian capitalism also grew up in the late nineteenth century, especially in the textile centers of western India (Holmström 1984:57).

The large Indian-owned companies modelled their management systems on those of the British, including the peculiarly

---

[2] Sir Charles Trevelyan (1838) (quoted in Stokes 1959:47) wrote:

The natives will not rise against us, we shall stoop to raise them ... The educated classes, knowing that the elevation of their country on these [European] principles can only be worked out under our protection, will naturally cling to us ... The natives will have independence, after first learning how to make good use of it; and we shall exchange profitable subjects for still more profitable allies.

British-Indian system of 'managing agencies'. A managing agency was not usually a holding company but one that raised capital for operating companies and appointed their managers, under an 'agency agreement'. The agency often maximized profits not by building up companies under its control, but by milking them of cash and by speculative transactions between the companies. Middle managers were appointed by the managing agency, often as a result of nepotism, and they sometimes spied on the senior managers for the agency. Labour recruitment and supervision were left to promoted workers, the jobbers. For employees at any level, job security and promotion depended on relations with sometimes capricious and corrupt patrons, tempered in places by violent clashes with trade unions. By the 1930s, the system's cost and inefficiency were obvious: it was gradually replaced by more stable management systems, with a strong paternalist ethic, and abolished after Independence.[3]

Indian-owned management agencies were private limited companies, usually controlled by a single family. The large conglomerates that replaced them have dominated much of the Indian large-scale industry since before Independence, sheltering behind tariff walls and restrictions on foreign companies, while chafing at other restrictions intended to check monopolies and encourage 'small-scale industries'. Their management practices became steadily more professional, as they tried to adapt western or Japanese management styles in their core business, while subcontracting more and more work to medium and small firms.

The managing agency system has gone, but has left its legacy in these hierarchically organized firms with diverse interests in manufacturing and commerce. Often each hierarchy is controlled by a tightly knit group, usually from the same family, caste or religion. These are the biggest and most successful examples of what Pierre Lachaier (1992) calls the 'industrial lineage firm', a system of patron–client relations typical of much Indian industry. The original company is divided and

---

[3] For an account of the managing agencies and their system of labour recruitment and supervision, see Holmström 1984:45–55.

subdivided among the founder's kin, who are bound to each other and to small-scale worker-entrepreneurs by complex subcontracting relations. Planning, marketing and assembly are carried on in the central unit under the direct supervision of the *karta*, the effective head of the family. Loyal employees are helped to set up ancillary firms; sometimes the distinction between employer and employee almost disappears.

Larger firms subcontract work to smaller ones not only for the usual reasons—flexibility, risk-spreading and so on—but to take advantage of government incentives to smaller firms, and to evade labour laws and social security by outsourcing work to nominally independent firms too small to be covered by the legislation.

The industrial lineage firm is bound together by a strong paternalist ideology, which the founding family and top management promote, and other employees may or may not share. Managers sometimes point to the fabled loyalty of Japanese employees, as an ideal rather than a reality in their own firms. For employees who share this ideology, employment in the modern company is akin to work as a religious duty in the *jajmāni* system (Holmström 1976:88–95, 126–7). Gérard Heuzé shows how nineteenth-century reformers gave a new meaning to the traditional value of *sevā*, which originally meant the 'service' or duty owed to one's superiors within the family:

> These ideas are still very much alive in many Hindu families, especially families of high status. They provide much of the ideological environment, and the context of social relations, in which young Indians first learn about work as a duty. Serving and being served means (among other things) *relating to others and reinforcing the hierarchy* through one's acts. It means belonging to chains of relationships which make you a human being (Heuzé 1992:12–13. My translation).

The new economic and administrative tasks, salaried and waged work, were justified and dignified as *sevā*, service to the organic unit, which was the family, caste or village, and is now the firm.

The industrial lineage firm's weaknesses have become more obvious in recent years. It is vulnerable to family quarrels over property and control of subsidiaries, and to personal tensions. Sons from the dominant lineage are sent abroad to study engineering and management, but can only supply a small part of the professional management and technical expertise required. Some of the biggest industrial houses, notably Tata, have always distinguished clearly between the top positions filled by the family, and all other posts filled by professional managers appointed strictly on merit and competence. Other firms have a reputation for nepotism, clientelism and favouritism, like the former managing agencies. Both kinds of firms offer a high level of job security to permanent employees at every level, but not to a large flexible work force of temporary, casual or contract workers.

In the period of licence-permit raj, foreign companies investing in India were subject to tight restrictions on majority ownership of Indian subsidiaries and repatriation of profits. The large Indian conglomerates, mostly organized as industrial lineage firms, had an obvious interest in maintaining these restrictions, which allowed them to make agreements for technical and financial collaboration if they could find foreign partners willing to invest on these terms.

Not all new or growing firms are industrial lineage firms. Entrepreneurs with a background in engineering or professional management find backing from other sources: government schemes to encourage technocrats, or financiers looking for profitable investments. For contracts, ideas and advice, these entrepreneurs have useful contacts in the private or public sector enterprises where they worked before setting up their own business. Long friendships between men who worked or studied together, who belong to the same clubs and aspire to the same managerial lifestyle, can replace family ties as a basis for trust and joint action.[4] Innovative small and medium firms can achieve a certain independence from the

---

[4] For an extended treatment of these networks in Bangalore's engineering and electronics industries, and the foundations and limits of useful trust between entrepreneurs, see Holmström 1997, 1998a.

large firms, especially if they can cooperate, formally or informally, in marketing, product development and subcontracting among themselves. This is a world of relatively self-contained management hierarchies, sometimes competing fiercely with each other, sometimes cooperating to a limited extent in the face of external competition, while jealously guarding their independence.

Nehruvian Socialism and Licence-permit Raj

All this has happened within limits set by the state, in an economy where the state was a major player as the regulator, customer and source of funds for investment. It is fashionable now to damn the whole Nehruvian project as an aberration from the market path, a lost opportunity to achieve outward-looking growth like the East Asian tigers, yet it had many positive achievements. The state did things the private sector probably could not have done in a desperately poor country with a largely illiterate population, and laid the foundations for a more open competitive economy.

Licence-permit raj could be regarded as a malignant growth on a reasonable project, Nehru's ideal of self-reliant development towards a 'socialistic pattern of society': not a command economy on the model of the Soviet-dominated socialist bloc, but a democratic pluralistic socialism designed to achieve rapid economic growth by building the infrastructure and heavy industry to support private sector development; to protect domestic industry, while preventing the excessive growth in size and power of the large Indian-owned conglomerates, by licensing and quotas where there was a lack of effective competition; to create employment in small-scale and cottage industries; to extend the protection of the social democratic state to as many groups as possible; and to achieve more immediate ends, such as raising the status of the Scheduled (ex-'untouchable') Castes and Tribes through reservations in education and employment.

An unintended consequence was to establish the state as an area fenced off from competition and insecurity, containing powerful fiefdoms: big firms sheltered by tariff protection, import quotas and licensing, which prevented fierce domestic competition; peasants and small-scale industries protected by subsidies, which sometimes ended up in the pockets of the rich; organized sector workers protected by labour laws and party patronage of politicized trade unions; employees in the overstaffed public sector, including a fortunate minority from the Scheduled Castes and Tribes. The closer you were to the centre of state power, the more protection and security you enjoyed.

The notion of the state sector as a moral area fenced off from competition and insecurity was not new, but it took new forms under the Nehruvian settlement. The job as *sevā*, service to a hierarchically organized group, and particularly as a piece of property to which some people are morally entitled, is a legacy of a society stratified by caste and wealth, modified to some extent by the requirements of an incomplete capitalism and a vague socialism, and by the equalitarian ideas that inspired the Independence movement and Gandhi.

The attempt to right wrongs and satisfy political demands by job reservations reinforced the idea that a job is property, especially a job in the public sector. The reservation of scholarships and public sector jobs for the Scheduled Castes and Tribes—about one-eighth of the population—was written into the Constitution as a special exception to meritocracy, a form of protective discrimination originally meant to be temporary. It has led to persistent and partly successful demands for similar concessions to much larger groups, the so-called Other Backward Classes (meaning castes). In the *jajmāni* system, the lowest castes—or at least those who were lucky enough to be clients of local landowners—had a recognized claim to subsistence. Leach (1960:6) even argues that this put the lowest castes in a privileged position: 'In a class system, social status and economic security go together—the higher the greater; in contrast, in a caste society, status and security are polarized'. This is a questionable view of the traditional caste system, but paradoxically it may have a certain truth now. The claim to a moral right to jobs is now made by those who were lower in the hierarchy—not just the Scheduled Castes who had first claim after Independence, but the Other Backward Classes each claiming to be more backward than the others. In the old days, of course, castes claimed *high* status if they could make the claim stick.

The notion of the job as property sits uneasily with a meritocratic ideology, the idea that hard work and integrity bring their own just reward: an idea that is not merely an import of western values. The British Empire was profoundly hierarchical; so were the attitudes of many British businessmen in India. Meritocracy has its own roots in traditional India, as in the work ethic of trading and artisan castes and of religious sects like the *Lingāyats*, whom the British called the 'puritans of the East'.

Licence-permit raj had its roots in a mixture of Nehru's Fabian socialism and Gandhian idealism, an attempt to build a harmonious rather than competitive society; for some enthusiasts, almost an attempt to restructure the *jajmāni* system on a national scale and to reconcile it with equalitarian and meritocratic ideals—a reply to Gandhi's emphasis on the village, and his attempt to restore and purify an imagined lost village republic, but now on a national scale. As licence-permit raj is gradually dismantled, the public sector is perhaps the last, rapidly crumbling redoubt of a moral order that began as an expression of worthy ideals before it was corrupted.

A Range of Business Systems Now

India now seems to have one dominant business system but a range of identifiable systems, each with its own rules and practices.

Discussions of Indian economic life often begin with a neat classification of the various types of organizations into pigeonholes. A set of dualistic distinctions roughly describe reality and bring some sort of intelligible order into it. These are entrenched in law, public policy and attitudes. They can be misleading, yet they make as good a starting point as any for a summary account of business systems.

Rural-agricultural versus Urban-industrial

This distinction is a broad value-laden view of two stereotyped ways of life. Rural 'firms' are farms, with unpaid family labour and some paid labourers, often seasonally employed and belonging to a low caste. Vestiges of paternalist obligation are left over from the defunct *jajmāni* system, but the relationship between landowners and labourers becomes steadily more mercenary and short term. Farmers are involved in the market economy but seldom compete directly with neighbouring farmers, except for status. There is more competition between rural traders.

The urban-industrial economy is commonly thought of as harshly competitive. The contrast between the rural and urban ways of life was always oversimplified and is now more misleading than ever, with the spread of capitalist farming. Agriculture becomes an investment for rural or urban capitalists, to be balanced against competing returns on other investments.

Public versus Private

The public sector is still enormous and its influence pervasive: the central and (regional) state bureaucracies, services such as education, nationalized banks and much of the manufacturing industry.

For many years Indian governments have tried to make public sector enterprises more competitive, market-friendly and even profitable, with varying success. This is still an area of secure employment for those regarded as deserving, but it is less insulated from market forces than before. The pace of change has speeded up since the economic reforms of the 1990s, with plans to cut waste, to reduce overstaffing by voluntary or compulsory redundancy and to find new products and markets, with some planned privatization. At its worst, the public sector remains a dumping ground for people with influence, political connections or recognized victim status. Other parts of the public sector show signs of revival and adaptation.

Organized versus Unorganized

The 'organized' and 'unorganized' sectors correspond roughly to the 'formal' and 'informal' sectors (though the notion of an informal sector is confusing, hard to define and of limited use: see Breman 1985; Joshi 1980). The organized sector consists of all public sector units and private companies employing over 10 permanent workers, who have been covered for many years by laws on unfair dismissal, trade union recognition, the Provident Fund Scheme for retirement, and Employees' State Insurance against sickness and unemployment. To avoid these laws, employers sometimes break up a firm into smaller units, each employing (on paper) not more than 10 workers, but all operating in the same building as an integrated factory.

In practice, especially in the smaller organized sector firms, these workers' rights can only be secured where the trade unions are strong. They do not apply at all to the large and growing number of temporary, casual or contract workers in firms of all sizes, who may work alongside permanent workers earning twice as much, and who may have little chance of acquiring permanent status (Holmström 1984:311–12).

If the public sector was a protected area for enterprises and employees, the organized sector—defined and regulated by the state—was almost an extension of it. Large firms enjoyed protection against imports. Some industries were dominated by oligopolies, with little incentive to innovate and little chance to expand, because their licensed capacity was limited to allow 'small-scale industries' to come up. For workers, the organized sector was a citadel of security: the important thing was to scale the walls, usually with the help of someone already inside. Once in, a worker could look around for a better job, but security almost always came first, because life outside was so grim. This partial and relative security is now threatened in the private sector and to a lesser extent in public sector enterprises.

Within the organized sector, there is a further important division into 'foreign' and 'Indian' firms. Foreign firms were allowed to operate only in certain sectors, usually as subsidiaries with a majority Indian shareholding. Repatriation of profits was restricted. These controls are now being swept away, but widespread suspicion of multinationals is still widespread across the political spectrum.

Large Firms versus 'Small-scale Industries'

Government policy since Independence has been to protect the small against the large through an array of subsidies, cheap loans, advisory and support services, and product lines reserved for small firms. Within the 'small-scale sector', 'tiny' or 'cottage industries' are singled out for special treatment.

While the organized and unorganized sectors are defined by the number employed, 'small-scale industries' are defined for official purposes by the amount of capital invested. This allows rich investors or large companies to buy up many small companies, or divide medium-sized companies into notional small ones and to pocket the extra profit and subsidies. Many really small entrepreneurs, on the other hand, have not asked for help because they prefer to remain unregistered, invisible to tax inspectors and other officials. Some of these subsidies and privileges, notably reserved product lines, are now being dismantled or have gone.

Blurring the Boundaries: The Present Restructuring of Indian Business

This habit of dividing the economic and social landscape into sectors made some kind of sense. From the point of view of workers, managers and entrepreneurs, the sector boundaries could be pictured as a series of concentric circles: the closer you were to the safe center—public sector employment—the more security you had. Outside the public sector, but still inside the organized sector citadel, employment in a large firm was almost as safe as in the public sector and better paid. Employees had less security and income in smaller organized sector firms; and even less in unorganized sector firms, including those that took advantage of the status of a small-scale industry, and which could be very profitable for employers. Temporary, casual and contract employees found work when and wherever they could. The outer circle of genuinely informal enterprises offered the least security of all to workers and petty employers, but not always the lowest incomes. Peasants are outside my scope, though they are the large majority.

Since the reforms of the 1990s got underway, this neat arrangement began to break down. Boundaries between sectors became blurred, with the gradual deregulation of business and opening up to the world economy. Fears that Indian industry would be swamped by aggressive foreign investors proved largely unfounded, but the now-welcome multinationals injected enough competition to raise the quality of Indian products. Management remained hierarchical and Taylorist in most companies. The organized sector citadel became less secure: people who had believed that they had a job for life, often one that could be passed on to a son or relative, were rudely disappointed. The government moved cautiously towards an 'exit policy', making it easier for bankrupt firms to close down and lay off workers. Though parts of the public sector were reorganized or prepared for privatization, it remained a relatively safe haven, more and more exposed to political pressures to employ members of the Other Backward Classes, in addition to the Scheduled Castes and Tribes who have enjoyed positive discrimination since Independence.

As the boundaries between sectors—large- and small-scale, organized and unorganized, even public and private—became blurred, the real boundaries of the firm also shifted. For many years the government has helped technocrats to set up high-technology, often capital-intensive firms in the 'small-scale sector'. With the easing of restrictions on large firms, the advantages of a small-scale status are decreasing: it makes more sense to let the firm grow. Many small firms are spin-offs from larger units, either industrial lineage firms or entrepreneurs who set up trusted employees in business as their suppliers. These small firms are effectively part of the decision-making hierarchy of the parent firm. However, some large firms now try to curtail old relationships with ancillaries, and shop around for alternative suppliers who can meet their requirements for price and quality. Small- and medium-sized enterprises increasingly have to fend for themselves.

In this situation, smaller firms can aim for independence, dependence or interdependence. They can design, make and market their own products: this is easiest if the technology is simple and the market local. They can do 'job work'—one-off, possibly repeatable, contracts to supply parts or services to other firms, large or small: an insecure source of income, but sometimes lucrative. Or, they can seek to become regular suppliers to the largest firms, including multinationals, sometimes displacing long-established ancillaries. The subcontracting small firm must work exactly to the designs and tolerances laid down by the buyer, which sometimes makes it necessary to buy expensive new equipment. It helps to have personal contacts with managers in the purchasing firm, who can pass on information about new plans; but this is generally a hard-nosed competitive relationship, rather than the old-style bond between patron and client. Since large firms try to avoid excessive dependence on a single supplier, subcontractors also look for alternative markets.

The third option is interdependence. Networks of smaller firms (usually, but not necessarily in the same industrial district) can complement each other to achieve economies of scale and scope. They cooperate on marketing, improving quality, developing new products and stages of production for which some firms have specialized machinery or workers. This allows them to do things they could not do if they were isolated in a jungle of competing firms. They are interdependent, and independent of the large firms when this is to their advantage.

This is the small firm variant of Piore and Sabel's (1984) 'flexible specialization' (Sabel 1982). Where this strategy is successful, as in north-central Italy, smaller firms can achieve economies of scale and scope that large firms achieve through centralization, while remaining more flexible, cheaper and more responsive to demand from even a few customers.

The chief obstacle is lack of trust. Flexible specialization requires some degree of trust between entrepreneurs, and between them and their workers. It could develop spontaneously, as local entrepreneurs see the advantages of acting together and develop effective sanctions against cheats and free-riders.[5] Yet most of Indian business has always been a

---

[5] Like those flooring tile manufacturers in Morbi (Gujarat) who use inferior materials for a quick profit, tarnish Morbi's image as a centre of tile manufacture and could force the other manufacturers to lower their standards unless they can act together (Das 1996).

jungle, where trust was limited to kin and a few close friends, or to close-knit moral communities bound together by religion or caste, such as the shoemakers of Agra (Knorringa 1991, 1994, 1998).

Effective networks of cooperation, capable of making India's smaller firms competitive on national and world markets, seem unlikely to take root without a push, a deliberate policy to encourage this kind of development. This happened in Italy, Germany, Denmark and Spain, where local or national governments worked with business associations, and sometimes with trade unions and universities, to provide what Italians call 'real services', such as training, consultancy and design, which single firms cannot afford to provide for themselves; and to encourage and support consortia or other local arrangements which gave clusters of interdependent small and medium enterprises access to wider markets.

Cut-throat competition, as well as older communal divisions, make Indian entrepreneurs too suspicious to share information or to develop stable forms of cooperation. Yet there are recently documented cases of local networks of firms, including innovative and successful ones in fast-developing industries, which have developed effective networks of informal cooperation, based on economic interest and personal friendship, sometimes cutting across communities of birth;[6] business associations of firms in the same industrial sector or simply in the same place, such as an industrial estate;[7] and, much more rarely, formal arrangements such as consortia for marketing or to develop new products.[8] There is some evidence not only that such forms of cooperation have developed spontaneously in some places, but that some—not all—of the real services provided by national and state governments, or by business associations, have been effective in helping smaller firms to do things

[6] See Tewari (1995, 1998) on Ludhiana's engineering industry, and Holmström (1994, 1998a) on Bangalore's electronic and engineering industries.

[7] See Benjamin (1993) and Benjamin and Bengani (1998) on the politics of industrial districts in Delhi; or Gorter (1996) on a business association in an industrial estate in Gujarat.

[8] See Holmström (1994:53–63, 1998a) on consortia in Bangalore and Coimbatore.

they could not do by themselves.[9] It seems likely that public provision of real services in India can not only make up for the lack of trust between entrepreneurs, but can sometimes *build* trust by demonstrating the advantages of consortia and cooperation, and by building up solid friendships and social networks, cemented in social clubs such as Rotary and Lions, professional associations of engineers or specialists, and the new culture of seminars and conferences that attract ambitious entrepreneurs and managers.

'Real services', then, can be useful both in doing what they are set up to do (training, help with marketing, testing, etc.) and indirectly, in building solidarity and trust, laying the foundations for useful cooperation and the networks of social and moral relations that make collective efficiency possible: not only in the relatively high-technology industries that face the stiffest international competition but also in more traditional industries.[10]

Concluding Remarks

The Indian economy is becoming more genuinely competitive, but the real competing units are not always individual firms, each with its own decision-making hierarchy. Nor are they giant conglomerates in long-term relationships of trust with dependent firms, as in Japan, in spite of the continuing strength of industrial lineage firms. Long-established relationships between the private or public sector enterprises and

---

[9] I have described the array of publicly provided 'real services' available to Bangalore's engineering and electronic industries (Holmström 1998a). Some, like the nationally funded Central Machine Tools Institute (now renamed the Central Manufacturing Technology Institute) and the Nettur Technical Training Foundation (a voluntary organization), provide valued services to smaller firms. Other services are provided—with varying success—by business associations and the state government, and nationally funded research institutes located in Bangalore because of its concentration of scientific talent and technologically advanced industries, especially since the Second World War. Such cities as Pune (Poona) and Hyderabad appear to have similar advantages.

[10] P.M. Mathew and J. Joseph (1994a, 1994b) and Mathew (1995) have shown how the right kind of real services could improve competitiveness, wages and conditions in traditional cottage industries such as Kerala's cane and bamboo industry.

dedicated ancillaries give way to more competitive sourcing, as customers seek better value and consistent quality. Management in large firms is often hierarchical, centralized and Fordist, with some gestures in the direction of Japan—participation, quality circles and so forth.

Among small- and medium-sized enterprises, forms of cooperative networking or 'flexible specialization' are emerging in places.[11] Where this happens, the boundaries between firms are blurred: an industrial district, or a geographically dispersed sector of industry, behaves in some ways like a large firm, with a presence in the market and common institutions to promote market-led innovation, yet decision-making is decentralized. The chief obstacle to this kind of development is lack of trust between entrepreneurs. However, some institutions to promote innovative small firms, run by government bodies or business associations, partly make up for this lack of trust and may also help to build trust.

For workers, the organized sector citadel of security disappears or is redefined. The labour market is polarized and is likely to remain so for a long time. A large part of the workforce, well educated and with access to training or experience with new technologies, has bright prospects and rising incomes: their security is the knowledge that they can easily find another job at least as good as the one they have. Many more workers— some well educated, most with little education—continue to find what temporary or casual work they can, in large or small firms. These workers can hope, at best, to learn a skill with some market value in small firms, paying perhaps half or one-third of the wages paid to regular employees in large factories. Surplus labour and the weakness of trade unions keep wages low, and encourage employers to go for cheap labour rather than building up workers' skills.

The impact of liberalization on Indian business has been modest. Licence-permit raj has been largely but not fully dismantled. The economy is more open to imports: this raises

---

[11] For a discussion of the potential and limitations of 'flexible specialization' in India, see Holmström 1993 and 1998b. Cadène and Holmström 1998 contains a collection of case studies: some encouraging and others less so.

the quality of Indian goods and helps to make them more competitive on world markets. Multinationals are welcome at last, but are feeling their way cautiously in the new environment: there is still widespread suspicion of them. These changes have not transformed the ways of doing business, but there are hopeful signs: big firms are more competitive and innovative, small ones show some capacity for networking and flexible specialization.

Some of these developments seem startling, even traumatic, by contrast with the immobility of decades. At least the logjam has broken: parts of Indian industry can move into the rapids of international competition. When this will lead to better work, incomes and welfare for the mass of Indian people is another question.

3

The Institutional Embeddedness of Inter-firm Relations in Indonesia[1]

Martijn F.L. Rademakers and Jos R. van Valkengoed

This chapter explores the merits of the market organization framework in the analysis of inter-firm relations in a single industry. The framework will be applied to describe and understand how arrangements of key social institutions affect the development of inter-firm relations in the Indonesian herbal medicine (*jamu*) industry.

The market organization framework has been derived from the broader business systems approach, in which the formation of dominant hierarchy-market arrangements is linked with the nature of nationally distinct institutions. The business systems approach was developed by Richard Whitley and his associates on the basis of studies in East Asian and European countries (see: Whitley 1990, 1991, 1992a, 1992b, 1994a). Up to now, however, business systems and in particular forms of market organization in South-east Asian countries have remained

[1] The background of this chapter is a research project that we conducted in Indonesia in 1994 and 1995. We are grateful for the supervision of Jules van Dijck and Sandra Schruijer, and for the invaluable support that we received from the people of the Management Education Institute, Pendidikan Pembinaan Manajemen (PPM) in Jakarta. Currently, Jos R. van Valkengoed works for GE Capital, London, UK, and Martijn Rademakers is Research Associate at the Rotterdam School of Management, Erasmus University, The Netherlands.

underexposed. Therefore, this chapter focuses on an industry in a genuine South-east Asian setting, addressing two major questions. First, what are the market organization characteristics of the Indonesian *jamu* industry? Second, do these characteristics correspond with the expectations that can be formulated on the basis of the results from previous business system studies in Asia and Europe?

Business Systems and Industry Studies

The business systems approach is particularly useful in cross-national comparisons of economic organization, particularly if we take into account its genesis, which is a comparative study of East Asian countries (Whitley 1990). This approach can also be applied in the analysis of industries (see Whitley 1992b:177–266). Such studies of industrial sectors imply the combination of analyzes both on the national level (i.e., the nature of key social institutions) and on the industry level (i.e., hierarchy-market arrangements). Regarding these different levels of analysis, Räsänen and Whipp (1992:47) argued that industry-specific business systems may emerge in a country. In addition, Whitley (1992b:177) noted that different business systems may develop in contexts characterized by a great variety of non-cohesive social institutions. Hence, the patterns of economic organization may vary between different industries in the same institutional setting. This variation, however, does not necessarily conflict with the existence of a dominant business system in a particular country. In addition, with respect to market organization analysis, evidence from a comparative study of the cotton textile industries in Hong Kong and Japan by Nishida and Redding (1992:264) supports the view that key social institutions, rather than industry-specific characteristics, influence the development of inter-firm relations. The textile firms involved in their study were embedded in different institutional environments and appeared to have developed distinct forms of market organization. Put briefly, this discussion leads to the conclusion that it makes sense to analyze an industry in its national context. The nature of key social institutions helps to explain the characteristics of inter-firm organization, but industry-specific influences may have to be taken into account as well.

The Market Organization Framework

In fact, the market organization framework constitutes a sub-system of the broader business systems approach (Whitley 1992b:9). The essence of the market organization framework boils down to four basic characteristics of inter-firm organization. In line with the business systems approach, these characteristics can be linked with the influence of key social institutions that inhibit or encourage particular directions of development. This section discusses both the market organization characteristics and relevant key social institutions. This will result in the construction of a matrix that provides an overview of the four market organization characteristics, linked with six key social institutions.

The first characteristic in the market organization framework comprises the ideal types of long-term cooperative inter-firm relations and spot-market relations (cf. Lane 1996). Both types have distinct features and can be seen as the extremes of a continuum. We regard a period of 3 years or longer as a safe indicator of a long-term relationship. In addition, cooperative elements of inter-firm relations are risk-sharing in the form of joint research, joint ownership and information-sharing that surpasses straightforward data exchange about prices, qualities and quantities. Spot-market relationships, on the other hand, are limited to particular transactions while the focus is on current options and outcomes. In other words, firms engaged in spot-market relations operate as 'islands in a sea of market transactions'. The firms do not intend to cooperate, and price–quality deliberations play a major role in the selection of suppliers or customers.

The second characteristic in the framework is the role of intermediary organizations in the coordination of transactions between firms. Organizations such as trading companies, banks and industry associations can play a significant facilitating role in creating and maintaining relationships between firms. Examples from studies on Japan (Whitley 1992a) and

Germany (Lane and Bachmann, 1996) show that these organizations can facilitate the exchange of information, goods and capital between firms.

The third characteristic deals with business groups as coordinating networks between autonomous firms. Based on Hamilton et al. (1990:118), four types of business groups with a coordinating function can be distinguished: the *kygyo shudan* type, characterized by horizontal linkages through 'president clubs' and/or mutual shareholding between independent firms; the *investment network*, which stands for horizontal linkages between firms, based on joint research and development programs, and joint investments in commercial activities; the *keiretsu* type, vertically linking firms in a supply chain by mutual obligations, subcontracting arrangements and mutual shareholding, and; the *distribution network*, where firms are linked together in a joint distribution channel. There are also two types of business groups that do not coordinate transactions between autonomous firms: the *conglomerate* model, characterized by a central actor owning a wide range of related and unrelated activities or firms; and the *chaebol* model, which stands for a central actor (a family or a group of owners) that has full authority over the activities of entire supply chains in different industries. Each type of business group can differ with respect to its scope (number of industries covered), size (number of different activities or firms involved) and stability (dynamics in growth and decline).

Finally, the basis of cooperative relations between firms is the fourth market organization characteristic. In fact, this characteristic reflects how economic actors deal with their uncertainty about the future behaviour of business partners. Inter-firm linkages can be based on personal ties (reputation or friendship) or on collective identities (kinship, ethnicity or religion), but relying on formal contracts is also an option. Each of these bases can provide firms with some degree of certainty in exchange relations. A combination of different bases can be used, but business partners in a specific institutional setting are likely to rely on one of them in particular. For instance, formal contracts need a well-functioning legal system before they can provide any certainty, but even in such a setting more 'relational' contracts may prevail, such as is the case in Japan (Sako 1992) and Italy.

The way inter-firm relations develop in an industry is influenced by 'background' and 'proximate' social institutions (Whitley 1990; Nishida and Redding 1992). Social institutions are regarded here as stable patterns of social action that are reproduced over time (cf. Lane 1996). Background social institutions reflect the cultural and historical background of societies and are reproduced through the family, religious organizations and the education system (Whitley 1992b:19). Proximate social institutions have emerged during the industrialization of nation-states. They are directly involved in economic activities as they at least partially control the availability and the ease of access to resources such as labour, capital and materials, together with property rights and political control (Whitley 1992b:269). The construction of a matrix is considered useful to create an overview of the key social institutions and their combined influence on market organization characteristics. Hence, we have 'scanned' the works of Whitley and other authors wherein the business systems framework was developed and/or applied (Whitley 1990, 1991, 1992a, 1992b, 1994a) and put the results in the matrix given in Table 3.1.

In the matrix presented in Table 3.1, six key social institutions are present, some of which are divided into two different types to gain a better overview. The role of the state can be 'dominant' or 'committed', the nature of the financial system is either 'credit based' or 'capital based'. Similarly, the level of individualism versus collectivism is presented as 'loyalty to collectives beyond the family' and 'the importance of individual rights, identities and commitments'. The contents of the matrix should not be interpreted as a collection of separate one-to-one relations between clear-cut variables. Rather, the symbols should be interpreted as positive (+) or negative (–) influences on the development of market organization characteristics and should be analyzed in connection with each other. The application of this matrix as a generator of expectations, will be demonstrated in the discussion of the Indonesian institutional context.

Table 3.1
The Influence of Key Social Institutions on the Development of Market Organization Characteristics

	Market Organization Characteristics			
	The extent of long-term cooperative relationships between firms	The significance of intermediaries for the coordination of transactions	The coordination of inter-firm linkages within business groups	The dependence of cooperative relations on personal ties
Background Social Institutions — Trust between non-kin	+	+	+	–
Commitment and loyalty to collectives beyond the family	+	+	+	–
Importance of individual identities, rights and commitments	–	–	–	
Formalization and depersonalization of authority relations				–
Differentiation of authority roles				–
Proximate Social Institutions — Business dependence on a strong state	–	–	–	
State commitment	+	+	+	
Credit-based financial system	+	+	+	
Capital-based financial system	–	–	–	

The Indonesian Institutional Context

Indonesian society is comprised of many different cultures, but two of them stand out: the Javanese dominate political life in Indonesia, while a small minority of Indonesians with a Chinese heritage are known to dominate business (Sato 1993; Hulst 1991:30). In the *jamu* industry, however, both the Javanese and Chinese Indonesians are active. This will be taken into account where relevant in the discussion of the background social institutions in Indonesia.

Family ties form an important basis of trust in the culturally diverse Indonesian society. The family involves social control among its members, which provides more certainty than the legal system in Indonesia. Clearly, the Indonesian legal system is not a very solid basis for trust between economic actors. The system is considered as antiquated, being in development yet and is affected by widespread corruption[2] (Schwarz 1994; Robison 1986). The lack of a reliable legal system means that reputation (past behaviour) is used as the primarily basis of trust between non-kin in Indonesia (Hofstede 1982:16; Kimman 1981:139).

At first glance, Indonesian society seems to have a very collective nature. According to Hofstede (1982:11), Indonesia can be found last in a ranking of levels of individualism among western and Asian countries. Moreover, if the Javanese *desa* (small village or 'micro society' as Muskens [1970:60] calls it) is taken as the unit of analysis, a high level of collectivism will be found. Collective decision-making processes (*musya-warah*), unanimous decision (*mufakat*), cooperation (*gotong royong*) and loyalty are important Javanese ideals. However, we argue that this high level of collectivism is restricted particularly to these Javanese micro societies and that it does not apply to the Indonesian Republic as a whole. Indeed, in the very diverse social environment comprised by Indonesia, membership of a particular group provides an individual

---

[2] This can be illustrated by the following practical joke. The Indonesian law, named Kitab Undang-Undang Hukum Pidana, is often abbreviated as KUHP. Some creative people gave this abbreviation with a new meaning: Kasih Uang Habis Perkara. This stands for: 'give money and the case is solved'.

security and protection (Mulder 1978:57). However, the assertion that a high level of collectivism exists between the many thousands of different *desa* or the hundreds of different cultural and ethnic groups is questionable at least. Rather, as the modern history of Indonesia comprises many disputes between different local, cultural and ethnic groups (Ricklefs 1993), it is obvious that social tensions exist. Thus, in Indonesia the degree of collectivism is regarded as being high *within* micro societies such as villages, but *between* groups or at the national level the degree of collectivism is low.

The level of formalization and depersonalization of authority in Indonesian society is very low. Authority in social units such as a family, a company or even the country itself can be traced back to a single person and is paternalistic in nature (Hofsteede 1971:52; Kartodirdjo 1972:77; Muskens 1970:59). In other words, authority in the Javanese society is strongly personalized. Also, among the ethnic Chinese, personalism characterizes social relationships (Redding 1990). The implication is that written contracts, formal rules and formal procedures to coordinate economic activities are less relevant: it are the personal deals with the one in authority that matter.

In line with this strong personalization of authority, the decision-making power in social groups is traditionally located with a single person in Indonesian society. Within families the father embodies the highest authority: all important decisions are made by him, and all family members have to obey the father figure (Mulder 1989:30).[3] This father figure, in turn, is obliged to take care of his subordinated group members (Mulder 1978:38). Strikingly, these paternalistic relations can be found at all levels of Indonesian society, ranging from the family to the President. Clearly, the differentiation of power in Indonesian society is very low.

The state, a proximate social institution, is closely involved in the development of the Indonesian economy. Since the New Order period, starting at the end of the 1960s, the Suharto government and its successors give economic development

---

[3] There are exceptions: in the Minangkabau culture on Sumatra for instance, the mother is the head of the family.

a 'prima donna status' (cf. Lubis 1993:47; Sato 1993:443; McIntyre 1992). State commitment to the development of the economy is propagated in a series of five-year plans, called *repelita*. These *repelita* among others involve state support to industrial sectors regarded as being of strategic importance. However, most strategic industries such as steel manufacturing and transport are dominated by state-owned companies or the military-industrial complex (Battacharya & Pangestu 1993). In practice, private firms cannot rely on any form of risk-sharing by a committed state. In fact, as an Indonesian scholar put it: 'there is a will but not a way'. Rather, the state-business relations are characterized by patronage practices. The most certain way to success is having the right relatives: entrepreneurs need to have political patrons who provide 'favours'. These favours include the provision of licences, contracts for state-financed projects, concessions and credit (Schwarz 1994; Hulst 1991:32, 35; Robison 1986:107, 212). These patrons belong to the bureaucratic and military élite that is governing the country, with, until 1998, President Suharto as the unchallenged leader at the top (Pangestu 1993:281; Robison 1986:211). The people with power have a remarkably high level of autonomy with respect to societal and other external pressures (McIntyre 1992; Pangestu 1993:281), and are involved in political as well as economic activities. Also, lower ranking state officials, even the street-level bureaucrats, have influence, notably over the small entrepreneurs. They have control over policy aspects such as how regulations are implemented, the granting of licences (required for virtually every industrial activity in Indonesia) and how industrial activities are monitored. Clearly, firms in Indonesia are confronted with the influence of a strong, dominant state.

The financial system of Indonesia is dominated by banks. By 1992, state-owned and privately-owned banks together represented 90 per cent of the gross assets of the Indonesian financial system (Nasution 1993:286). The national capital market is still in its infancy. For Indonesian firms, bank credit is the main source of external financing, both for long-term investment as well as for short-term working capital. Many of the private banks in the Indonesian financial sector are part of large business conglomerates (Price Waterhouse 1993). Although private banks have become more important in recent years due to deregulation and reforms, the state still has a strong control over the financial system. The state-owned commercial banks, which are led by the powerful Ministry of Finance, can be considered as 'arm's length extensions of the government bureaucracy' (Nasution 1993:290).[4]

The findings about the nature of key social institutions in Indonesia are incorporated in the matrix presented in Table 3.2. This leads to a profile of the expected characteristics of market organization in Indonesian industries.

The nature of the key social institutions in Indonesia and their combined influence on the development of inter-firm relations leads to the expectation that a low level of market organization has developed in the Indonesian industry. Relationships between firms are expected to have a predominantly short-term and non-cooperative character, because the nature of most social institutions is not very supportive of the development of long-term cooperative inter-firm relationships. In addition, the development of cooperation between non-family members is likely to be hindered because, apart from reputation, mechanisms to generate trust are absent or underdeveloped. Moreover, efforts to develop good relationships with powerful state officials is likely to prevail over the development of cooperative relations with business partners.

For the same reasons, intermediary organizations are not expected to play a role of importance in the coordination of transactions between firms, except if a state agency is involved that has assumed a coordinating role.

Business groups are not likely to be concerned with the coordination of links between autonomous firms. Rather, regarding the patronage relations between entrepreneurs and state officials, it is more likely that business groups have emerged

---

[4] The state bureaucracy in Indonesia has considerable influence on the financial system. For instance: officially the banks have to provide a minimum of 20 per cent of their total credit to small-scale enterprises (Nasution, 1993). For loans of 5 billion rupiah or more, a firm has to make an arrangement with a state-owned bank.

Table 3.2
The Nature of Key Social Institutions in Indonesia and the Expected Development of Market Organization Characteristics

		Market Organization Characteristics			
		The extent of long-term cooperative relationships between firms	The significance of intermediaries for the coordination of transactions	Stability, integration, and scope of business groups	Dependence of cooperative relations on personal ties
Background Social Institutions	Low level of trust between non-kin	−	−	−	+
	Low level of commitment and loyalty to collectives beyond the (extended) family	−	−	−	+
	High level of individualism beyond the extended family	−	−	−	
	Low level of formalization and depersonalization of authority relations				+
	Low differentiation of authority roles				+
Proximate Social Institutions	High business dependence on a strong state	−	−	−	
	Low state commitment	−	−	−	
	Credit-based financial system	+	+	+	

that revolve around individuals or families with good relations in the political sphere.

Inter-firm relations are expected to be based either on personal ties or on family ties. In family ties it is social control and in personal relations the experiences with people over time that substitute for the constrained Indonesian legal system as a mechanism of generating trust. In addition, the low level of loyalty to collectives beyond people's own micro society is likely to enforce the reliance on inter-firm ties based on direct, personal experiences. The development of personalistic inter-firm relations is further enhanced by the remaining two background social institutions. The high level of centralization and personalization of authority in Indonesian society combined with a low level of formalization of authority roles mean that decisions of any importance are made by the highest manager or owner of the firm. This implies that this owner or manager will be personally involved in inter-firm relations of any importance, and also that they will be reluctant to develop cooperative inter-firm relations that involve the sharing of authority over specific activities with business partners.

As can be seen, the influence of the credit-based financial system diverges from the other social institutions. However, regarding the strong influence of the state in the allocation of credit to firms, the influence of the state on the development of inter-firm relations is likely to prevail over that of the financial system. In addition, many firms have to rely on sources such as family capital or the informal circuit instead of official bank loans to meet their capital needs. This limits the positive influence of the credit-based financial system in the development of cooperative inter-firm relations.

The Indonesian *Jamu* Industry[5]

Before discussing the market organization characteristics in the *jamu* industry, we will introduce this genuine Indonesian

---

[5] The data sources used in this section are: our interviews with owners and managers of *Jamu* companies (1994–95), and with Dr. Djoko Hargono (Head of the Traditional Medicine Supervision Directorate, Ministry of Health), as well as a number of articles by Johannes Simbolon in the *Jakarta Post* (30 October 1994), and the Ph.D. thesis of Roy Jordaan (1985).

industry first. *Jamu* is the Javanese name for a wide range of herbal medicines. It can be used as a cure for several ailments, but people also use it as an energy stimulant, health maintainer, cosmetic or aphrodisiac. The *jamu* industry has developed on the basis of traditional knowledge about the healing power of herbs and both the wide variety and availability of this raw material in Indonesia. In earlier days, the recipes for *jamu* were secret and only shared among medicine men and royal families. Nowadays, there are thousands of street vendors (*warung kaki lima*) and shops (*toko*) that sell either industrially produced or home-made *jamu*. In addition, traditionally dressed women from poor areas in central Java hawk *jamu gendong*: a drink of several home-made herbal extracts that are mixed on the spot.

The *jamu* industry is relatively small but also genuinely Indonesian. In contrast to many other industrial sectors, such as pharmaceuticals and car assembling, no foreign firms are involved. Most firms in this sector are located on Java, where also a vast majority of the more than 200 million Indonesians live. In addition, all large- and some medium-sized *jamu* producers have an office in Jakarta. Although this industry was not taken very seriously earlier, at present it is receiving more attention. About 176 *jamu*-producing companies were registered in 1976. By 1994, this number had increased to more than 468, although just 14 large *jamu* firms dominate the market for pre-packed *jamu*. The large *jamu* firms in Indonesia employ hundreds of people and some even have more than one thousand employees. A few firms export their products to countries such as Malaysia, Taiwan and Saudi Arabia. Most *jamu*-producing firms are owned by either Javanese (*pribumi*), Sino-Javanese (*peranakan*) or Chinese (*totok*) Indonesians. The history of most firms reveals that they were set up by women who were able to make *jamu*, after which their children continued and expanded the business.

Since 1963, the Indonesian government has been involved in the *jamu* industry. The Directorate for Traditional Medicine Supervision of the Ministry of Health exercises control over this industry by, among others, issuing licences for *jamu* production and posing both quality and safety requirements.

Strikingly, the role of the Indonesian government in the *jamu* industry is quite ambiguous. On the one hand, it is very useful for firm owners to have access to a political patron who can help, for instance, in obtaining important licences. However, on the other hand, the government leaves the industry largely on its own. Because the *jamu* industry is not regarded as strategically important by the government, except from paying lip service no clear policy has been developed to stimulate its development.

The essence of producing *jamu* is mixing the right varieties of herb in the right amounts. Figure 3.1 provides an overview of the *jamu* supply chain, including the major activities and actors involved.

Figure 3.1
Activities and Actors in the *Jamu* Industry

Flow of activities ———→					
Growing herbs	Collecting the herbs	Washing, drying, cutting and processing the herbs	Mixing the herbs (in a pure, extracted or powder form), and packaging the resulting *jamu*	Distributing the *jamu* over Indonesia, export	Retailing the *jamu*

Firms involved					
Farmers	Herb collectors *Jamu* producers	Herb collectors *Jamu* producers	*Jamu* producers	Distributors, agents or wholesalers *Jamu* producers	Retailers

Thousands of small-scale farmers grow herbs for the *jamu* industry. Herb collectors (merchants) buy herbs from them and sell it, in bulk, to the *jamu*-producing companies. Like the farmers, these herb collectors are often small family firms. Strikingly, backward integration into growing or collecting herbs does not occur among the *jamu*-producing companies. There are three major reasons for this. First, herb growing is an agricultural activity involving the risks of fairly unpredictable harvests due to uncontrollable factors such as plant diseases, floods and rainfall. For the *jamu*-producing companies, it is advantageous that the farmers form a buffer against these risks. Second, the farms are small family businesses in which the members work long days for small returns. It would be hard for industrial firms to compete against these peasants. Third, the *jamu*-producing companies prefer to deal with herb merchants because they manage an extensive network of small farmers and bear the risk of damage until the herb is sold. On the contrary, the *jamu*-producing companies prefer to keep full control over all the steps involved in the actual production of *jamu*, so cooperative options such as outsourcing are rejected. In the *jamu* production process, herbs are either crushed, cut or extracted, mixed according to a secret recipe and then turned into pills, capsules, drinks, etc. The resulting *jamu* products are packed in bottles, sachets or boxes. Most *jamu*-producing companies keep the distribution of *jamu* under their own control. It is regarded as a crucial activity: a way to keep in touch with the market and a way to be sure that no distributor would pass important information to competitors. *Jamu* firms that cannot afford their own distribution system make use of multiple channels: they distribute their *jamu* to salespeople in the area near their factories and also make use of independent agents and distributors to enhance their geographical scope at reasonable costs. Finally, *jamu* is sold to consumers through many thousands of small kiosks, *toko* (small shops), supermarkets and street vendors.

The Market Organization in the *Jamu* Industry

This section uses the four market organization characteristics identified earlier in this chapter to describe the organization of inter-firm relationships in the Indonesian *jamu* industry. The findings are based on a series of in-depth interviews with the owners and managers from eight major *jamu*-producing firms. Additional information was obtained from interviews with officials from government and semi-governmental organizations, and with several scholars and management consultants. The interview protocol for the *jamu* firms was developed in collaboration with Indonesian scholars at the management institute PPM and further refined in three pilot studies at pharmaceutical firms in Jakarta. The interview results were fed back to the respondents, which led to minor changes made on the basis of their comments.

The relationships between *jamu*-producing companies, their suppliers (the herb collectors) and their customers (independent distributors, retailers and street vendors) have long-term nature. Most owners or managers of *jamu*-producing companies mentioned that they have been doing business with these supply chain partners for more than 10 years. Often, they have known these partners since the establishment of their firm. Despite this long-term orientation found at the *jamu*-producing companies, the respondents stated that the decision to do business with a particular supplier depends primarily on the price–quality mix offered. The *jamu*-producing companies have a strong bargaining position vis-à-vis the herb collectors because they can choose from many small firms that are involved in herb trading. Moreover, if necessary, the *jamu*-producing companies import herbs from other countries. By taking a closer look at these market relationships, it becomes clear that *jamu*-producing companies usually have long-term relations with a group of about ten to twenty herb collectors. For every particular transaction (generally the purchase of batches of different herb varieties by the *jamu*-producing company), the supplier who offers the best price–quality mix is selected to provide the main deliveries. Strikingly, the other in-group suppliers are then kept alive with smaller orders for herb deliveries. This arrangement seems to be a sort of compromise between either spot-market or long-term cooperative relationships. Strikingly, the long-term nature of the relations is grounded on paternalistic motives. All respondents involved expressed that they have 'a social responsibility' with respect to the small firms, which would need support and directions from the large *jamu*-producing companies to function well. This intermediate system of market relationships has clear benefits for the *jamu*-producing companies. This type of relationship is less labour intensive and less uncertain than a spot-market relationship, as the *jamu*-producing companies do not have to look for new suppliers constantly. Moreover, the prices for the herbs remain competitive and the supply of a range of different herbs is more certain. The *jamu*-producing companies are also in the position to refuse herbs that appear to be of poor quality, when delivered to the factory, because they can quickly switch to another (known) supplier. Despite their long-term duration, these relationships also have a clear spot-market nature given the lack of information-sharing, risk-sharing and shared activities, and the importance of price–quality deliberations. Most respondents of *jamu* firms explained the absence of cooperative relationships in the *jamu* industry by saying that, according to them, the industry was not ready for it yet. In fact, they recognized possible benefits of more cooperative buyer-supplier relationships, but they found that it was too early to invest in such relationships.

The relationships between *jamu*-producing companies with distributors and/or retailers are similar in nature. A long-term but straightforward relationship is preferred where the information exchange is mainly concerned with prices, qualities and quantities. In addition, *jamu* firms provide support and guidance to small shops and salespeople that sell their products. This includes short-term credits and guidelines about *jamu* storage and preparation. Usually, the very poor street salespeople are provided with utensils such as mugs and spoons, and in some cases the *jamu* firms organize transportation between their villages and the big cities on festive days.

Three intermediary organizations are active in the *jamu* industry: an industry association, a semi-governmental organization and a state agency. The official industry association for *jamu* producers is GP *Jamu*. Membership is compulsory, and this organization is supposed to promote the common interests of the *jamu* industry. A few times a year the Chairman of this association invites the owners of *jamu* firms to meetings to discuss the developments in their industry. Most respondents, however, view this association as a tool of the government '*to present its latest regulations for this industry*'. Kadin is the semi-governmental organization that is the official 'peak organization' of all the different industry associations in Indonesia. This organization has direct contact with the government but is regarded by the respondents as being very remote from what really happens in the *jamu* industry. Finally, the state agency involved in the *jamu* industry is the Directorate of Traditional Medicine Control of the Ministry of Health. This Directorate aims to guide the development of the *jamu* industry through regulations, instructions and monitoring the industry. However, a clear policy (i.e., objectives and means) to develop this industry is lacking. Some respondents noted that they did not really need the services of this department, but others demonstrated that they had very good contacts with this state agency. However, it became clear that this directorate played no facilitating or coordinating role with respect to inter-firm relationships. We have also checked the possible role of banks as intermediaries between firms. The owners and managers of *jamu*-producing companies explained that they do business with banks but that these organizations just provide loans.

Most *jamu* firms are part of business groups with a con-glomerate structure. Like most other business groups in Indonesia, they are strongly diversified into several unrelated industries. An owner of a *jamu*-producing company legiti-mized this high level of diversification with the saying: 'Never put all your eggs in one basket'. The respondents explained that *jamu*-producing companies prefer to spread their risks because there are both opportunities as well as uncertainties for entrepreneurs in Indonesia. This is due to the combination of a rapidly developing economy and the unpredictable behaviour of the government with respect to Indonesian indus-try. It is always uncertain which industry is most attractive to invest in, except if one has good relations with powerful state representatives.

The business groups involved in the *jamu* industry showed a remarkable stability combined with growth: new activities were added while none were sold or turned down. In short, we found that most firms in the *jamu* industry are part of relatively small but stable business groups that are loosely integrated and have a broad scope. These small conglomerates, owned by one person, a family, or a group of investors, are strongly self-reliant. They do not function as a coordinating network for autonomous firms.

Reputation and family ties are important bases of trust on which *jamu*-producing companies build their inter-firm relations. The importance of reputation was illustrated by an owner of a *jamu*-producing company who said: 'The relationship depends on trustworthiness ... we first try things out and then go further'. The other possible bases of trust—friendship, religion and ethnicity—were said to be irrelevant. Questions about the importance of family ties in inter-firm relations yielded evasive answers. However, our observations, informal talks, and interviews with scholars and consultants showed that family ties can be considered relevant in generating trust in inter-firm relationships as well. Dealing with family members such as sons, uncles and nephews, provides firm owners with some degree of certainty based on social control. Questions about the role of ethnicity in inter-firm relations also yielded evasive answers from the respondents. They explained that ethnicity is a sensitive issue in Indonesia and that it was not an important basis in generating trust in vertical inter-firm relations.

In sum, the results of our analysis of the market organization in the *jamu* industry show that long-term relations in this industry are common, but also that these relations are not cooperative in nature. These relationships combine spot-market characteristics and strong paternalistic elements: the maximum emphasis is on price–quality deliberations, while *jamu* firms to some degree take care of the survival of their suppliers and street salespeople. Intermediary organizations are present in the *jamu* industry, but they play no role in coordinating transactions. Most large *jamu* firms are part of conglomerate type business groups, which are not involved in the coordination of activities between independent firms. Finally, personal ties and kinship are considered important bases of the vertical relations between the firms in the *jamu* industry.

Conclusions

The market organization characteristics of the *jamu* industry reflect the mutually reinforcing nature of three key social institutions: authority, trust and the state. The high degree of

84   Martijn F.L. Rademakers and Jos R. van Valkengoed

centralization and personalization of authority in Indonesian
society apparently does legitimize the paternalistic behaviour
of *jamu* firms towards their weaker business partners. Since the
father figure (i.e., the *jamu* firm) makes all important decisions
in these relations but is also obliged to take care of his subordinates (i.e., herb suppliers and street vendors), the inter-
firm relationships involved are long-term but not cooperative
in nature. In addition, trust between non-kin in Indonesia is
largely based on personal ties, which goes well with the inher-
ently personal nature of paternalism in inter-firm relations.
Finally, paternalistic inter-firm relations have a chance to
emerge in an environment where spot-market relations are
considered impractical and the development of cooperative
relationships has no priority because it is more relevant for
firm owners to assure support from political patrons.

Strikingly, the market organization in the *jamu* industry
largely corresponds with the characteristics of the centrifugal
business systems type (Tam 1990; Whitley 1994a). The characteristics of this ideal type are: high isolation of firms, high
diversity of activities when large, low importance of private
intermediaries and high importance of personal inter-firm
connections. This business systems type is likely to emerge in
societies with low levels of institutionalized trust and weak
institutional mechanisms for managing market relations and
economic disputes (Whitley 1994a:173). This is much in line
with our findings about the Indonesian *jamu* industry and its
institutional environment. It is intriguing that, according to
Tam (1990), the centrifugal business system is exemplified by
the so-called Chinese family businesses. On the one hand, this
is remarkable because not only Chinese Indonesians, but also
Sino-Javanese and Javanese families are involved in the *jamu*
industry. However, on the other hand, the institutional environment in which Indonesian firms are embedded is
favourable for the development of this particular mode of
organization. Seen from this perspective, it is not very striking
that inter-firm relations resemble many characteristics of the
centrifugal business systems type.

Finally, industry-specific features may have also played a role
in the development of the market organization characteristics

in the *jamu* industry. Possible influences mentioned in the literature include technological complexity and the asset specificity of transactions (Willamson 1985; Smitka 1991). The *jamu* industry, like most of Indonesia's private industries, is involved in low-tech production and is capital extensive. However, it is not likely that these features would hinder the development of cooperative relations between firms. Rather, some owners and managers of *jamu* firms said that inter-firm cooperation would be preferable: vertical cooperation is needed to enhance product quality and horizontal cooperation in fundamental research is needed to develop more sophisticated *jamu* varieties. However, they find that the conditions are not yet suitable to initiate such relations. Aspects such as low trust between non-kin, uncertainties in the political sphere and the lack of skills among their suppliers and customers are considered as barriers to cooperation, rather than levels of asset specificity and technological complexity. It can be noted, however, that the lack of skills among their business partners helps to legitimize the paternalistic behaviour of *jamu* firms. Moreover, this industry-specific feature and the social institution authority are likely to enhance each other's influence on how inter-firm relations have been structured.

The market organization characteristics found in the *jamu* industry correspond remarkably well with the expectations drawn from the matrix constructed on the basis of business systems studies in East Asia and Europe. This demonstrates the relevance of taking into account the nationally distinct institutional context of an industry in the analysis of inter-firm relations. Despite this relevance, a bias towards deterministic applications of the framework should be avoided. Notably, the matrix combining market organization characteristics and key social institutions is limited, in the sense that it is suitable to generate broad expectations but not to make detailed predictions or prescriptions.

The market organization framework appeared to be a practical point of reference in our field study. It provided sufficient focus to avoid the risk of getting lost, while enough conceptual space was left to discover unanticipated features of the inter-firm relations under investigation. Moreover, the framework proved to be useful in a country such as Indonesia, where research is often regarded as a suspicious activity and where secondary data sources are very scarce or not available at all.

This chapter has drawn the market organization framework from the business systems approach and developed it further by interpreting and explicating its key notions. However, as a matter of learning by doing, some concepts may be developed further, as is the case with the social institution 'level of individualism versus collectivism' in the framework (see p. 69). This concept might benefit from further discussions with respect to the suitable level of analysis (cf. Nishida and Redding 1992:256). The same is true for possible connections between social institutions, such as 'mechanisms to generate trust' and 'the level of collectivism' in a society, and between 'the role of the state' and 'the financial system'. Future research would be helpful to shed more light on these issues.

Finally, we have found that the relations of both Javanese and Sino-Javanese *jamu* firms reflect Chinese family business characteristics. The question is whether this is also the case in other Indonesian industries and in other South-east Asian countries, such as Malaysia and the Philippines. Clearly, this calls for further business systems research in South-east Asia.

4

Business Systems and Sector Dynamics: The Case of the Malaysian Auto Industry

Peter Wad

Analyzing East Asian economic development and industrialization, neoclassical theorists have argued in favour of a market mechanism, with the World Bank taking a market-friendly approach, while statist explanations point to political governance of market forces, with neostatist theory emphasizing state–business interdependence (Weiss 1995) or embedded autonomy (Evans 1995). A third business system approach is presented by Richard Whitley, focusing on the diversity of economic organizations and institutional contexts in East Asia (Japan, Korea, and the overseas Chinese in Hong Kong and Taiwan).

Aiming for comparative analysis of economic organization in general (Whitley 1990, 1994a) and having been applied to the study of East Asia, North America and Europe (Whitley 1990, 1992a, 1992b, 1996c), the business system approach holds promise of a framework for the study of the second generation of industrializing countries in East Asia, i.e., Malaysia, Thailand and Indonesia, and developing business systems in general. These cases might simultaneously be used to test and revise Whitley's framework, addressing societies and nation-states that are culturally much more heterogeneous than

Japan, South Korea and Taiwan, and that are developing under different international conditions than these societies.

Taking the Malaysian automotive industry as its focal empirical point, this chapter intends to critically assess the business system approach in order to improve understanding of Malaysian industrialization and business dynamics. The question is whether the business system approach provides an appropriate knowledge-enhancing framework for the interpretation of post-colonial Malaysian economic and business transformations, or does it need to be revised, extended or rejected as a relevant analytical tool addressing the complexities of industrializing Malaysia?

This chapter starts with a critique of the business system approach, followed by a proposal for a dynamic sector or cluster business approach, analyzing the interplay between units at various levels (enterprise, industry, sector or cluster and macro) and systems (ethnic, national and international). This dynamic framework is applied to the changing Malaysian auto industry, which is described and assessed as a cluster business system. The problem area of explanation is then addressed, questioning the explanatory power of the institutional, the business logic and the international framework in relation to the evolution of the Malaysian auto industry and its potential as a mode for a national business system, with conclusions at end the chapter.

A Critical Assessment of the Business System Approach

The Business System Approach

Criticizing mainstream economic approaches for neglecting productive enterprises as economic actors in market economies, Whitley (1987:126) attacked neoclassical economics as well as Marxist political economics while rejecting the new institutional economics on hierarchy-markets, based on transaction–cost rationalism (Coase 1937; Williamson 1975). Inspired by DiMaggio and Powell (1983) in general and Hamilton and Biggart (1988) in particular on East Asian business organizations, Whitley coined the concept of business systems, grounding empirically his theory on three East Asian hierarchy-market configurations, which represented clear-cut constructs (Whitley 1992a, 1994a:178). Being particular business systems they, too, turned out to be stable, resilient systems even within a changing and turbulent international economic context (Whitley 1996b)—at least until the East Asian financial crisis of 1997.

By integrating economic, cultural and political institutions Whitley constructed an explanatory model of hierarchy-market configurations that went beyond both transaction cost analysis and Hamilton and Biggard's authority explanation. Positioning himself as a new institutional sociologist, he shares an epistemological interest in contextual explanations, or 'a middle-level analysis', as Hamilton and Biggart (1988:210) advocated, rejecting both a narrow efficiency explanation and a general cultural explanation. He also makes use of concepts and approaches familiar to the broader paradigm of 'new economic sociology' (Granovetter and Swedberg 1992), which contends that economic activities are social activities, that economic activities are socially situated and that economic institutions are social constructions.

However, Whitley elaborates neither his understanding of economic development nor his concept of business system effectiveness. He presumes that he is dealing with successful economic systems (for a critical assessment of the so-called East Asian miracle before the crisis of 1997, see Krugman 1994; and for a critical assessment of South Korea, see Dieter Ernst's chapter in this book). Like many other economic sociologists and economists, Whitley thereby abstains from bridging sociological and economic analysis and performing a much-needed integration of sociological and economic analysis of business activities (Ingham 1996).

Conceptual Issues

One of Whitley's crucial contributions to economic sociological thinking is that he combines the two spheres of hierarchy (organization) and market (relations between buyers and sellers, producers and customers in terms of firms) into one concept:

business system, thereby contrasting with neoinstitutional economists, who explain hierarchies, markets and quasi-markets by transaction cost factors.

Whitley defines business systems as 'relatively cohesive and stable ways of ordering firm-market relationships that develop interdependently with dominant social institutions' (Whitley 1994a:175), adding sometimes the criterion that they have 'developed, and remain, effective in particular and separate institutional contexts, typically within the nation-state' (Whitley 1992b). However, in spite of the lack of analysis of 'business system effectiveness' the measurement of effectiveness must be placed in a context following the logic of Whitley's approach.

The key characteristics of a business system are provided by three factors: the nature of the firm, the market relations and the system of authoritative coordination and control, eventually incorporating or adding a fourth factor: employment and personnel practice (Whitley 1992a:74 versus 80). While these three components appear rather consistently throughout Whitley's writings, their substance varies from time to time, leaving a few characteristics more important than others.

Concerning the core constituent element—the nature of the firm—a few factors recur (referring to Whitley 1996c:50 and, in parentheses, Whitley 1992a:80 respectively): (1) the scope of economic activity (diversity of activities and capabilities coordinated through authoritative communication, or homogeneity of expertise and similarity of activities); (2) the principal-agent aspect of capital (owner control or delegation of control to salaried managers); and (3) sharing of economic risks (isolation of economic actors from other organizations and agencies, or risk sharing through mutual dependence among actors). Termed 'the extent of decentralization of economic power to private interests' (compare Whitley 1994a:157 with Whitley 1996c:50) the dimension of state versus private ownership, which is an aspect of crucial importance in analyzing developing economies, disappears and reappears in Whitley's writings, but state owned enterprises are not out of reach in a business system perspective (lately Whitley has written extensively on East European business systems, e.g., Whitley and Czaban 1998).

The underlying problem hinges on how one defines the very unit of the business system (the firm as an economic actor) and demarcates the boundaries of the system (the firm-market configuration). Whitley turns to Penrose (1959), conceiving firms as 'collections of productive resources that are coordinated and transformed into services by administrative organizations which impart a cohesive character to the activities of the people working within them' (Whitley 1987:131). Hence, what makes a difference is neither financial nor legal relations but organizational control of economic resources, disqualifying by implication holding companies and investment trusts from being firms, when they do not make use of their capital leverage for controlling the management. Hereby, Whitley discloses two points. First, he confines his focus to productive enterprises (economic actors), excluding financial institutions while including trading companies. Second, he socializes his concept of law and overrules it by concepts of power and control, arguing that legally independent enterprises are one economic actor (firm) when they are controlled by the same person due to non-legal power (e.g., family network, as is the case among Chinese family business groups).

In practice, Whitley does not consistently apply this concept when he treats, e.g., the Chinese family business: the Chinese family business unit is specialized (Whitley 1990), diversified (when large, Whitley 1994a) or highly specialized in firms while medium in families (Whitley 1992a). If the Chinese family business, defined by control, the head of the family is in control without necessarily being the formal or legal owner of all companies; in consequence, the firm is normally diversified and not specialized, because the individual legal entities (business units) specialize in different undertakings in various sectors such as manufacturing, property, trade and finance. To complicate the matter: the holding company is normally the apex of the Chinese family business (Machado 1997). In sum, part of the problem regards the conceptualization of the firm as coordinator of economic resources: Is the firm the coordinator of labour resources (employer) and daily production (operational management) or the coordinator of investments (strategic management)?

The business system is also defined by its marker organization, i.e., modes of inter-firm coordination. Again, this presents problems in specifying these markets. Are they about coordination of goods, of capital, of labour, of information or of services? Is it goods in general or particular goods? What defines the market? Theoretically speaking, Whitley treats these questions in a vague manner, but in practice he externalizes capital, information and labour markets from the concept of business system, treating them as part of the institutional context (financial, labour and educational institutions).

Moreover, Whitley talks about vertical and horizontal market coordination. How is this to be understood: in terms, of authority (power to decide, i.e., one firm) or in terms of production linkages (supplier-customer, i.e., productive units)? The Korean *chaebol* is described as highly 'vertically coordinated' (Whitley 1990) and as lowly vertically integrated (Whitley 1992a). The first picture makes sense when we understand the concept in terms of production linkages within the firm (*chaebol*), while the second picture is realistic when we think in terms of production links between firms (between *chaebols*).

Finally, Whitley delimits the market to the typical national market (a market with the same currency), assuming that differences in product and process technology do not matter for organizing economic activities (an indirect attack on traditional contingency theory). According to Whitley, specific business systems cross industries and sectors within a particular institutional context, and this context is supposed to be primarily national, or even better, confined by the nation-state, indicating the hegemony of a particular and interdependent national cultural and political system.

The inconsistencies of Whitley's business system concept surface when he tries to establish a typology of specific business systems. In an early article Whitley outlines four business systems: the Japanese *kaisha* system, the Korean *chaebol* system, the Chinese family business system, and the United States system of diversified corporations (Whitley 1990). These four business systems can be differentiated by using variation in horizontal and vertical market organization. By implication, a theorist, adhering to the principle of simplicity or parsimonious explanations, would skip the other dimensions. Later on, Whitley describes five types of business systems

(Whitley 1994a:174) and then six major types (Whitley 1996b):
the (Italian/Danish) coordinated industrial districts, the
centrifugal (Chinese family business), the (Anglo-Saxon) partitioned system of diversified corporations, the (continental
European) collaborative system, the (post-Second World War
Japanese) state-coordinated system, and the (South Korean)
state-dependent system. Recently (Whitley 1998), he is back at
five types; fragmented, coordinated industrial districts, compartmentalized, collaborative and highly coordinated.

Beside adding types (the industrial district and the collaborative, both European) and eliminating types (merging the
state-coordinated and the state-dependent types) of business
systems, Whitley also changes the specification of the systems
in relation to their horizontal and vertical axes in such a way
that these factors co-vary in new ways. In fact, in 1996 the same
market organization is found among several types where that
criterion differentiated all (four) types in the earlier version
(Whitley 1990), making the low degree of horizontal or vertical
coordination held by the centrifugal, the partitioned and the
state-dependent systems, the medium degree by the coordinated industrial districts and the collaborative system, and the
high degree by the state-coordinated system. The only consistent classification regards the partitioned system in the United
States and the Japanese state-coordinated system, until Whitley
changed again in 1998.

In sum, Whitley deals with markets and business systems at
the national level, neither at the international or global level,
nor at the subnational, local or ethno-cultural level, or at the
industry or sector or cluster level. He gives primacy to
the institutional context and not to the defining criteria of the
firm: economic control of economic resources, within a local,
industry, sector, national or transnational setting. This decision follows from his explanatory logic, taking the institutional
context as the conditional set for the evolution of a distinct
business system, and the state as the primary conditional institution. However, some of his conceptual and typological problems relate to the same explanatory logic. Finally, using a
classification system with 16 dimensions with two values for
each dimension makes 2^{16} possibilities. Empirically, Whitley

has identified much fewer—not more than six types, posing questions: Are these types the effective business systems, and the rest the ineffective systems, and why? This is again a matter of theory, explaining the causes, conditions, constructions and consequences of particular types of business systems.

Explanatory Issues

The ongoing problems of defining firms and particular business systems in consistent ways indicate that Whitley's theoretical thinking is ambiguous—or they reflect Whitley's inductive research strategy. In fact, explaining the constitution and change of business systems opens for three theoretical logics:

- the internal logic of the business system, i.e., the internal dynamic between its core components: the nature of the firm, the market organization and the organization of work;
- the external conditioning or determination of the business system by its institutional context; and
- the dual of dialectical logic of internal and external conditions and the dynamics of the business system.

Whitley chooses mainly the second option, leaving the first and third ones more or less unexplored (Whitley 1992a:245, 1994a:167). This decision is paradoxical, considering Whitley's opening statement about bringing the firm back in as economic actor. Although Whitley speaks about coherence and interdependence among business system characteristics, he treats them as descriptive (dependent) aspects rather than explanatory (independent) factors (see the simplified diagrams of explanations, Whitley 1992a:Chapter 6).

Following the 'new institutionalist' sociology, Whitley argues that business systems are conditioned by two sets of institutions; background and proximate institutions. Background institutions covers political systems, economic systems, legitimacy and village and family organization, including trust between non-kin, loyalty to non-family collectivity, the importance of individualism, depersonalization and formalization of authority relations, differentiation of authority roles, reciprocity and distance and the scope of authority relations (Whitley 1992a:105,

1992b:20). Proximate institutions include; business autonomy or dependence on a strong and cohesive state, economic policy (developmentalist or not), the financial system (a capital market or a credit-based bank system), the education and training system (a unitary or dual system), the strength of trade unions and the private or public system of skill certification (Whitley 1992b:27). This institutional complexity might be simplified a bit, turning the background institutional set-up into three dimensions; trust and loyalty to non-kin people, individualism or collectivism and power or authority culture (cognition, norms and values regarding non-repressive power and politics), while proximate institutions may be reduced to four; the political and state system, the financial system, the educational and training system and the industrial relations system (see also Whitley 1992a:231).

Whitley's explanatory exercises are very complex and also rather unclear as he mixes historical and structural explanations. In a diachronic perspective, he makes use of an evolutionary model in which background institutions are understood as the cultural legacy of the past, while proximate institutions condition the formation of the business system during industrialization. In a synchronic perspective, he provides a static, institutional model in which background and proximate institutions directly (and indirectly too for background institutions) condition the particularity of the business system.

Addressing the evolution of contemporary business systems, Whitley seems to stick to a political theory of his own, making the political system and the state the core structure and agency during industrialization, shaping the state–business relations that influence the evolution of the business system. The political system during industrialization varies according to state autonomy and implementation capacity, commitment to state-led industrialization, state cohesion and executive power, and domination by an external elite (Whitley 1992a:141). The state–business relations are described in terms of business subordination, discretionary state intervention, state ownership of industry, state ownership of banks, state control of financial system, state promotion of heavy industry, state promotion of general trading companies, state control and suppression of organized labour and state support for agriculture and rural industry (Whitley 1992a:161). The factors of political system and state–business relations merge into a set of consequences in terms of: the importance of state approval and support, the bargaining power of firms, their dependence on banks, state risk sharing, the encouragement of large firms, dependence on general trading companies, the strength of organized labour and the urbanization and concentration of workers (Whitley 1992a:163). All these factors do affect some but not necessarily all characteristics of the business system.

The institutional approach, applied by Whitley, implies that changing an established, integrated business system requires change in core institutions—and the reverse: without such changes, no profound transformation of the business system will take place (Whitley 1992a:249). More specifically, Whitley seems, in fact, to hold that the transformation of contemporary business systems is conditioned primarily by changes in political systems and state-business relations.

This hypothesis may be influenced by the constituting empirical reality of Whitley's framework, the particularly successful East Asian market economies and their developmental states (Whitley 1992a). But it leaves several problems: (1) the problem of understanding other East Asian countries with large and influential sectors of foreign direct investment; (2) the problem of analyzing business in developing countries that takes place not necessarily within an established, national system, either because it is changing from one system to another, or it is internationalized and appears as a truncated, peripheral system, or it is still part of a local or regional economy; and (3) the problem of explaining institutional change.

Whitley boldly rejects the contemporary fashion of discourse of internationalization, globalization and convergence. He acknowledges that the world economy does change with the establishment of distinct global systems of coordination and competition, the internationalization of leading firms and managerial structures and practices. However, these changes will not become institutionalized unless strong cohesive international institutions arise and national institutions are weakened. The ongoing internationalization of firms and markets will not alter the characteristics of contemporary business systems (Whitley 1994b). And if changes are forced upon particular business systems as the International Monetary Fund is trying during the East Asian financial crisis, not least in South Korea, Whitley condemns the IMF for neglecting the particularities of the Korean business system and for pressurizing South Korea to accept elements of a different (United States) business system (in the Danish newspaper *Politiken*, 17 December and 21 December 1997).

The hard core of Whitley's theory is that:

- a strong interrelated institutional structure generates one particular business system, meaning, for example that if several countries have the same coherent institutional context, the same business system evolves in these countries;
- less integrated, pluralistic institutional contexts further several distinct and non-dominant business systems (or no business system at all);
- the prevalent institutional context of business systems is the nation-state because it has direct bearing on social practices (through the legal and administrative system) and influences key institutions (legal, financial, educational and industrial relations); and
- the internationalization of national economies is not supposed to change business systems as long as no international (political) institution subordinates national political institutions.

Methodologically speaking, Whitley's (1992a:211–15) explanatory model makes use of multiple causality, limited reversibility and non-exhaustive sets of explanatory factors. This means that the influence of background institutions is normally reinforced by proximate institutions, providing more than one factor of explanation for every core business system characteristic. Moreover, the relationship of causation does not correspond with correlation between variables. Finally, the explanation of a particular business system will often be incomplete, meaning that one might provide for necessary factors of explanation without being able to identify both sufficient explanatory factors or the whole set of sufficient and necessary explanatory factors.

In sum, Whitley does not claim to deliver the paramount explanation of patterns of effective coordination of economic activities, i.e., business systems and their variety. However, does his framework suffice for improving the understanding of business in developing economies such as Malaysia? Or is Whitley's approach either irrelevant, empirically flawed or theoretically deficient to the point of logic inconsistency and empirical invalidity?

The Dynamic Business System Approach

Reconsidering the Business System Approach

Although Whitley's conceptual and theoretical framework highlights important characteristics, diversity and institutional contexts of business systems among late industrializers and the industrialized countries, the foregoing review indicates that the business system approach also has theoretically inconsistencies and inappropriate delimitation for analyzing changing firm-market configurations in developing countries. Three problems of primary significance have been identified:

- Business systems are understood as stable systems of economic organization, but developing economies, constituted by firms and markets, might always be considered in a dual perspective of system stability and changing dynamics. How are business developments or transformations to be conceptualized and explained? How is the problem of structure-agency handled? How are we to move analytically to and from the micro-world of the firm, the macro level of the nation-state and the global level of the international economy? How do we handle business without systems, or systems without (effective) business?
- Business in developing countries is not necessarily incorporated into a national economy or confined to a (nation) state. Business activities are probably more or less internationalized, and/or they might be more or less localized and ethnicized, too. Taking the nation-state as the paramount

explanation (and holistic frame) may derail the very task of business system analysis from the very beginning.

- The institutional approach is overwhelmingly unilateral and structuralist in the sense that institutions condition the business system, while the actors of the business system— the firms—do not shape its own institutional context. A more reversible and pluralistic understanding of the interplay between social actors, existing, business systems and dynamic changes seems to be preferable, providing space for economic actors as agents of transformation and system maintenance. This would soften the deterministic flavour of the business system framework.

These challenges can probably be met, not necessarily by superseding the business system framework but by adhering to its very premise: taking firms serious as economic actors (Whitley 1987). Doing so requires elaborating the interplay between firms and markets at the industry and sector level without bypassing their institutional contexts, adding that firms are not only economic but social actors productively applying technology and generating goods and services. They are not only formed by and adapted to, but actively influence or reconstruct the very conditions for their economic activities. They act in terms of economic, cultural and political rationality—to repeat the claim of the new economic sociology.

The Sector Approach

Whitley's nation-state perspective has been challenged by Räsänen and Whipp (1992), who propose an alternative sector approach. They question the institutional approach when it excludes the technological and economic factors (Räsänen and Whipp 1992:53), proposing that the institutional, technological; and market conditions are combined in order to understand the formation of business systems.

They define a sector as 'an historical formation of complementary, interlinked and co-evolving business activities' (Räsänen and Whipp 1992:47–48). The sector concept differs from the industry concept, meaning a cluster of interrelated industries rather similar to, for example, Porter's cluster of industries (Räsänen and Whipp 1992: note 1). A sector is a contradictory entity of economic actors with different types of logic, making up a whole with or without a common business recipe. In the strong sense, a sector exists when four criteria are fulfilled: an extensive cluster of complementary and co-evolving economic activities in regular transactions; a social network connecting or coordinating the various parts of the cluster; a common and unifying cultural identity among the actors of the cluster; and a common political representation of the sector towards the state and international agencies (Räsänen and Whipp 1992:50).

These sector characteristics are compatible with the business system concept; the extensive cluster of economic activities parallels a vertical related market organization of production and value chains (upstreams and downstreams), the social network of the cluster overlaps with the constituent characteristics of the firm and the organized market (capital-management-operation, risk sharing and coordination of inter-firm relations), and the cultural identity of the actors relates to the cultural institutions, especially relations of trust. The sector concept does not include work organization, except as a form of technology, nor the institutional context, except for the factor of political representation. Thereby, it is not focusing on the national context in the same way as Whitley's business system approach.

Räsänen and Whipp's argument is also in line with the new economic sociology, stressing contradictory power and cognitive relations between economic actors: 'Sectors are historically evolving wholes of interrelated economic and political relationships. Sector-specific business recipes are the logics by which conflicting rationalities of the various actors are fused on the basis of changing relations of power within the sector'. (Räsänen and Whipp 1992:49). Moreover, the national business system evolves out of sector-specific business systems, formed by interacting firms: 'These processes of contestation between and inside the sectors constitute the dynamics through which the national business systems evolve' (Räsänen and Whipp 1992:49). Finally, Räsänen and Whipp agree indirectly and partly with Whitley's institutionalist approach by stressing the paramount importance of state-business relations and the historical process of business system formation, but they do also emphasize sector-specific aspects such as technology and market competition.

The proposed sector approach fits more or less with Whitley's framework. By focusing on the subsystem or sub-national market segments, they make use of technology and production linkages as integrating and differentiating criteria of firm-market configurations. By opening up for multiple and even conflicting sector recipes within and across sectors, they make it possible to understand the generation of system recipes as a process involving economic, political and cultural considerations. By downplaying external institutional factors (except nation-state power relations), they open up for exploring the explanatory opportunities related to the sector dynamics, a dynamic conditioned by firm, market and technology factors, or simply a system of production and distribution. They unlock the missing logic of Whitley's approach, i.e., the internal dynamic of the business system, loosening the deterministic grip of the institutional context.

Although Räsänen and Whipp argue that successful clusters of industries are interlinked by social, cultural and political networks and hegemonic business rationalities, they do not specify or explain how clusters of industries might be more or less internationalized, regionalized or globalized on the one hand, and culturally divided on the other hand, forming sub-state ethnic business systems or cross-state, regional ethnic business systems (such as the overseas Chinese business networks).

Business Systems versus Global Commodity Chains

Räsänen and Whipp do not address the question on internationalization, but this is done by the global commodity chain theory, which takes a sector approach to the understanding of international coordination of economic activities.

Based on a world-system theory perspective (Hopkins and Wallerstein 1986), Gereffi (Gereffi 1996a, 1996b; Gereffi and Korzeniewich 1994) contends that global commodity chains explain the various positions, characteristics and dynamics of economic sector activities in different countries. Acknowledging that institutional contexts condition the organization of economic activities and thereby further the evolution of similarities across commodity chains within the boundaries of a nation-state, Gereffi argues that:

> Sectoral analysis is a useful point of departure for studies of global capitalism. Rather than taking the nation-state as the basic unit of analysis in order to identify how domestic institutions shape the interplay between markets, policies, and national development outcomes, the premise of sectoral analysis is that fundamental differences exist between industries in terms of technology, competitive structures, and labour-intensity, and these play a primary role in explaining industrial governance structures and the strategies countries should pursue in order to succeed in global markets. (Gereffi 1996b:433–34)

Contrary to this view, Whitley argues that the international context is presently less constitutive for distinct business systems than their national context because of lack of dominant international institutions and, if dominant, they are generated by dominant nation states and their business systems. The resolution is simply to interpret global commodity chains in a business system perspective:

> From a business systems perspective, global commodity chains are particular ways of coordinating economic activities cross nationally which have become institutionalized in different industrial sectors. They are therefore analyzable in much the same way as any other system of economic coordination and control. (Whitley 1996a:422)

For Whitley, the point is that each global commodity chain (such as car production and distribution) shows a variety of cross-national coordination systems. This implies that there are several nationally contextualized business recipes within a global commodity chain, limiting the evolution of standard recipes for particular global commodity chains (except under special circumstances like the oil industry) (Whitley 1996a:422).

Without abandoning his institutional framework of explanation Whitley accepts that there might be an internal dynamic within particular market segments and related firms that can be described by the theory of global commodity chains:

> it seems, in practice, more realistic to focus on the processes by which different kinds of cross national coordination and control develop and change in specific sectors, and the institutional factors which help to explain this. Such studies would combine the dynamic and international concerns of the global commodity chain approach with the institutional and systemic focus in different business systems framework. (Whitley 1996a:422)

In fact, such a dynamic should comprise the internal logic of business systems (defined by specific product markets and their enterprises), which Whitley has bypassed more or less so far.

Although Whitley and Gereffi seem to disagree in significant ways, they do agree that their frameworks are complementary instead of competing of contradicting. They disagree primarily in two ways. First, Whitley sticks to a theory based on institutional and contextual explanation, while Gereffi prefers explanations within international industrial and transaction-cost theories. Second, Whitley focuses on the nation-state as the proper conditioning context of business system formation, while Gereffi turns to internationally linked sectors in terms of global commodity chains. This divergence implies that Whitley, in contrast to Gereffi, holds that there are normally multiple sector-specific recipes in internationalized sectors and only one national business recipe, provided that the national institutional context is coherent and resilient. In between Whitley and Gereffi, we find the position of Räsänen and Whipp, acknowledging the multiplicity of business recipes and their ongoing interaction, eventually and periodically dominated by particular recipes within particular sectors.

In sum, the institutional and the international approaches need to be combined, and the sector approach seems to fit both parties if revised handsomely.

The Dynamic Sector Business Approach

Revising Whitley's business system framework requires that the basic logic of the system approach be explained systematically and coherently. Confining the problem area to capitalist market economies, the rationality of a sector business system is assumed to be understood as a dynamic between a business context, structure and agency comprised of interdependent organizational systems, based on the control of three core resources of business organization: capital, labour and non-capital/labour (sociocultural business relations, such as trust). Moreover, it is assumed that the driving agency of the system is the capital organization (capital ownership and capital management), i.e., power relations based on capital ownership and its delegation or transformation into management author-ity and risk-sharing practices, implying that the core power-holders and actors are the owners and executive managers acting in accordance with certain institutions (common regula-tive, normative and cognitive understandings). Furthermore, it is assumed that the capital organization forms the commodity organization (management-labour relations) in order to add and accumulate value (the value chain) by way of producing commodities or services (the commodity chain). The produc-tion of the various commodities (goods, technical services, and financial services) are principal types of commodity organiza-tions (such as plants, consultancies and banks). Within the com-modity organization the control and deployment of labour, including knowledge and technology, turns the operative man-agement and collectives of employees into core powerholders. The market and market segments are constituted by the exis-tence and interaction of many capital and commodity organi-zations, whereby two other systems are constituted and sustained; the cluster organization, which is a coordinated system of goods, money, labour and services, based on the interfaces of the value and commodity chains, and hence with the suppliers, customers, financiers and servicers as the pri-mary powerholders, and the cultural organization of communi-cation and interpretation of information among powerholders of the capital, production and internally and externally, where the powerholders are the people in control of the means of business communication (language, media, codes, symbols and trust). Finally, it is assumed that the various actors only have incomplete knowledge and control, i.e., that the various organizations are more or less articulated into a coherent business organization and that there is not a perfect match but ongoing adaptations and conflicts between these organizational components, based on the interaction of the actors concerned (such as owners, managers, staff, workers, suppliers, customers, financiers, corporate communicators, trade unions, etc.). In sum, the structure and dynamic of the sector business system are constituted and changed in accordance with four more or less interdependent rationalities: capital valorisation (adding value), commodity technology, cluster opportunities (exchange of goods, services and money) and business identity and cultural meaning.

With regard to terms, the proposal is that Whitley's firm be redefined as a corporation in terms of capital relations, being the company in ultimate control by virtue of controlling the equity ownership of other companies. The 'nature of the firm' is delimited to mean the 'capital organization' of the corporation, i.e., capital-management relationships in terms of ownership control (owner-manager versus professional manager, private versus state, domestic versus foreign), investment pattern (specialized versus diversified) and risk-sharing (internal and external risk-sharing, private and state investments). Whitley's market organization is divided into the capital network (such as capital alliances, joint ventures and crossholding ownership), and the cluster organization in terms of vertical (primarily within the corporation) and horizontal (primarily between corporation) production and commodity chain upstream or downstream, plus the competitiveness of the market structure (monopoly, oligopoly or competition). 'Authority relations' are redefined into commodity (or work) organization, i.e., the operational management-labour relations in terms of technology level (intensity of labour, capital, information), production flexibility (scale and scope), management of labour (authoritarian versus cooperative individualistic versus collectivistic), employment (temporary versus regular, internal versus external labour flexibility) and industrial relations (unionized versus non-unionized, collective agreement versus no agreement; cooperation versus militant). Finally, the concept of a 'business recipe' is to be understood as the cultural organization of the corporation, meaning common understandings among business actors on how to do business with whom about what and why (strategies, principles of organization, corporate identity, basis of loyalty and trust relations). A sector business system is therefore constituted by several more or less integrated or coupled organizational systems and dynamics within a particular sector, defined as a competitive field of business corporations within the same commodity market segment.

The above revision converges partly with Whitley's latest attempt to outline the characteristics and typology of the institutional structuring of business systems (Whitley 1998) in the sense that he more clearly than before differentiates between ownership relations, interfirm relations and employment relations and furthermore also splits the ownership and inter-firm sets of relations integration within or across production chains. However, he does not yet understand these sets of relations as separate and interrelated organizational systems having more or less separate actors and dynamics.

Taking stock of the complexity of business organization and business institutions in the wake of the sector and global commodity chain discussion, my view is that it is better to assume from the outset that there might be several subsector (industry), sector and nationwide business recipes and business systems and that they might interact in ways that might or might not generate dominant sector, national and/or international business recipes.

The proposed analytical method is based on three assumptions. First, if a national business system exists it will also exists in core industries or sectors, contending that the argument does not necessary hold vice versa. Second, national business systems evolve from sector business systems that come to dominate the whole national economy. Third, such sector business systems are explained by the interplay between social actors located within their domestic business, institutional and international contexts.

In terms of methods, the analysis starts by selecting core industries or sectors and analyzes the specific industry or sector in order to identify dominant organizational actors, internal and external structures and business dynamics. The analysis addresses the question of characterizing the object of analysis by the three core component of the sector or cluster business system, acknowledging that they are supposed to have internal business interdependence and be situated within an external institutional context and related to international dynamics. If dominant processes, perceptions and patterns are revealed, a cluster of sector business system and recipe have been identified. Following the description, the evolution of this cluster system and recipe is explained and its momentum and its development potential within a particular institutional and international context is assessed. In so doing, three types of explanatory logic are considered:

- the rationality and dynamics of business system components (organizations);
- the institutional political and nation-state system, supplemented by legal, industrial relations, educational and sociocultural institutions, and
- the international aspects of business activities, not least their relations to transnational companies and international business networks.

Aiming for an understanding of changing business patterns in Malaysia, this analytical method prescribes that a specific core industry of high priority to economic development be selected. e.g., the auto industry, its core corporations, structures, dynamics and cluster linkages, institutional context and international aspects be assessed and, finally, the results be synthesized in the terms of the dynamic sector business approach. Then, the business, institutional and international dynamic that might sustain the present state of affairs or drive the auto business towards a new and distinct sector business logic is examined. Finally, the relationship between the industry, the auto cluster and other core industrial clusters within the particular developing economy must be analyzed, assessing interdependence between patterns and dynamics and an eventual overarching logic that might either generate a more encompassing and national business system or fragment business activities into divergent international business recipes or simply accumulate contradictions among business actors and relations, implying devolution and failure of the particular business organizations.

Due to limited space, this chapter does not address two important aspects. First, the question of corporate and sector business effectiveness (viability), where effectiveness is crudely understood as the market share (of particular firms or sectors), indicating the relative competitive (or protected) position in a given context. Second, the question of the impact on socioeconomic development (e.g., dynamic efficiency; see Wad 1996a, 1996b for discussion of this phenomenon in a capital-labour perspective).

The Dynamics of the Malaysian Auto Industry

The Evolution of the Malaysian Auto Industry

Following rising Malaysian regulation of car imports in the 1960s in line with the government's policy of import substitution industrialization, major western and Japanese auto transnational corporations transferred assembly activities to the Malaysia from 1967 onwards. Western auto makes dominated the market in 1960s, but this changed during the 1970s, as Japanese cars gained increasing market shares and came to dominate the market in the early 1980s.

In the late 1960s, the auto manufacturing transnational corporations relied on regionally well-established western auto traders (Inchcape Holdings, Wearne Brothers and Syarikat Fiat Distribution) or domestic Chinese-owned companies (Cycle & Carriage and Capital Motor). Holding the franchise for selling and producing the makes, sales companies forged capital alliances between sales companies and assemblers, making the assembly company a subsidiary of the sales company, or part of a holding company, including the sales company (Torii 1991). Transnational auto manufacturers only invested directly in assembling companies in two cases out of seven. In both cases, European auto transnational corporations participated; Peugeot in alliance with a Japanese auto transnational corporation (Mazda), and Volvo with domestic capital (Federal Auto Company).

In the early 1970s, US General Motors took control of the domestically owned assembly company, divesting again in 1980, whereby a joint venture of domestic Chinese capital (Oriental Holdings) and Japanese capital (Honda) acquired the company. This reflected a situation whereby Japanese cars became dominant on the Malaysian market, making domestic Chinese distributors and assemblers dominant market players in joint venture alliances with Japanese auto transnational corporations (Nissan-Tan Chong 1976, Toyota-UMW 1982 and Honda-Oriental Holdings). Western transnational corporations were relegated to secondary positions and only kept a stronger position in up-market segments (luxury cars).

During the early 1980s, transnational auto manufacturers changed their global sales and investment strategies. In Malaysia this implied that western companies sold assembly equity to domestic capital while Japanese companies formed joint ventures investing minority capital in domestically owned assembly companies. By 1986, nine out of 11 Malaysian auto assembly companies were majority controlled by domestic interests. Only the Volvo joint venture remained in business in the mid-1990s, while the company controlled by the Mazda-Peugeot ceased operation in 1989. By the end of the 1980s, two companies had closed down, and nearly all remaining assembly companies were joint ventures between domestic controlled sales companies and transnational auto manufacturers. Besides a new dominant auto manufacturer had appeared, based on an alliance of the Malaysian state and a Japanese auto transnational corporation.

Having outlined a strategy for increased localization of components and parts production, employment generation and local Malay ownership of and participation in the auto industry in the early 1970s, the government provided new licences in the mid-1970s in order to increase Bumi participation and expand local production. At the end of the 1970s, the industry was still characterized by low levels of local supply manufacturing and weak Malay capital involvement (Doner 1991).

Dissatisfied by unfulfilled targets, the Malaysian government decided to establish Malaysian car production within a broader strategy for heavy industrialization during the 1980s. Based on a conglomerate of state-owned enterprises, with HICOM being the holding company, the government in 1983 formed a joint venture, PROTON, with a Japanese auto transnational corporation (Mitsubishi) that had a weak market position in Malaysia. Mitsubishi, holding 30 per cent of share capital, would provide entrepreneurial and management expertise to start production of a Malaysian car by the mid-1980s, and then the Malaysians would take management control. A sales company, EON, was founded independently of PROTON, with HICOM as a minority shareholder and controlled by UMW, the domestic Chinese-owned corporation that held the Toyota franchise (Machado 1989/90). In the late 1980s, the national car company had captured about three-fourths of the passenger car market, but due to production and sales problems during the economic crisis in 1985–86 and the concomitant slump of the car market, the Japanese regained management control for the period 1988–93. The Malaysian government hoped that the Japanese might spur the export of Malaysian cars, while Mitsubishi accepted management responsibility, allowing it to pursue its complementation program for the ASEAN region (Hill and Lee 1994; Machado 1994). The Japanese renegotiated the deal between PROTON and EON, rectifying the very favourable deal EON had acquired in the mid-1980s. Meanwhile, UMW had been acquired by a Malaysian Bumiputera trust company, PNB, and HICOM had become the ultimate shareholder of EON.

In 1994, PROTON and DRB (a private Malay owned company) allied with a French auto transnational corporation (Citroën) for the production of a third Malaysian make. This paved the way for capital restructuring of the state-led auto industry. In 1995, HICOM was privatized and the controlling share acquired by DRB, owned and managed by Jahaya, a wealthy Malay with auto engineering experience and strong political connections. With DRB in control of HICOM, PROTON and EON came under managerial control of the same company and person. The new owner and top manager of PROTON wanted to promote technological upgrading, productivity improvements and high quality standards. Before he took over, he challenged Mitsubishi's resistance to producing a three-door hatchback by his auto company (Master-Carriage) and succeeded without much assistance (*Far Eastern Economic Review*, 2 May 1996). He continued to expand PROTON and started rationalizing the industry. A new PROTON City was launched. The top management of PROTON was changed. Vendors were threatened in order to slash prices. And a serious step to establish Malaysian controlled design capacity was taken with the acquisition of a British company (Lotus Sports Car). However, the situation changed dramatically with the death of Jahaya during a helicopter crash in March 1997, followed by the outbreak of the financial crisis in Malaysia from mid-1997, which also threatens the viability of the DRB-HICOM corporation (*Far Eastern Economic Review*, 19 February 1998).

Before these events took place, a second Malaysian car company, PERODUA, had been established in 1993 as a joint venture between a state-controlled enterprise, UMW, and another Japanese auto manufacturer (Daihatsu, affiliated with Toyota), and it had started production of small cheap cars in 1994. When another Malay businessman sought to acquire this successful company, controlled by PNB, a state fond in trust of the Malay community, the creating of a private Malay-owned and -managed auto industry by privatization was contested and postponed. Some critics feared that the 'juvelries' of Malay corporate capital went to a few individuals, leaving ordinary Malays with the crumbs (*Far Eastern Economic Review*, 30 January 1997).

During the rise of Malaysian car manufacturing, the transnational corporations did not resist the Malaysian policy. Instead, assemblers allied with transnational corporations moved up-market (luxury cars), scaled down or ceased operation. Besides, domestic auto components and parts producers multiplied, and some assemblers allied with transnational corporations turned into original equipment manufacturers for Japanese transnational corporations, while others took up sub-assembling or component manufacturing for PROTON, forging a new alliance between Chinese and Bumi-controlled corporations.

A Distinct Auto Sector Business System in the Making?

Does the evolution of a Malaysian auto industry then force us to talk about a transformation of the sector from one particular sector business system to another?

Let us first take a view of the transformation of the capital organization. During the 1970s, the auto industry of Malaysia changed from a western-controlled industry, involving foreign and domestic distributors and assemblers, into a Japanese-controlled and domestic Chinese-owned and -managed industry, both in sales and assembling activities. With the implementation of the two National Car projects during the 1980s and 1990s, the Malaysian car industry changed to a transnational corporation-allied state-dependent, private (PROTON) or collective/trustee (PERODUA) Malay-owned and -controlled manufacturing industry (adding the AMI majority owned by the Sime Darby corporation). In sum, the shifts in capital organization relate to dimensions of capital alliances and inter-cultural alliances, not to the formation of an auto industry independent of transnational corporations; at first, joint ventures of domestic manufacturers, distributors and auto transnational corporations were the preferred capital structure, and then, dominant western–Chinese and then Japanese–Chinese cooperation became replaced with dominant Japanese–Malay cooperation.

The commodity organization of Malaysian assembling companies was formed on the precondition of a small, protected and competitive market, providing for the same company to assemble several makes and many models. The business effectiveness was based on economies of scale in the transnational corporation home country and economy of scope in Malaysia. First, it moved from completely built-up car imports to domestic completely knocked-down assembling. Then it moved from completely knocked-down assembling to domestic manufacturing (local body stamping, die and engine making, local components and parts production). The third move into design and development is ongoing with the acquisition of the UK Lotus sports car manufacturer, but design capability has not yet been achieved, implying that makes and models carrying Malaysian brand names (PROTON, KANCIL, TIARA) are in fact modified transnational corporation designs.

With the initiation of the Malaysian car project (the PROTON company), market conditions were changed by state intervention, providing opportunities for mass production and economies of scale for the state-owned companies and worsen conditions of scope for other companies, intensified by the economic recession of the mid-1980s. This structural shift, initiated by the Malaysian state, was based on an expected rationalization of the industry into first monopoly and later oligopoly, and it was accompanied by the establishment of a more advanced work organization, including more capital-intensive production methods, mechanical assembling lines designed for teamwork, quality control circles and production on order. Moreover, recruitment of the labour force was ethnically based, providing employment and in-house training for Bumi employees. Finally, enterprise unionization (or no unionization) developed with the support of management, and industrial relations were settled in-house, providing wage and work conditions equal to or better than the auto industry in general.

The changing cluster organization of the Malaysian auto industry relates to its capital and commodity organization. Malaysian manufacturers have increased their sources of technology, and by establishing huge conglomerates (HICOM, PNB and Sime Darby), they are able to coordinate the commodity chain vertically as well as horizontally (within the same ethnic business community), aiming for just-in-time manufacturing with nearby located suppliers and customers. Besides, during the Jahaya interlude, the PROTON corporation moved towards establishing a strong financial business unit within the business group.

By the mid-1990s, global transnational corporation auto manufacturers still controlled design technology and partly management capability, delivering high-value core components and production machinery for Malaysian manufacturers while low-value components are manufactured by multiple local producers, divided into two ethnic business communities consisting of Malay and Chinese businesspeople respectively. And the industry moved again from monopoly-like market conditions to oligopoly-like conditions with three Bumi transnational manufacturers (PROTON, PERODUA and AMI) while several foreign transnational corporations (Toyota, Nissan, Volva, Honda, Daimler Benz) are staying in the market.

Finally, the cultural organization of the industry has changed at a general level. At first the corporations were divided in terms of foreign nationality, which again changed from western to Japanese nationality, and internally from Chinese to Malay ethnicity. In the end, dominant corporations were established with ethnic homogeneity in Bumi-owned companies and inter-firm cultural pluralism between these companies and their transnational corporation partners. Besides, intra-organiza-tional cultural pluralism evolved in Chinese controlled corpo-rations with Malay workforces. This cultural composition created different conditions for the construction of corporate culture, identity and loyalty. The reasoning on business expan-sion and upgrading has changed from diverse transnational corporation recipes via Chinese family business recipes to emerging Malay business understandings, based on ethnic Malay and UMNO party priorities (political business), imita-tion and adaptation of Japanese and Korean business recipes moving towards the understanding that Malay business should be a blend of best practices, irrespective of their origin, and recently even opening up to learning from the Chinese.

In sum, a new fragile sector business system evolved before the financial crisis broke out. It is dependent on the state and multiple transnational corporations and designed along the model of Japanese lean production, i.e., the most competitive recipe of the auto industry in the 1990s (Womark et al. 1990). It is formed as an ethnic (Bumi) business system, supported by the Bumi-controlled state and allied with transnational corporations while domestically competing with a Chinese business comm-unity. It achieved market dominance to the point of monopoly in targeted market segments, adding another state-owned Bumi auto manufacturer allied with another Japanese transnational corporation. However, the advanced principles of organization have yet to been fully implemented (cluster coordination), and when implemented by Malaysian management, they do not operate smoothly. They are to be carried out, not by company multi-skilled, experienced workers having facilitative managers and work station autonomy, but by authoritarian and ethnically based ways of mobilizing semi-skilled workers, generating a hybrid in technology and work organization (Rasiah 1996a). By chance, the paramount owner-manager of DRB-HICOM died before he could publicize how he would develop the industry in the long run or how he could reorganize the huge diversified conglomerate in practice. And the financial crisis emerged when this dominant corporation was beset with a leadership vacuum and conflicting interests trying to take over the conglomerate.

Can this emerging configuration be described in terms of Whitley's typology of business systems? Probably not. The *zaibatsu*-type presumes that the market is coordinated horizontally by general trading houses (*sogo soshas*), and they have not been viable in Malaysia. *Kaisha*-type business presumes that the dominant auto company (PROTON) is re-privatized into interlocking capital and directorships within a business group, which is currently against the privatization policy of the government. *Chaebol*-type business was possible due to the dominance of private auto companies and ongoing privatization on the one hand, and strong political business and state-business risk sharing for Bumi companies on the other hand (Gomez 1995, 1997). However, the very diversified investment strategy of *chaebols* is partly lacking, as is the strong state control and dirigism of private business (Rasiah, 1997). In the Malaysian auto industry, finally, the death and the financial crisis forced a return of state control of the dominant player while the second player was held by an ethnic trust fund, ultimately controlled by the state. Chinese-family business is indeed the counterpoint of Malay business, but the policy for the emerging Malay businesses is focused on large corporations (the prime minister required people to think big). Besides, the government faced enduring difficulties in creating viable small- and medium-sized companies— the prototype and underwood of Chinese family businesses.

No existing business system in East Asia fits the Malaysian auto business sector, but western types might go too, due to the Western colonial and post-colonial context of Malaysia. The Anglo-Saxon system with share capital dominance is not compatible with ethnically designed restructuring as it will make the

Malay-owned companies open for hostile (Chinese and trans-national corporation) acquisitions. The German system of corporate governance (state and social stakeholder cooperation) is also far from the Malaysian political culture, where labour and part of the business community are excluded at the outset. Finally, the industrial district business system is locally based and incompatible with a Malaysian society without strong local governments and local state-business cooperation for small- and medium-sized companies (except in a few Chinese-dominated areas).

In this way, it is possible to talk about an emerging distinct sector business system, depending on and allied with trans-national corporations, demonstrating effectiveness within a protected domestic market, but not yet viability (Japanese management recurs) and international competitiveness (a protected domestic market and subsidized exports). Whether it will develop into a distinct and effective system in domestic and global terms (international competitiveness) is probably too early to determine, and the answer depends on the understanding of the past evolution, the impact of the financial crisis 1997 onwards and the future dynamics within changing institutional and international contexts.

Explaining the Changing Malaysian Auto Business

In order to explain the character and changing forms of sector and national business systems, three interdependent types of logic of sector business dynamics have been outlined: the business logic (of capital, commodity, cluster and cultural organization), the institutional logic (of cultural, political, legal, educational and labour institutions) and the international logic (of global markets, commodity chains and international production networks). Whitley advocates the second type of explanation, so I will begin with that.

Institutional Explanations

The short history of the Malaysian auto industry provides evidence in favour of the institutional explanation, indicated by the significance of ethnic political and state power in conflict and cooperation with other domestic and foreign economic actors. The auto industry was transformed in line with the overall ethno-economic policy of the New Economic Policy and the strategy for heavy industrialization. Hence, explaining the changing auto industry calls for an explanation of the New Economic Policy, which provides the common ethno-political rationality and resources for the Malaysian Car Project.

In a business system perspective, post-colonial Malaysia before 1970 included three types of economic organization: a foreign (British)-owned sector of export manufacturing and wholesale trading companies, managed by agency houses; a Chinese family business system operating small- and medium-sized firms in the urban areas within manufacturing (retail) trade and services; and a subsistence and petty commodity sector of Malay peasants, farmers and fishermen. These partly interlocking and yet distinct economic systems evolved during British colonialism, which created a plantation and mining industry based on immigrant (Chinese and Indian) labour and a subsistence and petty commodity agricultural system operated by Malays. The British governed the multi-ethnic colony through indirect rule, leaving cultural issues for self-governance (Malay Sultanates; Chinese 'captains' and 'towkays'), and keeping national economic and labour affairs under central colonial administration with as little use of force as possible.

The Malaysian development policy changed dramatically after bloody ethnic riots in 1969. The Malay powerholders, organized in UMNO, achieved hegemonic state power, based on an enlarged inter-ethnic coalition. A New Economic Policy went for the eradication of poverty and restructuring of corporate ownership and employment in order to abolish the relationship between ethnicity and economic position. This implied that the workforce of domestic-market companies should change reflecting the ethnic composition of the population (55 per cent Bumis), that ownership relations should include at least 30 per cent of share capital for Bumis (predominantly Malays), and that a new Bumi Commercial and Industrial Community became established. The Industrial Coordination Act of 1976 provided the means (licensing,etc.) for implementing the New Economic Policy targets in the corporate sector, based on local resources or the domestic market. Export industries based on foreign direct investment had been privileged since the late 1960s and was further supported by the establishment of export processing zones since 1971.

With the New Economic Policy 1971 to 1990, the Malaysian state entered the market economy as a new economic player, intervening selectively in the dominant business activities controlled by Chinese family businesses and transnational corporations aiming towards the formation of a Bumiputera Commercial and Business Community. State-initiated heavy industrialization began in 1980 including transport equipment, steel and cement. Then, the government announced a Look East policy, taking Japan as the model of development, a policy for state-business cooperation (Malaysia Incorporated), a management policy (leadership by example) and a privatization program. The economic crisis of 1985–86 marked a watershed in Malaysian development policy. The Look East policy was downplayed, Malaysia Inc. was promoted, and state-business relations developed further with the liberalization and deregulation of private business from 1986 and the increased incentives for foreign direct investment independent of its nationality. Privatization was reconsidered and given higher priority, but it was not before the 1990s that privatization accelerated, creating wealthy Malay businesspeople in large numbers.

Hence, Whitley's new economic historical sociology makes sense in the way that the state and governing ethno-political groups managed to transform the ethno-economic structure of Malaysian society. However, it does not explain why the auto industry was singled out for New Economic Policy-intervention, why the government kept intervening even during the economic recession of 1985–86 but in general has deregulated foreign direct investment since then. Nor does it explain which kind of sector business system is emerging.

Business Logic

State intervention in the auto industry was conditioned by the failure of domestication and Bumi-equity participation in the privately owned auto business, controlled by transnational corporations and Chinese domestic capital. State-led capital restructuring with transnational corporation technology-transfer and management assistance was deemed to be necessary. It would not come about by itself or by way of market-friendly mechanisms, because these mechanisms operated against the entrance of new Bumi entrepreneurs. Why?

Torii's (1991) analysis of the Malaysian auto industry provides tentative answers. He argues that the auto industry in developing countries follows production stages of domestic cluster development: (1) import and sale of completely built-up cars (Malaysia 1896–1966); (2) assembly of completely knocked-down parts and domestication of parts production, subdivided into *(a)* parts replacement production (Malaysia 1967–78), *(b)* domestic original equipment manufacturing production (Malaysia 1979–), and *(c)* domestic original equipment manufacturing of core components (engines); (3) domestic production of materials for cars and components (not reached by Malaysia, except for rubber); and, (4) domestic design for car bodies and components (not reached by Malaysia).

Although such phase models are questionable, the fact is that the Chinese auto companies evolved along the same path as the Malaysian industry. They began as sales companies, linked up with the upcoming Japanese auto manufacturers and gained control of distribution during the 1970s, moved into assembling and controlled car assembly companies during the 1980s until PROTON took over after 1986, and finally they expanded into original equipment manufacturing production and assembly for PROTON and foreign auto manufacturers in the 1990s. The Chinese companies were family owned and managed but structured as joint ventures, adjusting to the New Economic Policy of Bumi minority participation and the business strategy of Japanese companies for minority equity participation.

Assuming that the lack of improvement for localization and equity restructuring was caused by the alliance between transnational corporations and Chinese capital, the option left for the government was to ally with a weaker auto transnational corporation that might be manageable by state agencies and would provide the technology and management needed. Mitsubishi was that kind of auto transnational corporation. After having formed the state–transnational corporation alliance, the

Malaysian car project was able to survive the economic crisis of the mid-1980s and even overtake Chinese family companies (UMW) as well as western controlled companies (AMI).

The government strategy proved partly right. Playing the weak transnational corporation card, the government surpassed tough competition and entrance deterrence of domestic Chinese family business, but the price to be paid was ongoing dependence on transnational corporations (e.g., the return to Japanese management of PROTON 1988–93), although this dependence was increasingly diversified.

Hence, the Malaysian auto industry changed due to established capital structures of the domestic auto industry, the production dynamics of the industry, the changing domestic market conditions and competition, shifting strategies of investment and technological cum organizational developments within the global car industry. The difference between the Malaysian industry and the known business systems of East Asia (Whitley's *kaishas* and *chaebols*) is that it is strongly interlinked with auto transnational corporations and constituted within rival ethno-economic business communities.

Completing the picture therefore requires looking into the international aspects of the car industry, not least in order to understand the options for the future development of the Malaysian auto industry beyond the state regulated domestic market.

The Global Position of the Malaysian Car Industry

The ultimate weakness of the whole Malaysian auto business is its dependence on huge auto transnational corporations and the globalization of the auto industry. The auto industry has been dominated for long by western and Japanese auto transnational corporations. In fact, South Korea has been the only country that has developed a dynamic national car industry that has competitive strength in export markets (Dicken 1992:304–6). Before 1997, Korea had three important car manufacturers: Hyundai (domestic capacity 1.5 million units), Daewoo and Kia (each with a domestic capacity around 1 million units), but a fourth, Samsung Motor, a subsidiary of the largest *chaebol* of South Korea, has planned production for 1998 with a capacity of 30,000 units (*Far Eastern Economic Review* 13 June 1996). Facing a sluggish domestic market and rising imports from Japan and the United States, all three Korean automakers turned to the Asian markets, with Hyundai and Daewoo focusing very much on India and Kia on Indonesia. In 1997, Kia faulted and is now under restructuring, with Hyundai and Samsung as competing bidders and Ford/Mazda holding a share in Kia large enough to influence the future ownership of the corporation.

Comparing Malaysian and South Korean automakers, Hyundai is the only Korean-majority owned car manufacturer that managed to form its own technology from many sources, to gain significant global market shares and invest directly in the industrial world (Canada) (Dicken 1992; Kim and Lee 1994). Similar to Malaysia, Mitsubishi has been Hyundai's joint venture partner with minority shares, providing the design for Hyundai's second car model. In the mid-1980s, Hyundai exported 300,000 units to North America, pursuing a strategy to outcompete Japanese cars in a narrow market segment through low pricing. However, at the end of the 1980s, Hyundai faced steep problems in North America due to a poor reputation caused by low-quality cars.

The Malaysian automakers have had a capacity well below the Korean ones, but they planned to expand very much with the accomplishment of the PROTON City. Malaysian PROTON seems to be developing along the Hyundai path, having the same Japanese partner and working towards diversified technology sourcing (Mitsubishi, Citröen and Lotus), while concentrating on the domestic market and then expanding to export markets. However, Malaysia will probably be forced to liberalize imports faster than Korea due to the World Trade Organization, reducing its local content requirement (45–60 per cent) and completely built-up quota at 5 per cent (*The Sun* 14 May 1996). The Malaysian motor traders' association held that Malaysian car exports will be dependent on the reduction of barriers to foreign exports to Malaysian (*The Sun* 14 May 1996). This might come true due to the present excess capacity of auto production worldwide, making car companies producing at 73 per cent of capacity in 1996 (*The Economist*

10 May 1997). The financial crisis and declining growth rates in Malaysia did at first reduce the queuing to buy a PROTON car and reduced the delivery date considerably.

The Malaysian Auto Industry: A Recipe for a National Business System in a Globalizing World?

The options for the development of a national business system in Malaysia are different from the conditions prevailing before and during the development and consolidation of the business systems of Japan, South Korea and Taiwan. In institutional and historical terms Malaysia has not been an isolated and socio-cultural homogeneous society. In market terms, post-colonial Malaysia has been an open economy to foreign investments and transnational corporations, combining a dual policy of import substitution and export promotion and creating a dual economy (Jomo and Edwards 1993). During Malaysia's forward leap to achieve industrial status by the year 2020, the world market will probably become more and more liberalized through the institution of the World Trade Organization, while the regional (Association of South East Asian Nations [ASEAN]) market might open up even faster, forcing the Malaysian auto industry to become more competitive at home as well as abroad.

The restructuring policy of the auto industry is being applied across the various industries and sectors. The Second Malaysian Master Plan 1996–2005 for the manufacturing sectors seems to outline an industry-cluster approach, inspired by Michael Porter's thinking (*Malaysian Industry*, April 1996): Malaysia is positioned in between the factor driven and the investment driven phase of national competitive development, and at the lower range of the value chain: assembly and original equipment manufacturing. The Master Plan proposes the creation of intensified links between industries to achieve a critical mass of inter-firm integration in order to lift up, thereby developing industries from being home-based world production centers to own brand manufacturing centres with ongoing technological innovation and development.

The industry-cluster strategy fits with the privatization strategy of picking a few outstanding Malay businessmen and making them Malay billionaires. The owner-manager of PROTON was one out of several Malay businessmen who were selected by the political powerholders (i.e., Mahathir and the former Minister of Finance, Daim Zainuddin) in order to create Malay millionaires in control of business groups that could achieve world-class standards (*Far Eastern Economic Review*, 21 December 1995). To name a few beside Jahaya (*Far Eastern Economic Review*, 21 December 1995; *Malaysian Industry*, May 1996): Halim Saad in charge of the Renong group focus on construction activities; Tajudin Ramli with the Technology Resources Industries in the telecommunication business and later buyer of Malaysian Airlines (MAS); and Mahathir's son, Mirzan, investing heavily in shipping and haulage with his KPB. Shamsuddin Kadir, owner of Sapura Holdings, bid for UMW and thereby for the controlling share of PERODUA (*Far Eastern Economic Review*, 30 January 1997), which however, did not mature. Many of these big Malay businessmen are now facing tremendous problems due to the financial crisis (*Far Eastern Economic Review*, 19 February 1998).

The political formation of a Bumi business elite has been named crony capitalism, creating Umnoputras businessmen instead of Bumiputras businessmen (*Far Eastern Economic Review*, 21 December 1995). Others point to the tight connections between political and business leaders (Gomez 1995, 1997; Gomez and Jomo 1997), the huge costs of the Bumi restructuring policy in general (Gomez 1995) and heavy industrialization policy with PROTON in particular (Jomo 1994b; Rasiah 1996b). Jesudason (1989) found that the New Economic Policy objective of a strong Bumi commercial community was accomplished to the point that it turned the prosperous Malaysian economy of the 1960s and 1970s into recession in the mid-1980s, escaping the trap only by liberalizing the economy for foreign direct investment to the benefit of the transnational corporations, but without concessions to the Chinese business community.

My contention is that the Bumi Commercial and Industrial Community policy of the New Economic Policy failed until the 1990s. At that point state intervention had transformed the transnational corporation–Chinese nexus to a Bumi–transnational corporations coalition, and privatization could succeed with the formation of an ethno-national Bumi business system, based on the development of selected sector business systems, united by the Malay political business community under the hegemony of UMNO, the coordinating role of the state, and links to various transnational corporations. The costs have been huge, but at least until 1997 the benefits were impressive in a global perspective in terms of socioeconomic development (eradication of mass poverty), near full employment and political stability (avoidance of ethnic violence and civil war). (Jesudason revised this argument in 1997, arguing that the Malay–Chinese inter-ethnic conflict during the 1990s became superseded by the shared interest for high growth and business cooperation.)

The Malaysian auto industry is a playing ground for the overall development strategy of ethno-economic restructuring and has been rather successful so for, subordinating or leveling the pre-existing domestic transnational corporation–Chinese-controlled car makers to minor market segments. No definite sector business system has evolved yet, but the overall political strategy for a business recipe is outlined: the creation of a Bumi business system, incorporating the best practices of domestic and foreign companies through joint ventures with multiple transnational corporations.

The future development of the auto sector business of Malaysia into a sector business system and a recipe for a national Malaysian business system depends on the three earlier delineated types of logic and dynamics. One scenario is that two transnational corporation-related ethno-business systems evolve (the Bumi political business system and the Chinese (less political) business system, both in alliances with transnational corporations. Another scenario is that the distinct domestic ethno-business systems interlink to form an inter-ethno-cultural Malaysian business system. The departure from a Japanese transnational corporation–Chinese auto business system seems irreversible, but the evolution of a multi-ethnic auto business system, incorporating Chinese business families in component manufacturing and distribution, presumes that a shared cultural identity develops among the Malay and Chinese business communities. This is not impossible, but it will probably take a very long time. In fact, it is assumed that it can be accomplished within the long-term strategy for Malaysia's industrialization: Vision 2020, which calls for Bangsa Malaysia, i.e., Malaysia of Malaysians (Mahathir 1991).

The financial crisis since 1997 might have turned a third scenario into a more likely outcome than before the crisis. That is the scenario in which the Malaysian ethno-business systems are subordinated to the global strategies of the dominant transnational corporations within the auto industry as well as other industries. However, it is too early to definitively assess the viability of the Malaysian auto industry.

Conclusion

The chapter has considered important contributions to the business system debate and then applied a dynamic sector business approach, based on a triple explanatory logic of business, institutions and international business actors (transnational corporation) aiming for an understanding of the changing Malaysian auto industry and its potential as a business recipe for the overall Malaysian economy.

In terms of theory and methods the business system approach revealed strengths and weaknesses. The approach took the debate on East Asian industrialization beyond the state-market contradiction, focusing instead on the characteristics of different modes of economic organization and the broader institutional context as explanatory devices. Neglecting the importance of the international dimension of business in developing countries, the approach is inappropriate for analyzing business in post-colonial societies, where foreign capital held strong positions, and it will also be inappropriate in the future due to increasing economic internationalization. Moreover, ignoring technology and production issues, the approach is unable to understand the industry and cluster specificity of industrialization and the types of internal business dynamics and logic formed by the interplay between organizing relations of capital, labour and non-capital/labour aspects.

Taking notice of the key strengths and weaknesses of the business system approach, a sector or cluster perspective was proposed in order to transform a rather static approach, although historically and sociologically informed, into a more dynamic approach. This revision opens for the integration of the international dimension and contributions from theories on, for example, the new international division of labour, global commodity chains and new competition theory. It also makes Malaysian business development more comprehensible as a developing business configuration composed of several and interacting ethno-economic systems and dynamics.

The auto industry has been selected as a core sector for Malaysian economic development. Analysis of the Malaysian auto industry disclosed transformational processes in ownership, management, industrial structure and economic organization within a period of three decades. An industry formerly dominated by western transnational corporations and then controlled by Japanese transnational corporations and Chinese has been transformed into a state-led private owned auto complex, allied with and dependent on Japanese transnational corporations. The strength and strategies of the key actors: the Malaysian government/state, the domestic Chinese family business and the transnational corporations, conditioned the transformational processes, influenced by technological factors and market trends. Moreover, chance, in the form of the recent death of the owner-manager of the dominant car corporation, added to the complexity of understanding, stalemating the development of a private Malay owner-managed auto empire. The financial crisis across some months later, and created a new situation for the political economy of Malaysia and its social actors.

Leaving the crisis aside, the Malaysian auto industry will increasingly face international competition at home and abroad, with Malaysian auto manufacturing capacity surpassing domestic market demand, rising liberalization of the home market and excess capacity in world auto manufacturing. Until now, only Korean automakers have managed to become world market players in a market dominated by western and Japanese auto transnational corporations. Malaysians are following the path of South Korean Hyundai, linking up with the same Japanese auto transnational corporation within an overall political economic framework inspired by and congruent with the Japanese trajectory. But such a strategy cannot be replicated under similar circumstances, nor is Malaysia's political economy and society similar to South Korea's.

A transnational corporation-dependent Malaysian sector business system has been in the making which again links up with other emerging sector business systems in the rapidly growing economy. The auto industry business recipe, initiated by the government, is consistent with the broader ethno-economic restructuring of the Malaysian economy from a system controlled by transnational corporations and Chinese into a Bumi-controlled and state-coordinated business system, based on selected alliances with transnational corporations. The government has succeeded, at great cost, in establishing state-owned companies in key industries, later to be privatized and formed into clusters of industries. Several outcomes are open, but the new Bumi political business network has come to stay. The ethno-economic business system of the past has been reproduced in the present, adding a Bumi business system in the making, strongly related to and supported by state power, and increasingly attracting Chinese businesspeople and companies.

In sum, the changing Malaysian auto industry indicates that state-led construction of a national business system challenges and is challenged by domestic and international forces, not least private domestic and transnational firms. In order to grasp this dynamic, Whitley's business system approach need to be expanded and made dynamic, incorporating a focus on internationally linked industrial clusters, internal business rationalities and diverse ethno-cultural institutions and actors. The regional financial crisis erupting during 1997 makes a dynamic and international analysis even more necessary.

5

Technology Management in the Korean Electronics Industry: What Factors Explain the Dynamics of Change?

Dieter Ernst

Probably the most important contribution of debates that centre on distinctive features of national business systems is that they have opened the door for a revisionist research agenda that allows movement beyond the popular convergence hypothesis of neoliberal economists.[1] In the business systems approach, firm organization and strategies are shaped by peculiar sets of institutions and hence are unlikely to converge.[2] In this view, nothing is predetermined about the impact of globalization. It is argued that distinct differences exist in how Japanese, United States, Korean and various European models of capitalism adapt to globalization and that these differences are especially pronounced when looking at individual firms.

---

[1] The neoliberal convergence hypothesis argues that, as firms face similar constraints, resulting from the spread of globalization, they will converge in their organization. A key assumption, which, however, remains implicit, is that convergence means convergence to the United States model of international production. For a widely quoted example of this neoliberal globalization doctrine, see Ohmae 1991. For a critique, see Berger and Dore 1996; Ernst 1996a, 1996b.

[2] '... [A] key task in organizational analysis is to understand how different kinds of business organization and economic rationalities develop and become effective in different institutional contexts.' (Whitley 1992a:1)

It is attractive to apply this concept to developing countries. A focus on firm organization and strategies could help in moving beyond the old debate on whether the market or the government should play the leading role in economic development.[3] Yet, the concept of business systems has also important weaknesses that need to be made explicit. To paraphrase Peer Hull Kristensen (1992:117), much of the debate has focused on 'ideal or stereotypes of business systems', neglecting the dynamics of change. Whitley (1992a:23–24) acknowledges that changes occur. In his view, 'such changes are relatively slow' and hence do not deserve priority attention.[4]

This proposition does not square well with the findings of research based on the assumptions of evolutionary economics: the speed of change in economic institutions and firm organization has accelerated, and this has happened in response to the combined effect of globalization and information technology.[5] Business system analysis thus needs to integrate the dynamics of change.

This chapter uses the example of Korea, one of the earliest applications of the business system concept, to demonstrate the importance of the dynamics of change. I focus on the organization of technology management as one essential characteristic of the Korean business system. Key features of the Korean way of building technological capability have been shaped by a broad congruence of interests between the government and the leading *chaebols* that gave rise, over the 1960s and 1970s, to a

---

[3] Prominent protagonists in this debate include the World Bank 1993; Amsden 1989; Balassa 1981 and Wade 1990.

[4] '... [T]he identification of distinctive forms of business organization in East Asia does not imply that they are unchanging products of stable and homogeneous culture .... [I]t is entirely possible that certain features of, say, the currently dominant Korean conglomerates ... will alter .... However, the examples of Western Europe and North America do suggest that such changes are relatively slow ...' (Whitley 1992a:23–24).

[5] Carlsson and Stankiewicz 1991; Christensen 1996; Dosi et al. 1998; Foray and Lundvall 1996; Foss 1996; Llerena and Zuscovitch 1996; Lundvall 1992, 1998; Malerba and Orsenigo 1996; Maskell 1996a, 1996b; Nelson and Winter 1982; Penrose 1959; Teece et al. 1995. For an application of this theoretical approach to research on developing countries, see Ernst and Lundvall 1997.

very close and reasonably consistent interaction between both actors.[6] This became a powerful recipe for mobilizing huge investment funds and for channelling them into a few sectors and product groups that were identified as priority targets. It enabled large firms to emerge and to practice a particular form of oligopolistic market competition: incessant, octopus-like diversification across sectoral boundaries replaces a focus on continuous innovation in both quality improvements and product differentiation. Since the late 1980s, this traditional Korean model of late industrialization has come under increasing pressure: exposed to the increasingly complex requirements of global competition, Korea is now searching for new approaches that would enable it to upgrade its national system of innovation.

This chapter traces the evolution in the Korean approach to technology management. I first analyze how Korean electronics firms have developed their technological capability in the context of export-led industrialization and review some of the causes for the initial success and for the emerging new constraints to the Korean way of building technological capability. I then show how Korean electronics firms were able to develop sound production, investment and adaptive engineering capability by integrating into the increasingly complex international production networks of United States, Japanese and some European electronics companies.[7] By building technological capabilities through original equipment manufacturer arrangements, Korean firms were able to avoid the huge cost burdens and risks involved in research and development and

---

[6] For a detailed analysis, see Ernst 1994c.

[7] The concept of an 'international production network' is an attempt to capture the spread of broader and more systemic forms of international production that cut across different stages of the value chain and that may or may not involve equity ownership. This concept allows analysis of the globalization strategies of a particular firm with regard to the following four questions: (1) Where does a firm locate which stages of the value chain? (2) To what degree does a firm rely on outsourcing? What is the importance of inter-firm production networks relative to the firm's internal production network? (3) To what degree is the control over these transactions exercised in a centralized or in a decentralized manner? (4) How do the different elements of these networks hang together? For details, see Ernst 1992, 1994a, 1994b, 1996a, 1996b, 1997a; Ernst and Ravenhill 1997.

in setting up international distribution and marketing networks and thus could substantially accelerate their capacity and international market share expansion. In the third part, I document how the leading Korean semiconductor producer Samsung Electronics was able to enter the manufacturing of computer memory, despite the existence of substantial entry barriers, and assess the strengths and weaknesses of the technological capability accumulated in this process.

In the concluding section, this analysis of the Korean approach to technology management is placed into a broader context, i.e., some fundamental limitations to the Korean model. New competitive challenges are reshaping the patterns of competition in the world electronics industry, and I ask under what conditions Korean electronics firms will be able to meet these new challenges and sustain their international market share expansion. I argue that, although an overriding concern with production, investment and adaptive engineering capabilities made perfect sense during the technological catching-up phase, it has become an important constraint now that the limits of catching-up have been surpassed.

Building Technological Capability the Korean Way

The best way to highlight some of the peculiarities of the Korean case is to compare it with the earlier Japanese approach to technological capability formation in this industry. When Korea began to enter the international electronics markets in the late 1960s, its main concern mirrored that of the Japanese electronics industry in the early 1950s: master as quickly as possible the types of production technology that would enable it to capitalize on its low labour costs and, at the same time, to reap economies of scale. Logically, this implied a focus on rapid capacity and market share expansion. Almost by definition, this in turn implied that the growth of the electronics industry would have to occur primarily on the basis of borrowed technology.

Absorbing Foreign Technology

The Korean way of building technological capability in the electronics industry resembles the Japanese model most closely in its utilization of foreign technology. Rather than letting foreign firms establish local subsidiaries and decide on the speed and scope of technology diffusion, Korean firms focused on learning and knowledge accumulation through a variety of links with foreign equipment and component suppliers, technology licensing partners, original equipment manufacturing clients and minority joint venture partners. By licensing well-proven foreign product designs and by importing most of the production equipment and the crucial components, Korean electronics producers were able to focus most of their attention on three areas:[8]

- the mastery of production capability, initially for assembly, but increasingly also for related support services and for large mass production lines for standard products;
- some related minor types of change capability, ranging from 'reverse engineering' techniques to 'analytical design' and some types of 'system engineering' capability that are required for process re-engineering and product customization; and
- some investment capability, especially the capacity to carry out at short notice and at low cost investment in the expansion of capacity and/or modernization of existing plants and in the establishment of new production lines.

In order to succeed, Korean electronics firms had to develop the knowledge and skills that are necessary to monitor, unpackage, absorb and upgrade foreign technology. Equally important was a capacity to mobilize the substantial funds for paying technology licensing fees and for importing 'best practice' production equipment and leading-edge components.[9] Most Korean electronics producers arguably would have hesitated to pursue such high-cost, high-risk strategies had they not been induced to do so by a variety of selective policy interventions by

[8] For the underlying conceptual framework of capability formation, see Ernst et al. 1998a. See also the excellent analysis in Bell and Pavitt 1993.

[9] Already in the 1970s, most Korean electronics firms had to pay on average roughly 3 per cent of their sales for technology licensing fees, a share which since then has increased to more than 12 per cent (Lee 1992:132, 139).

the Korean state. Getting relative prices 'wrong' (Amsden 1989) has been important. By providing critical externalities such as information, training, maintenance and other support services and finance, the Korean government has fostered the growth of firms large enough to hurdle high entry barriers.

It is due to these particular and, as we know today, historically conditioned circumstances that Korea's electronics firms were able to reverse the sequence of technological capability formation (Dahlman et al. 1987). Rather than proceeding from innovation to investment to production, they could take a shortcut and focus on the ability to operate production facilities according to competitive cost and quality standards. Production capability was thus used as the foundation for developing capability in investment and adaptive engineering, while product and market development and process innovation were postponed to a later stage of development. Through judicious 'reverse engineering' and other forms of copying and imitating foreign technology and by integrating into the increasingly complex international produc- tion networks of United States, Japanese and some European electronics companies, Korean electronics firms were able to avoid the huge cost burdens and risks involved in research and development and in developing international distribution and marketing channels.

How Industry Structure Shapes Capability Formation

There are, however, also important differences that distinguish Korea's approach from the Japanese model. Arguably the most important difference is the extreme degree of concentration which is much higher than in Japan (Kohama and Urata 1993:152). Korea's electronics industry is controlled by four companies—Samsung, Goldstar, Hyundai and Daewoo. In 1988, 56 per cent of the country's electronics production came from these four groups, with the first two alone accounting for 46 per cent of production (Bloom 1992:12). The figures are even more remarkable on an item-by-item basis with Samsung, Lucky-Goldstar and Daewoo accounting for 100 per cent of the VCRs, microwave ovens, refrigerators and washing machines and 82.2 per cent of the colour TVs produced locally (Bark 1991:32).[10]

Sellers' concentration ratios in the domestic market are even higher: until the early 1990s, Samsung, Goldstar and Daewoo had control over roughly 70 per cent of the Korean market (author's interviews). For colour TVs, VCRs, microwave ovens, refrigerators and washing machines, the Big Three's domestic market share came close to 100 per cent. Due to the gradual liberlization of the domestic market for consumer goods and industrial electronics, this tight control of the domestic market is now beginning to erode. Yet while the *chaebol* may lose control over final product markets, their dominant position in components, and especially DRAM memory, may last much longer. In 1992 for instance, the total semiconductor and electronics sale of one company alone, Samsung Electronics, accounted for 20 per cent of the Korean electronics industry's exports.[11] None of the big electronics groups in Japan comes close to such an overwhelming position of dominance. In short, the Korean electronics industry retains a structure that is no longer supposed to exist according to textbook wisdom; a tight national oligopoly controls both domestic production and the domestic market.

This has given rise to a peculiar form of competition strategy focusing on incessant product diversification, often into technologically unrelated areas. Each time a *chaebol* has reached the limits of 'easy' capacity and market share expansion for a particular product, it moved on to a new product group promising rapid market expansion. Rather than using diversification as an instrument for deepening their involvement in a particular sector or group of related products, the *chaebols* have typically used diversification as a short-cut to rapid market share expansion, without much concern for the depth of the production system that can be generated by such shallow forms of diversification. This 'octopus-like' diversification has made it very

[10] Hyundai, a latecomer to the electronics industry, has concentrated on components and industrial electronics and has no activity in consumer electronics.

[11] *Dataquest*, Vendor Profile Samsung Electronics Co. Ltd, 20 September 1993, p. 1.

difficult for most Korean electronics companies to accumulate systematically a broad range of technological capabilities for a given set of products.

Here lies one of the most important differences between *chaebol*-type business strategies and those pursued by the Japanese electronics firms, which typically have been reluctant to engage in product diversification. A survey of the 200 largest Japanese industrial firms undertaken by Fruin shows that only 40 per cent engaged in a limited amount of diversification, with 41 per cent of new goods being in the same two-digit SIC category as the firm's established products (Fruin 1992:318).[12] Gerlach (1992) has also shown that Japanese diversification has predominantly resulted in the 'spinning-off' of new subsidiaries that retain a certain degree of decision autonomy from the parent company. At least for the electronics industry, there are grounds for challenging Amsden's claim that constant '… diversification into many technologically unrelated mature product markets was one of the essential "pillars" of Korea's successful late industrialization and that, in doing so, it was dutifully following the earlier Japanese example' (Amsden 1993:17–18).

The dominance of *chaebols* in the electronics industry also has had a negative effect on the role of small- and medium-sized firms engaged in the supply of parts and components and other complementary support activities. Although formally independent, most of them are tightly integrated into the production networks of one of the four major *chaebols*. Until the early 1980s, this had resulted in an industry structure in which the leading *chaebol* tended to produce almost everything in-house, from electronics components and electrical accessories to transistors, semiconductors and precision engineering parts (Kam 1991:53). Since then, they have been forced to increase their reliance on domestic subcontractors for two main reasons. As a result of the proliferation of labour disputes since the famous wave of strikes in June 1987, the

---

[12] The latter figure would in fact be higher—46 per cent—if the United States SIC code did not classify computers in a different category (35) from other electrical devices (36 and 38).

chaebols are now eager to shift the burden of increasing labour costs onto the shoulders of formally independent domestic suppliers. At the same time, the growing sophistication of Korea's electronics production has increased the demand for local support industries and services. With intensifying price competition, the *chaebols* are now more willing to outsource some of these activities. One peculiar feature of the Korean electronics industry is that subcontractors work only for one manufacturer and are thus locked into a fairly closed production network controlled by a particular *chaebol*. Small- and medium-sized suppliers have very limited decision-making autonomy, which significantly limits any attempts to improve their international competitiveness.

In recent years, the government has started to give greater attention to the promotion of small- and medium-sized enterprises capable of developing their own component designs. This has led to a variety of new policy instruments designed to improve the competitive conditions for innovative start-up companies.[13] Most observers agree that such policies have had only limited success. A recent survey by the School of Small Business at Soongsil University indicates that 70 per cent of government-allocated credit goes to a few relatively large small- and medium-sized enterprises with strong ties with the leading *chaebols* through subcontracting arrangements.[14] One particularly ironic finding is that many of these small businesses are becoming 'mini-*chaebols*' by branching into various businesses but keeping each of the companies small to maintain access to cheap credit.

The independent small- and medium-sized enterprise sector will probably remain weak and vulnerable for some time

[13] For example, the government has designated 205 business territories, the so-called 'SME sanctuaries', where neither *chaebols* nor their affiliates may intrude. Attempts are being made to increase the share of total commercial bank loans for small- and medium-sized enterprises to 35 per cent through the so-called 'compulsory lending ratio' and the government has initiated aggressive venture capital funding for product development by small- and medium-sized enterprises.

[14] These findings were reported in *Far Eastern Economic Review*, 19 November 1992, p. 70.

to come. This sets Korea apart from the Japanese production system, with its sophisticated multi-tier supplier networks, where small companies can be found at all levels with sound design and engineering capability for components and materials. This lack of a strong domestic supplier network of small and medium-sized enterprises also marks a major difference with Taiwan, where highly flexible domestic subcontracting networks based on small- and medium-sized enterprises have played a crucial role in the development of Taiwanese electronics exports (Ernst 1997b).

Squeezed in between the *chaebols* and the myriad of small- and medium-sized enterprises are a handful of independent, medium-sized second-tier firms, each of which is basically organized again as a mini-*chaebol*. Typical examples of these second-tier firms include the Anam group, with Anam Industrial as its flagship company, and Trigem Computer. In an industry dominated by *chaebols* with their privileged access to government bureaucrats, both companies are able to survive only by identifying smaller, but lucrative niche markets that the *chaebols* have neglected. An additional prerequisite, it seems, has been a long-term relationship with a foreign company: Trigem Computer through its joint venture with Seiko Epson, and Anam through its link with its United States marketing affiliate, Amkor, the original founding company of Anam Industrial.

While Japan's electronics industry includes a number of originally small- or medium-sized, highly innovative start-up companies such as Sony, Kyocera, Canon, Minebea or Uniden, the tight oligopoly governing the Korean electronics industry has made this almost impossible. A telling example of the constant frustration that innovative start-up companies encounter is that of a small computer design company run by a group of eight engineers and computer scientists who knew each other since high school and who no longer wished to work in the highly regimented environment of the *chaebols*. After trying, without success, to sell some of their designs for pen and pocket computers to the *chaebols*, they ended up selling them to a second-tier Taiwanese PC assembler which, at least for a few months, is reported to have made healthy profits with these machines (author's interviews, Korea, November 1993).

Consumer Electronics—Trade-offs Involved in Original Equipment Manufacturing

How did Korean firms build their technological capability in consumer electronics? This is an industry in which economies of scale are critical. For reasons of quality and reliability, production requires automatic component insertion machines. Such machines have very high throughputs and can be effectively utilized only in connection with high-volume assembly operations. The minimum efficient scale for a colour TV plant, for instance, typically exceeds 400,000 sets per year, with minimum investment thresholds ranging between $15 million and $40 million. Minimum efficient scales are even higher for TV picture tubes, starting from a minimum capacity of 1.4 million tubes per year, with an estimated $75 million to $90 million as the investment threshold (Ernst and O'Connor 1992:183–85). Rapid expansion of market share is thus an essential prerequisite for successful late entry strategies in consumer electronics. In Korea, the domestic market was clearly insufficient to exhaust the relevant scale economies. The main focus thus had to be on exports. For a long time, Korean consumers had to subsidize the learning costs of their consumer electronics producers, paying substantially higher prices for lower quality products.

Korean consumer electronics manufacturers have entered exports by focusing on the final assembly of mature and proven imported product designs. Attempts to deepen the industry structure were postponed to a later stage. This specific industrialization pattern gave rise to a particular pattern of technological capability formation: the focus was on the development of production and, linked to that, the capability to reproduce similar investment projects. Production capability was primarily developed for the different stages of final assembly, most of it related to the insertion of components onto printed circuit boards. From the mid-1980s onwards, this was complemented by the development of component manufacturing, especially for picture tubes and some semiconductors. Yet very little progress has been achieved in product design.

As a result, Korean companies are very much followers of the latest product designs developed elsewhere, mostly in Japan. They lack the capacity to generate such new designs and to collect early on the relevant information on new market trends and customer preferences.[15] This applies to TV sets, VCRs and audio equipment as well as to household appliances, in which Korean companies continue to depend to a considerable degree on original equipment manufacturing arrangements to keep up with the rapidly changing international markets. 'We used to take Sony, Hitachi and Matsushita as our natural benchmarks without ever asking whether we could do it better.'[16]

Historically, it made all sense to start with a focus on assembly based on borrowed technology and to enter international markets with the help of powerful foreign original equipment manufacturing clients. Rapid expansion of capacity and international market share would have been impossible, if Korean firms had tried to start off with a more integrated production system. And original equipment manufacturing arrangements have proven to be one of the most cost-effective methods for acquiring core capability in production and investment. Original equipment manufacturing arrangements provide the supplier with a high volume of business, which permits the realization of scale economies. The often tedious and grueling qualification process that potential suppliers have to pass before they can aspire to get a contract opens up a variety of learning possibilities about its organizational deficiencies and technological weaknesses. In addition, the customer often provides technical assistance in engineering and manufacturing processes in order to ensure quality and cost efficiency. This applies in particular to capabilities in tooling (e.g., plastic molds), the lay-out, use and adaptation of automated insertion,

---

[15] This contrasts sharply with Taiwan's PC industry, in which early access to market intelligence enables firms to accelerate speed-to-market and to continuously upgrade their products. For evidence, see Gee and Kuo 1998; Ernst 1997b.

[16] Interview at Goldstar, November 1993.

soldering and assembly equipment, and specialized equipment for coil winding and other operations required for various subassemblies, for instance, of a TV set. At the very least, the customer must supply detailed technical 'blueprints' to allow the supplier to produce according to specifications. The most important immediate advantage is that the customer takes responsibility for marketing and distribution, saving the original equipment manufacturing supplier substantial investment in these areas.

Learning through original equipment manufacturing arrangements was not confined to the consumer electronics industry. Substantial spillover effects occurred into other segments of the electronics industry and the manufacturing sector at large, as some technologies used in consumer electronics products are similar to those used in industrial and professional electronic systems. Korea is relatively well placed to reap such spillover effects due to the highly concentrated structure of its consumer electronics industry, which is dominated by a handful of large, vertically integrated *chaebols*. A second factor conducive for strong spillover effects resides in the tendency of these *chaebols* to engage in constant product diversification across market segments and sectoral boundaries. Picture tubes generated such spillover effects. Throughout most of the 1980s, computer monitors used to be built around the same cathode ray tube technology that is used in TV sets. As a result, Samsung and Goldstar could use the technological capabilities accumulated in the production of picture tubes for TV sets to establish a strong position in computer monitors.

Original equipment manufacturing arrangements, however, can also have substantial drawbacks. A firm may become 'locked into' an original equipment manufacturing relationship to the extent that it is hindered from developing its own independent brand name recognition and marketing channels. Profit margins are substantially lower in original equipment manufacturing sales than in own brand name sales, which in turn makes it difficult for the Korean companies to muster the capital needed to invest in research and development that eventually might lead to the introduction of new products. This constraint, however, is of limited importance, as long as sales volumes through original equipment manufacturing contracts are large and fairly well predictable so that, despite low profit margins, total earnings may be substantial.

Original equipment manufacturing exports continue to account for a substantial share of Korea's consumer electronics exports. In 1988, about 50–60 per cent of all Korean exports of colour TV sets and VCRs were carrying original equipment manufacturing brands (Jun and Kim 1990:22). And four years later, in 1992, the original equipment manufacturing share of consumer electronics exports was reported to have increased to nearly 69 per cent.[17]

Over the last few years, Korean companies have moved out of low-end original equipment manufacturing arrangements (e.g., for standard, small-sized TV sets) and strengthened their position for products that require more demanding production capabilities (e.g., VCRs and computer monitors). In earlier original equipment manufacturing arrangements the Korean company was basically restricted to printed circuit board assembly and had to purchase most components from the foreign client. More recently, however, Korean companies have qualified for more demanding original equipment manufacturing arrangements in which they supply not only the components but are also responsible for detailed design or for design modification.[18]

During the late 1980s, everyone in Korea began to talk about the necessity to move beyond the original equipment manufacturing trap, and expectations were running high that, given the substantial amount of accumulated technological and organizational capability, this could be done without much pain. All three major consumer electronics manufacturers of Korea have since then tried to increase their brand name recognition abroad and have made huge investment to build

[17] Interview at the Korean Institute of Economics and Technology (KIET), November 1993.

[18] For an analysis of the increasing variety of original equipment manufacturing arrangements and the impact on technology diffusion, see Ernst 1994a, 1994b.

up an overseas marketing, distribution and service network. In some cases, such attempts have worked quite well, as for Samsung's TV sets and VCRs for the low-end market segments in the United States, and for Daewoo's microwave ovens in France. In most cases, however, the transition to original brand name strategies has been rough and full of pitfalls. After years of heavy advertising and public relations promotion, Korean electronics firms must still contend with an image that their products are of inferior quality and reliability.

Product development is still primarily conceived as a gradual improvement of a given Japanese product design. Strategic marketing continues to play a marginal role in the Korean innovation process. The goals of innovation are set by the established foreign benchmark firms. Almost no attempt has been made until very recently to identify still undiscovered customer needs and to use this knowledge to develop new markets. It should be mentioned, however, that, over the last few years, all three *chaebol* active in consumer electronics have identified this passive acceptance of foreign product designs as a major barrier to sustained competitiveness. All three are now considering or have started to implement important organizational reforms that should enable them to link together more closely strategic marketing and innovation management. All three also claimed that they have now interdisciplinary product teams working on original product designs. The fact that top management is now more willing to spend substantial resources on original brand design may help to break at last the old passive design mentality. Such a change is overdue. As consumer electronics today has become almost a fashion industry, competitive success increasingly depends on whether a firm is able to rapidly adapt its product designs to the changing requirements of the main international export markets.

Building Technological Capability in Semiconductors

Korea's involvement in the semiconductor industry began in the late 1960s as a low-cost assembly base for export-oriented semiconductor multinationals. At the time, assembly was a highly labour-intensive process. The more skill- and capital-intensive design and wafer fabrication stages of production were performed exclusively in OECD countries. Very little change occurred until the early 1980s, and competing in the international semiconductor market as a fully integrated producer seemed to be well beyond the reach of even the most powerful *chaebol*. Since then, important changes have occurred, and Korea has moved to the forefront of international competition in this industry.

By that time Korea had reached a stage where a handful of its *chaebols* had become serious contenders in the world electronics industry for a variety of consumer goods. While on the surface everything seemed to go well, two dark spots did not escape the attention of the *chaebol* strategists. The first concerned Korea's heavy reliance on component imports, especially from Japan, which, in the words of one of my interview partners who was personally involved in the relevant decision-making, '... reminded us that here we were serving as a low-margin final assembler for the Japanese component guys who had licensed us dated technology and were able to keep for themselves most of the cake'.[19] Entering the semiconductor industry was perceived as a vehicle for repairing this fundamental weakness, by broadening the domestic supply base for electronic components.

A second reason why the *chaebols* began to shift their attention and investments to computer memory resulted from intensifying international trade conflicts. In reaction to earlier market penetration by Japanese firms, protectionist measures began to proliferate in OECD countries against consumer goods, and it was clear that they would soon also target Korean exports. *Chaebol* planners thus felt it was time to consider further product diversification. Semiconductors were considered to be an ideal candidate, since their production requirements (high capital intensity; mass production of standard products) matched well with the strengths of the *chaebols*.[20] Decision-makers in the

---

[19] Interviews with the Samsung Group, November 1987.

[20] Note that this rather mundane interpretation of Korea's entry into semiconductors, offered by people involved in the original decision-making, contrasts with much of the academic debate on Korea's role in semiconductors, which continues to talk about 'leap-frogging' into a 'leading-edge', 'high-tech' industry.

chaebols thus were confident that they would be able to leverage their mass-production capability to quickly establish a strong position in this sector and reasonable profits.

The shift into the mass production of computer memory was spear-headed by Samsung and Goldstar, with Hyundai in the role of the aggressive latecomer. In 1983, the government introduced the Semiconductor Industry Promotion Plan that, in addition to a wide range of tax incentives, was to provide substantial policy loans to '... activities related to the development of domestic wafer fabrication'.[21] In the same year, Byung Chul Lee, the founder of the Samsung Group, announced that Samsung would spend $1.5 billion on the company's entry into the mass production of computer memory (DRAM) and indicated that Samsung was prepared to take a long-term view and follow up with additional huge investment outlays.[22] The goal was to enter mass production of 64K DRAM computer memory as quickly as possible in order to reap the high profits typical for the early product innovation phase.[23] This was a challenge even for a cash-rich conglomerate like Samsung that could only be met due to a number of very specific circumstances.

A first prerequisite for success was that Samsung decided to rely on a proven foreign chip design and that it was able to find a foreign company willing to license such a design. Both for the initial 64K DRAM and for the next generation of 256K,

[21] Quoted from *Dataquest* 1987, 'History of Semiconductor Industry—South Korea', p. 2. Policy loans are a specific Korean policy innovation that are designed to accomplish various social objectives of the government. For details, see Okyu (1994).

[22] Details on Samsung's entry strategy into DRAM are based on interviews with Samsung in November 1987. I have chosen to focus on Samsung as it represents the most sophisticated approach to the formation of technological capabilities in this industry, while at the same time nicely illustrating some of the main weaknesses of the Korean approach to technology management. For information on the DRAM entry strategies of Goldstar and Hyundai and why Daewoo decided to stay out of this race, see Jun and Kim 1990; Bloom 1992; Ernst and O'Connor 1992.

[23] For an analysis of the economics of semiconductor manufacturing, see Ernst 1983, 1990.

Samsung licensed the design from Micron Technology. This medium-sized United States DRAM producer, based in Boise, Idaho, was the only survivor, in addition to Texas Instruments, of the successful conquest of the DRAM business by Japanese semiconductor majors. For Micron, licensing technology to a potential low-cost competitor to the dominant Japanese DRAM oligopoly was very attractive for two reasons: it generated desperately needed cash and it could help to establish a low-cost second source, which could act as a buffer during periods of rapid demand growth, enabling Micron to keep its own investments at a minimum.

A more important challenge was to develop the sophisticated process technology. Process technology and not design is the key to success in DRAM competition. Integrated circuit fabrication consists of a great variety of extremely complex chemical processes—for the 64K DRAM for instance, 309 individual manufacturing steps are required. Each of these different processes sequentially defines the circuit elements on the silicon wafer by introducing and diffusing the appropriate impurities into the defined areas. Many of the steps occur at high temperatures (approaching $1,000°C$), and all involve the precise repetition of almost identical, but slightly different, steps. Since there are over 1,000 variables to be set, handling them all requires some knowledge of the distribution pattern of the result of changing each variable. Yet, such knowledge is still at a very rudimentary level. Frequently, engineers have only limited ideas of what each step will bring. Improving yields, i.e., the number of saleable devices as a percentage of devices started, thus requires an extremely tedious process of trial and error, which often borders on alchemy rather than scientific engineering. Moving from a circuit design to mass production thus normally requires a lot of time and effort, with little control over whether the deadlines for market entry can be effectively met.

This posed a major dilemma for Samsung's goal of rapid market entry. In order to speed up time to market, Samsung licensed process technology from Sharp (Japan). Sharp, an innovative consumer electronics and appliance producer that had pioneered the world's first liquid crystal display (LCD) in 1973, was willing to license such technology, presumably for the following reasons.[24] Sharp has been a long-term producer of DRAM with excellent process technology. Yet, with a world market share of hardly more than 3 per cent, its strategic focus was quite different from that of the Five Sisters (Toshiba, NEC, Hitachi, Fujitsu and Mitsubishi), the core members of the Japanese DRAM oligopoly. For Sharp, the world market leader for leading-edge LCD, the main purpose of its involvement in DRAMs was not market share expansion but to use the process technology developed for DRAM in order to improve the yields of its LCD production. Licensing its DRAM process technology to Samsung thus was very attractive for Sharp, as it generated cash required for the tremendously capital-intensive LCD production, while at the same time it helped to erode the overwhelming dominance that the Five Sisters had established over the world DRAM markets.

The most important step, however, was the decision to hire on fairly attractive terms a group of young engineers that had just graduated from leading United States universities who had been trained in semiconductor process technology and to assign independent foreign consultants to assist in their in-house training and in their integration into a highly motivated project team. Provided with an unusual degree of decision autonomy, these young engineers were willing to work around the clock and thus were able to finish the project in the record time of six months. Equally important, Samsung was able to construct the wafer fabrication line in six months, substantially quicker than the normally required 18 months. As a result, Samsung succeeded in starting mass production of the 64K DRAM chip for export to the United States and Europe as early as the spring of 1994.

In late 1984, the 256K DRAM was developed, and production was started in 1986. This time, Micron's design was submitted to extensive reverse engineering. Samsung pursued a dual strategy by carrying out simultaneously the development work at its headquarters laboratory and at its affiliate in Silicon Valley. In contrast to the initial 64K generation, development

---

[24] Based on interviews with Sharp Corp., Tokyo, November 1993.

was not restricted to process development; it included chip design. The explicit goal of combining reverse engineering with a parallel effort of chip design was to maximize in-house learning possibilities and to move as quickly as possible to a situation in which Samsung would be able to rely on its own design capabilities. This strategy worked extremely well: the headquarters team completed its task in record speed, but the Silicon Valley team produced a qualitatively better design, both in terms of performance features and manufacturability. The actual production then utilized the design of the Silicon Valley team.

In a nutshell, this small example tells us a lot about some of the strengths and weaknesses of the Korean way of building technological capability. Within the highly regimented environment of a *chaebol*, an absolute dedication to fulfil a target and to do it at breakneck speed could be taken for granted, at least until very recently.[25] At the same time, however, there is a seemingly deeply entrenched habit of following the benchmarks set by the technology leaders and very limited efforts to try and attempt new and unconventional solutions. The quality of the domestic development results thus cannot compare with those undertaken in a United States-style research environment, whether in the United States itself or in Taiwan or Israel. Our example also tells us a lot about the pragmatic approach of Korea's strategic planners, who realize the aforementioned weaknesses and try to come up with innovative solutions that could help to bridge the time needed to build up the necessary capabilities at home.

The 256K DRAM development was a breakthrough. From then on Samsung was able to rely on its own design efforts for DRAM devices. In 1987, it began the production of 1 Mbit DRAM and has been able to catch up since then with the Japanese industry leaders NEC and Toshiba. While in June 1990, Samsung was still reported to be about 1 year behind

---

[25] While many of the established authoritarian organizational and behavioural patterns are currently being challenged by increasing demands for grassroots democratization, a recent case study of the Samsung group (Janelli and Yim 1993) shows that old habits die hard, and that serious reform attempts will face substantial barriers.

NEC and Toshiba, in April 1992 it claimed to have drawn even with its 16 Mbit design. My own assessment would be a bit more cautious. The real issue today is the variety of designs that a company can offer for any particular DRAM generation, and here NEC clearly continues to be in a leading position. This has also been acknowledged by both companies when they announced their agreement for the joint development of 256 Mbit DRAM in March 1994 (Computergram, 3 February 1994).

However, these are minor details compared with the unprecedented pace and scale of the capacity and market share expansion of Korea's semiconductor industry.[26] How was it possible that Samsung, together with Goldstar and Hyundai, were able to enter the DRAM market at record speed and to erode the once seemingly watertight grip that a tight Japanese oligopoly had come to impose on this industry since the mid-1980s?

Two external factors need to be mentioned upfront, before discussing how the Korean way of building technological capabilities may have contributed to this success. I have pointed out elsewhere (Ernst 1987) that one of the probably unintended, yet very consequential side effects of the September 1986 United States–Japanese agreement on trade in semiconductors was that, due to the unrealistically high price floors set for DRAM imports into the United States, Korean producers were able to outprice their Japanese rivals at price levels that, in 1989, began to generate substantial profits. A second external factor has been the strategic decision of United States semiconductor producers and computer companies to create an alternative, low-cost source of DRAM in order to tamper the oligopolistic pricing and supply behaviour of the Japanese majors (Ernst and O'Connor 1992). It is plausible to assume that, without these two external factors, Korea may have had a much harder time entering the DRAM market segment.

As for the Korean contribution, the first factor to mention is the willingness and the capacity to spend huge amounts of money on investment and technology acquisition.[27] Between 1983 and 1989, the three *chaebols* are reported to have invested

---

[26] For details, see Ernst 1994c: Chapter 2.

[27] If not indicated otherwise, the following figures are provided by the Korea Semiconductor Industry Association (KSIA).

more than $4 billion on production equipment. This amount can be considered to be the original entry fee. However, while catching up is already quite costly, keeping up and getting ahead leads to an even higher fixed capital cost burden. Since 1987, annual capital spending has increased from $800 million to an estimated $1.350 billion in 1993, which in that year equaled more than 20 per cent of the world's total semiconductor facility investment. In the same year, Samsung alone had the third largest capital expenditures of production equipment ($930 million), after Intel ($2.1 billion) and Motorola ($973 million), but well ahead of Toshiba ($519 million), NEC ($482 million) and Hitachi ($409 million). Even Goldstar's and Hyundai's capital expenditures, $417 million and $401 million, came close to or even surpassed that of their Japanese rivals.[28]

In order to get an impression of the tremendous overall cost involved in Korea's entry into semiconductors, let us first compare, for the five years between 1988 and 1992, cumulative capital spending with cumulative sales. We find that on an average Korean semiconductor *chaebol* had to spend nearly 51 per cent of their semiconductor sales on capital investment, $5.7 billion out of a sales total of $10.2 billion.[29] As if this would not already be enough, we need to add the quite substantial licensing fees that Korean semiconductor producers have to pay for United States and Japanese technology. It is estimated that in 1992 and 1993, the Korean semiconductor industry had to spend 14 per cent and 16 per cent of its annual turnover on royalty payments (KSIA 1993), i.e., $281 million and $322 million respectively. It is reported that 85 per cent of these payments went to the United States semiconductor industry, which provides an interesting and somewhat surprising contrast to Korea's otherwise high dependence on Japanese technology, especially for consumer electronics.[30]

A second important prerequisite of Korea's successful entry into semiconductors relates to the specific nature of the

[28] VLSI Research figures, quoted in *Electronics New*, 12 June 93, p. 4.

[29] Sales figures provided by *Dataquest*, September 1993.

[30] This raises interesting questions concerning earlier (probably inflated) estimates of Japanese technological superiority in semiconductors, which I have addressed elsewhere (Ernst 1994b, 1996b).

technology acquisition strategies pursued. These strategies were based on a judicious combination of three main elements that enabled the *chaebols* to participate in international technology networks and to maximize their internal learning possibilities. First, all of them established early on subsidiaries in Silicon Valley that served as listening posts for intelligence gathering on technology and market trends. As we have seen before in the case of Samsung, these subsidiaries were also used for research and development activities that complemented and helped to direct or correct similar efforts at home. A second element of technology acquisition has been a pervasive reliance on 'second-sourcing' agreements in which the *chaebols* were licensed by leading United States and Japanese semiconductor producers to manufacture some of their DRAM designs.[31] The *chaebols* also used a third approach to technology acquisition through contract manufacturing, the so-called silicon foundry services provided for leading United States application-specific integrated circuit companies such as LSI Logic and VLSI Technology. Based on the gate array or standard cell designs received from these foreign companies, the *chaebols* used their strength in process technology and their capacity to rapidly improve yields to produce such devices at short notice. Being forced to comply with the stringent design rules typical for States application-specific integrated circuit devices, the *chaebol* thus were able to deepen their knowledge about necessary process improvements.

More recently, there has been a tendency to combine these different individual approaches into somewhat broader package deals aimed at cross-technology sharing. As the *chaebols* expanded their share in international DRAM markets, they were able to strengthen their bargaining position with regard to licensing agreements, as a result of which we now witness an increasing trend towards cross-licensing and mutual patent swaps, which today link all of the *chaebols* with the leading Japanese semiconductor producers. More and more, the

---

[31] Examples of such second-sourcing include the following link-ups: Goldstar with AT&T (for 256K DRAM) and Hitachi (for 1 Mbit and 4 Mbit DRAM); Hyundai with Texas Instruments (for 256K and 1 Mbit DRAM); and Samsung with Micron Technology (256K DRAM), and Intel (microcontrollers, microprocessors, DRAM and EPROM—erasable programmable read-only memory).

chaebols get involved in international technology sourcing networks, which include links with other firms (inter-firm networks) and attempts to tap into and use key elements of the national innovation systems of other countries (inter-organizational networks).[32] These networks now typically cover a great variety of arrangements, ranging from second-sourcing and fabrication agreements to technology licensing and cross-licensing, patent swapping, joint product or technology development, the exchange of researchers and guest engineers, and standard coalitions (e.g., for RISC [reduced instruction set computing] and flash memory). Within a few years, technology acquisition approaches pursued by Korean semiconductor producers thus have experienced major changes, moving from the reverse engineering of licensed chip designs to much broader and increasingly systemic forms of international technology sourcing.

It is now time to assess more closely the nature of the achievements that have resulted from all these efforts and to identify some important weaknesses. As before, I will concentrate on DRAM. Let me first clarify the nature of the technological capabilities required for the production of these devices. Five of them can be discerned: wafer production, circuit design, wafer fabrication, assembly and packaging, and testing. In a nutshell: Korea has excellent assembly capability over a broad range of products. Its wafer fabrication capability is excellent or good for a limited number of products, i.e., DRAM, SRAM (static RAM) and ROM (read-only memory). Other than that, very little has been achieved, and there continue to be glaring deficits, in particular for circuit design.

Of much greater importance, however, is the fact that Korea's semiconductor industry is based on an extremely weak foundation in terms of the materials and production equipment required. In 1991, 90 per cent of the production equipment had to be imported, with 50 per cent originating from Japan. It will be extremely difficult to reduce this dependence. Only joint production with leading overseas manufacturers is likely to help. There is some evidence now that this pragmatic

---

[32] For details, see Ernst 1994c.

strategy may work. As Korea has become the 'hottest market' for semiconductor production equipment, leading United States producers such as Applied Materials, Lam Research and Varian Associates have concluded such joint local ventures.[33] This, in turn, may help to overcome the deeply ingrained resistance of Japanese equipment manufacturers, especially Canon and Nikon, to establish similar joint ventures with Korean partners.

Levels of import dependence are also quite high for semiconductor materials, particularly for high-value special materials. Korea's current annual consumption of semiconductor materials today is approximately $600 million, with 70 per cent of total consumption being imported (40 per cent from Japan and 20 per cent from the United States). Some progress has been made in the domestic production of silicon wafers, using foreign technology obtained either through licensing or joint ventures. Most domestic production, however, is still restricted to relatively simple materials such as lead frame, bonding wire and packaging materials for chip assembly.

Probably the most important weakness, however, relates to circuit design and the weak capacity of Korean firms to broaden their product portfolio and to develop new products and markets. Beyond DRAM and some other types of memory such as SRAM and erasable programmable read-only memories (EPROM), Korean firms have played no role at all in international semiconductor markets. In other words, Korean firms are only able to compete in a particular segment of the world market, DRAM, that currently generates roughly 22 per cent of worldwide semiconductor revenues.[34] Korea's competitive position in semiconductors thus remains highly fragile. The three leading Korean semiconductor producers in fact all heavily depend on computer memory: 80 per cent of Samsung's semiconductor revenues come from memory, and in the case of Goldstar and Hyundai, this share is even higher, i.e., 87 per cent and 90 per cent. It is this heavy dependence on memory,

---

[33] Author's interviews in the Korean electronics industry, March 1996.
[34] *Dataquest Annual Report*, 1996.

and especially on DRAM, that clearly distinguishes the Korean semiconductor industry from its international competitors and keeps it in a highly vulnerable position. This vulnerability results from the fact that the demand for DRAM is highly volatile, while investment thresholds continue to grow rapidly. In the case of the largest Japanese semiconductor producer, NEC, for example, only 35 per cent of its semiconductor revenues were generated by metal oxide on silicon memory.

The key issue today for the Korean semiconductor industry is whether or not it will succeed in broadening its product portfolio and move beyond computer memories. As technology management is still overwhelmingly dominated by a production bias, I am somewhat skeptical to what degree and how fast design and product development capability can be developed. If such changes in the product mix do not come soon, this may have quite negative consequences. The absence of Korea from most international semiconductor markets has led to a very unbalanced international trade structure, which may not be sustainable for long: Korea continuously has a huge trade surplus for memory chips, while at the same time accumulating equally huge deficits for microprocessors, application-specific integrated circuits and video image chips.

The narrow focus on memory products also has very negative implications for the overall structure of the electronics industry at large. Korea keeps exporting more than 90 per cent of its total semiconductor output, while at the same time importing more than 87 per cent of its domestic demand. Such an extreme imbalance between supply and demand makes it very difficult to broaden and deepen forward and backward links within the electronics industry and to place it onto a more viable basis. It is probably fair to say that Korea's semiconductor industry represents today a modern version of the classical mono-product export enclave, characterized by a minimum of links with the domestic economy. There is, however, one important difference: as shown before, the cost of entering the semiconductor industry is horrendously high and certainly exceeds that of entering the plantation industry.

One final issue should help to understand better the nature of Korea's entry strategy into the semiconductor industry and to place it into the proper context. While catching up in this industry has been a major achievement, it should not be interpreted to imply that Samsung, Goldstar and Hyundai have been able to move beyond their strength in mass production and that they have now established a firm foothold in highly research and development-intensive forms of industrial production. The very high entry barriers typical for DRAM are due less to the research and development intensity than to the capital intensity, very high economies of scale and the extremely volatile nature of demand for these devices. The minimum efficient scale for producing these devices is now more than $1 billion of annual sales. This implies that only firms that have reached the critical threshold of 5 per cent of world production can compete successfully.[35] Competition in DRAM centres on the capacity to invest in huge mega-plants churning out a limited variety of standard products and on the capacity to improve as quickly as possible yields and productivity. Wafer fabrication lines thus are typical examples of mass production.

In contrast to microprocessors, logic and analogue devices, DRAM designs are not complex at all. The main focus is on improving process technology and thus learning economies and yields, primarily through continuous improvements on the shop floor and tedious trial and error. DRAM designs need to be simple, repetitive and safe enough to minimize the risks and complications entailed in producing these devices with complex process technologies. The device should be easily testable in order to isolate defects. With progressive miniaturization, this last requirement becomes even more important—the circuits become so tiny that if defects cannot be located by electrical testing, finding them becomes prohibitively expensive. To compete in the DRAM market, a firm must be able to mobilize huge investment funds, implement complex investment projects quickly and at low cost and have sufficient financial clout to discount the periodic huge losses that result from extremely volatile demand and the periodic emergence of

---

[35] For a detailed analysis of entry barriers in different sectors of the electronics industry, see Ernst and O'Connor 1992.

huge surplus capacity. Once these fundamentals are in place, a firm needs to organize its production in such a way that it can rapidly improve yields and be the first to the market as the lowest-cost supplier.

The *chaebols* are particularly well placed to cope with such entry requirements. They have access to 'patient capital' and ample opportunities for internal 'cross-subsidization' and thus are among the few firms worldwide that can cope with the demanding financial requirements of the DRAM business. They also have been able to accumulate increasingly sophisticated production and investment capabilities, both in typical mass production industries such as cars and consumer durables and in resource-intensive process industries such as the steel industry.

It is thus probably fair to say that Korea's entry strategy into semiconductors did not fundamentally differ from its earlier entry into shipbuilding, the steel industry or the production of picture tubes for TV sets and monitors. What DRAM shares with these other industries is that success does not require a strength in research and technology development, at least not during the initial entry phase. Rather, the success of the *chaebols* has been primarily a result of their capacity to raise incredibly many funds for high-risk investment into huge mass-production lines for standard products. High risks in this case do not result from technological uncertainty but from the extremely volatile nature of demand and from the periodic emergence of huge surplus capacity.[36] In other words, competition in DRAM is of a fairly conventional nature, with size, economies of scale and first-mover advantages being of primary importance. Korea's success in this particular segment of the semiconductor industry should thus not be construed to indicate that Korea is now able to compete in the so-called new industrial paradigm industries. This, on the other hand, should not belittle our appreciation of the impressive achievements that Korean companies have made in the mass production of computer memory.

---

[36] For an early model of the volatility of demand and recurrent periodic surplus capacities in semiconductors, see Ernst 1983: Chapter 1

Limits to the Korean Model

We have seen that the Korean electronics industry was tremendously successful as long as the goal was catching up. Today, catching up has been largely achieved, albeit at the cost of some fundamental weaknesses in the existing industry structure and business organization. In order to overcome these weaknesses, substantial changes will be required in firm strategies and in the policies of the Korean government.

It is simply no longer possible for Korean electronics firms to continue to rely on mass production of low-end commodity products. Radical changes are now overdue in the choice of product mix and in technology management. It will be very difficult to implement such changes as long as a few *chaebols* continue to dominate the domestic market and as long as they control the financial and human resources of this industry. As part of a tight domestic oligopoly, the *chaebols* have a strong tendency to rely on incessant diversification across sectoral boundaries. Such octopus-like diversification prevents continuous, long-term accumulation and deepening of technological capability for a given set of products. It also leads to a neglect of selective and gradual product differentiation within a given product category. Furthermore, it frustrates any serious attempt to move from product to technology diversification, which is defined as '... the expansion of a company's or a product's technology base into a broader range of technological areas' (Granstrand et al. 1992:291).

Technology diversification strategies differ substantially from the so-called 'high-tech' product innovation strategies which focus on products with a high research and development content (i.e., high intensity or high value-added from research and development) in that they focus on products that are based on several crucial technologies that do not have to be new to the world or difficult to acquire. Given Korea's limited capacity to create generic technologies and to develop new products and markets, any attempt to follow the United States focus on 'breakthrough' technologies would clearly be unrealistic, with the possible exception of semiconductor memory products. In most cases, Korean electronics firms would be well advised to pursue technology diversification strategies, which would enable them to build up gradually their capabilities for product and market development.

Overcoming the weaknesses of the Korean electronics industry also requires a major shift of government policies away from sectoral targeting to more diffusion-oriented policies. It also requires an opening up of Korea's still considerably closed economic system. This does not imply an indiscriminate shift to laissez-faire, open-door policies. The increasing importance attached to industrial and technology policies in the United States and other OECD member countries clearly indicates that market opening needs to proceed in a gradual manner, using corrective policy interventions to guarantee eventual success. It is with this caveat in mind that I would like to advance two final propositions.

The first one relates to a possible future role of inward foreign direct investment as a vehicle for technology diffusion. It would certainly be unrealistic to expect such an effect for leading-edge technology that no foreign company is willing to give away.[37] This type of knowledge cannot be accessed through traditional inward foreign direct investment. The only alternative is to gain it through participation in technology cooperation networks with foreign firms. Yet inward foreign direct investment continues to matter, especially for the transfer of 'best practice' organizational techniques related to production and investment. Here outdated policy instruments that focus on excessive restrictions continue to be an important constraint. Recent moves to streamline foreign investment regulations have not been very convincing.[38]

My second proposition relates to fundamental changes in the organization of technology management, an important element of the Korean business system. Korea's innovation system continues to be dominated by a handful of *chaebols*: they can recruit the best scientists, engineers and managers,

---

[37] As shown by Kogut and Zander (1993:43), '... the choice of transfer mode is explained by the tacitness of technology: ... the more tacit the technology, the more likely technology will be transfered within the firm.'

[38] For an assessment from a United States perspective, see Graham 1994.

and their strategies determine the country's research agenda. Serious problems have been detected with regard to the effectiveness of the *chaebols'* innovation management.[39] While external technology sourcing strategies are highly sophisticated, the organization of innovation within these firms remains rather ineffective, and there is a huge potential for reorganization and productivity improvement. Organizational conservatism continues to prevail. If changes occur, they follow an outdated centralized research and development model. In contrast to the progressive decentralization of research and development which is typical today for Japanese, United States and European firms and which has led to an increasing outsourcing of technological development, '... the Korean manufacturing industry is still at the stage of establishing centralized research and development laboratories with the objective of concentrating scarce resources in R&D' (Kim and Chung 1991:6).

This is true in particular for the leading electronics companies. As they face growing restrictions in the international technology markets, these firms have shifted to quite extreme forms of centralized in-house technology generation. Successful innovation, however, requires continual and numerous interactions and feedbacks among a great variety of economic actors and across all stages of the value chain (OECD 1992: Chapters 1–3). Organizing research and development in a centralized manner is bound to produce rigid procedures concerning information management and decision-making, with the result that product design cycles and speed-to-market become much too long. In addition, centralized research and development organizations are ill equipped to coordinate the complex requirements of innovation. Feedback loops across the value chain thus remain weak and unreliable, and design, marketing and manufacturing often proceed in an asynchronous way.

---

[39] See in particular H.S. Kim 1991, 1993; Linsu Kim 1993, Kim 1995; Kim 1996; Kim and Chung 1991; Kim and Kim 1991. While Bloom (1992) shares much of the diagnosis with the authors mentioned above, he proposes a quite different therapy. For him, strengthening the *chaebol* would be the safest way to upgrade technological capabilities to the new competitive requirements.

A bias in Korea for centralized research and development organizations also has quite negative implications beyond the boundaries of the firm. It is probably one of the main reasons for the still very weak status of domestic technology networks among the different actors involved in the process of technology generation and diffusion. This applies in particular to linkages between the large electronics manufacturing companies and their suppliers of parts and components. Most of these links are either with foreign companies or are internalized by the leading *chaebols* (Bloom 1992). Both links have considerable disadvantages. Reliance on imported components not only contributes to a continuous foreign exchange drain but has also reduced substantially the local value-added and the learning possibilities involved in the design and manufacturing of the relevant components. In the second case, excessive vertical integration leads to very high fixed capital cost burdens and limited flexibility. As long as components are only for in-house consumption, chances are low that they will correspond to 'world-class' standards.

There is now a rich body of theoretical and empirical literature that shows that both end product manufacturers and component suppliers can reap substantial benefits from vertical production networks.[40] Such networks make possible a shift to a new division of labour in research and development: they enable manufacturing firms to concentrate on system design and final assembly and thus to restrict their research and development primarily to product design and process innovations for final assembly. Suppliers, in turn, can focus their limited resources on product and process innovations for parts and components and thus can aspire to accumulate specialized technological capabilities.

A further important weakness of the Korean innovation system, paradoxically enough, relates to the established educational system. Its heavy focus on the training of mid-level managers, engineers and technicians has been an important

---

[40] Antonelli 1989; Antonelli and Foray 1991; Bieber et al. 1991; Bongardt 1991; Ciborra 1991; Doleschal 1991; Ernst 1994a, 1994b; Imai and Baba 1991; OECD 1992: Chapter 3; Sabel et al. 1991.

prerequisite for success during the catching-up phase. Yet today, as the focus shifts to research, product design and market development, the educational system is poorly equipped to cope with these new requirements.

In short, as a result of its earlier success, Korea's innovation system is now faced with new challenges. It is characterized by a number of structural weaknesses, which by now have been well identified and extensively debated within both the government and management circles. Yet the inertia resulting from previous success and established power structures appears to constrain Korea's ability to adapt to the new competitive environment. The search for a new policy doctrine and new corporate strategies remains constrained by a highly unequal distribution of economic and political power.

Most of the current problems of Korea's electronics industry can be traced back to some peculiar features of the Korean export model, which focused on rapid export expansion based on imported technology and on 'octopus-like' diversification strategies. This pattern of growth has limited the formation of a broad set of domestic technological capabilities, especially for system and circuit design, market development and software engineering. As the globalization of competition has drastically increased barriers to entry into the electronics industry, such bottlenecks in Korea's technological capabilities have now become a major constraint to a further expansion of electronics exports. This has given rise to an intensive debate in Korea on what changes are required in government policies and the competitive strategies of Korean electronics firms.

A radical paradigm shift is overdue, as Korea has reached the limits of the old export-led industrialization model with its emphasis on standardized mass production, original equipment manufacturing exporting and a catch-up mentality. These limits are rooted in fundamental changes in the nature of international competition and in the inability of the traditional Korean growth model to cope with these new challenges. They are systemic in the sense that, with only limited variation in timing, they apply with roughly equal force to different sectors of the Korean economy. The international environment in the 1990s is not nearly as welcoming to latecomers as that of the 1970s and early 1980s. Competition has globalized and become more knowledge-based, making it more difficult for firms to identify market niches and to grow with them. Competition centers around global standards that are set by a handful of powerful technopolists, such as Intel and Microsoft. Korean firms can no longer focus exclusively on price competition but must simultaneously match best practice in quality, product innovation and speed to market. Under these competitive conditions, the static comparative advantage on which Korean firms have based their export success erodes more rapidly. Probably the most dramatic warning sign for a country that is heavily dependent on trade is the dramatic increase of Korea's current account deficit, which is estimated to have reached a record $23 billion.[41] The largest in the world after the United States, the deficit is now almost 5 per cent of Korea's gross domestic product.

Moving beyond these limits will require a number of fundamental changes in the Korean business system. This is true for government policies and industry structure as well as for firm organization and strategies. In order to simply keep up with the new challenges of global competition, Korea needs to move ahead with technological deepening that involves strong product innovation capabilities, closer attention to client needs and the development of new markets. Strengthening the financial and technological capabilities of domestic small- and medium-size enterprises is a second essential element of such a paradigm shift. Third, in order to improve their scope for learning and knowledge creation, Korea's *chaebols* need to open up their hierarchical and centralized governance structures. Fourth, a selective liberalization of imports and inward foreign direct investment is essential for improving access to generic technologies and core components through closer participation in international technology networks. Finally, Korean electronics firms need to move beyond export-led international market penetration and to improve the balance between the location of their markets and production sites by expanding and

---

[41] *Financial Times*, 9 January 1997, p. 11.

upgrading their international production networks in the United States as well as in Asia and Europe. While Korean firms and the state understand that such changes are long overdue, they have yet to take the necessary actions needed to fully make this transition.

Conclusions

This chapter has shown that nationality is just one among various factors that shape industrial dynamics. The main determinant of firm behaviour is competitive dynamics and not national origin. Nationality matters, which implies that an economic analysis that excludes history and the development of institutions is ill equipped to address the question of globalization. But nationality is just one determining factor among others, and its relative importance is likely to decline over time as firms learn to develop their capacity to manage technology.

By choosing an evolutionary perspective, this chapter discards some popular misconceptions. This applies in particular to Whitley's comparative-static theory of national business systems and its claim that there is a unified Korean approach to the organization of international production networks. Equally misleading is the claim that the Korean business system is largely resistant to change. An evolutionary perspective can help to improve our understanding of the importance of nationality. Peculiar features of Korea's institutions have certainly shaped the development of Korea's approach to technology management. However, so have other factors that result from industry-specific features and from the dynamics of competition.

6

Institutional Context of Ghanaian Firms and Cross-national Inter-firm Relations

Olav Jull Sørensen and John Kuada

Recent studies by economic sociologists have shown a growing awareness of the diversity of successful business strategies and economic development recipes and have drawn attention to factors hitherto ignored in economic analysis of market based economies. The dichotomy of socialism and capitalism has been replaced by a search for national characteristics that shape the development of economies and a refinement of yardsticks for measuring economic success. It has been argued on the basis of evidence from western economies as well as the economies of selected Asian countries that national recipes of successful economic development emerge on the basis of an irreplicable chain of fortuitous local circumstances. Each recipe is therefore unique and non-transferable across socio-cultural boundaries (Whitley 1991, 1992b, 1992c; Schultz and Pecotich 1997).

A notable characteristic of these studies is that they focus on the national context of business systems and engage in comparisons between countries. The impact of national contexts on international business relations has received limited attention. Furthermore, business systems of African countries have not as yet received any attention in the current studies. The fact that African economies have not chalked up the same degree of success so evident in Asian economies in recent decades makes the study of special research interest. Finally, the issue of change has not been explicitly introduced into the models such as Whitley's that have guided many of the studies. However, since the main goal of market economies is to secure continuous growth and development of the respective countries, the capacity of business systems to promote change is of a vital concern.

These observations have informed the present study. An understanding of business systems in Africa requires an insight into the social institutions, popular expectation and political as well as economic experiments in post-independent Africa. Most African countries south of the Sahara attained political independence in the 1960s. Independence was ushered in with jubilation by the societies, which considered the event as a harbinger of economic prosperity throughout the continent. The expectations of socio-economic development were, however, belied. On the one hand, the imported economic models and institutions proved ineffective within the social context that surfaced after the colonial administrators left the scene. On the other hand, the post-independence politicians realized that the world has changed to such an extent that reinstating traditional modes of organizing production and distribution could not meet the requirements of their societies. Above all, no viable synthesis between the old and new could be immediately provided. Several leaders found the socialist model of the Soviet bloc and China an appealing (albeit tantalizing) alternative and tried to carve an African version for their societies, but without distinctive economic success. The structural adjustment program of the mid-1980s sponsored by the International Monetary Fund and the World Bank is an attempt to dismantle the vestiges of the economic experiments of the 1960s and 1970s.

The Ghanaian political economic experience discussed in detail in this chapter epitomizes the general situation in many African countries. It illustrates how the combination of state entrepreneurship, politically inflicted economic mismanagement, as well as the dominant sociocultural structures and values have produced a complex institutional context resulting in decades of economic decline.

The choice of Ghana as an illustrative case of the African situation is appropriate for the simple reasons that Ghana was the first African country of the south Sahara to gain political independence from European colonial administrators, and was judged to have a good base for rapid economic development in the late 1950s and early 1960s. The economic derailment in Ghana, caused partly by the factors mentioned above, has been repeated in several other African countries with minor modifications. At the same time, Ghana was one of the first African countries to adopt the structural adjustment program. The liberalization of the economy started already in 1983. The current attempts to revive the economy are discussed in this chapter, with a focus on the impact of global integration and cross-national inter-firm relations as well as the Ghanaian way of redefining the role of the state and the relationship between government and business.

The empirical evidence on which our arguments are based derives from a review of the literature on post-independence economic policies and activities in Ghana as well as recent studies conducted by the present authors into the internationalization process of Ghanaian firms (Kuada and Sørensen 2000). The discussions are undertaken at two levels: (1) the national context of business activities, and (2) the relationship between firms based in different (and apparently disparate) business systems.

The foundational concepts in the chapter are *perception* and *interaction*. Briefly explained, the concept of perception addresses the basis of human behaviour in encounters with other social actors. It is generally acknowledged that human perceptions are informed by prior experiences, knowledge, expectations and understanding. In fact, people perceive more than they actually see in any given situation, since people tend to use previous knowledge and experiences to ascribe meaning to what the senses register (Crossley 1996). Most often, we hold firmly to our perceptions, believing them to be right.

Viewed in terms of the central issues in this chapter, it will be argued that the perceptions that Ghanaian business people and institutional actors have of each other influence the responses they manifest in the course of their interaction. Their behaviour towards each other, in turn, influences the subsequent development of the Ghanaian business system. Similarly, the perceptions Ghanaian and foreign business people have of each other do influence their interaction.

The chapter is organized as follows. First the Whitley framework is unfolded. Then, in three sections, the Whitley framework is used to describe the Ghanaian business system and its institutional context with a focus on international business links and government-business relations. The last section provides the theoretical reflection on the empirical evidence: First the dominant business systems model is suggested, then the government-business relationship is modelled explicitly and the framework is extended to include the interaction between different business systems. Our foundational concepts of perception and interaction are discussed and related to Whitleys framework. The discussion here emphasizes the understanding that business systems are social constructions that emerge dynamically as a result of the daily and strategic interaction between actors within the business system itself as well as the interaction between the system actors and those of the institutional context.

An Overview of the Business Systems Concept

The concept of Business Systems is used by Whitley (1992b:6) to cover arrangements of hierarchy-market relations that become institutionalized and relatively successful (or unsuccessful) in a particular context. This is in contrast to the hitherto dominant pure market approach to the analysis of the behaviour of economic actors (Hamilton and Biggart 1988). The market approach follows the rationalities underlying neoclassical economic thinking, which holds that wherever the market principles are introduced, the logic of competition will prevail and, eventually, all economies will be alike. In contrast, the business systems approach considers the sociocultural context within which economic actors operate as well as the political and power relations that govern the coordination and control of economic resources in a given country.

Whitley divides the market economy into a two-sector system, i.e., the enterprise subsystem that he conceptualizes as the business system and the institutional subsystem. The business system is described in terms of a set of features, divided into three groups, and the institutional subsystem is divided into two, one revealing the basic cultural values within society and the other comprising the institutions and actions of everyday life, in Whitley's terminology, the background and proximate institutions respectively. The two main subsystems are shown in Figure 6.1.

Concerning the relations between the subsystems, the background institutions constitute a stable base on which the business system develops. The position of the proximate social institutions is less clear. First, Whitley groups the labour market and the financial market under the proximate institution. Although these two markets are structured differently from the markets included in the business system, it can be strongly argued that they also belong to the business system. Second, the proximate institutions also form part of the state and, as will be shown later, Whitley considers the state to be the boundary of the business system because it both influences the institutional arrangements and shapes the business system.[1]

Whitley's model has become a dominant model in studies of business systems. It has therefore been used in this chapter to guide our discussion of the Ghanaian case as well as the theoretical reflections we undertake at the end (see Figure 6.1).

Key Features of the Ghanaian Business System

The post-independence economic history of Ghana, as well as of other African countries (Hyden 1994), has been characterized (until recently) by a remarkable consistency in a political mistrust of private capitalism and the market system. Under the Nkrumah government (1957–66), the state was ideologically considered the most legitimate custodian of national wealth

---

[1] For a more detailed meta-theoretical discussion of the business system model, see Wad 1997.

Figure 6.1
A Framework for Business Systems Analysis

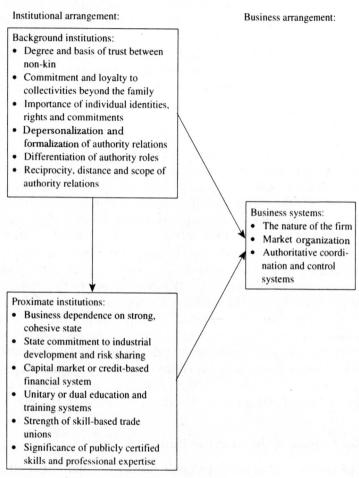

Institutional arrangement:

Background institutions:
• Degree and basis of trust between non-kin
• Commitment and loyalty to collectivities beyond the family
• Importance of individual identities, rights and commitments
• Depersonalization and formalization of authority relations
• Differentiation of authority roles
• Reciprocity, distance and scope of authority relations

Business arrangement:

Business systems:
• The nature of the firm
• Market organization
• Authoritative coordination and control systems

Proximate institutions:
• Business dependence on strong, cohesive state
• State commitment to industrial development and risk sharing
• Capital market or credit-based financial system
• Unitary or dual education and training systems
• Strength of skill-based trade unions
• Significance of publicly certified skills and professional expertise

Country framework

Source: Adapted from Whitley (1992b).

and a guarantor of collective social benefits for the variegated constellation of ethnic groups that form Ghana. Successive governments during the 1960s and 1970s (except for the Busia government, 1969–72) showed similar distrust for markets as an effective and fair resource allocating mechanism. Thus, development plans and economic policies formulated during this period placed strong emphasis on investment in projects with low private but high social profitability (Huq 1989). However, the allocation of economic resources through administrative mechanisms has been fraught with serious weaknesses. This, as numerous analysts have observed, accounts, to a considerable extent, for the decline in the economy from mid-1960 to mid-1980 (Hutchful 1995; Green 1987). This section provides detailed discussion of economic policies and results during the period. It also draws attention to the sociocultural and political institutions that constituted the organizing context of entrepreneurial activities in Ghana.

State Ownership and Entrepreneurial Activities

The Nkrumah government's policy of using the state as an authoritative instrument of industrial growth led to the establishment of over 100 state-owned light manufacturing enterprises during the first half of the 1960s. Most of these enterprises were located in the Accra-Tema metropolis with less than 10 per cent of the country's population at that time. They were to form the core of the formal sector of the economy, but accounted for only 12 per cent of the gross domestic product in 1974 (Kuada 1980). The geographical concentration of the factories encouraged rural–urban migration, thereby depleting the rural agricultural sectors of the needed workforce and frustrating the social mobility aspirations of the youth who arrived in the urban areas only to find themselves unemployed as the absorption capacity of the factories was below the migration rate. Furthermore, being import-substitution factories, they relied mainly on imported inputs and technology and therefore exerted severe strain on the foreign exchange resources of Ghana. The industrial sector became grossly inefficient and remained a drain on the country's resources for several decades. In a recent study, Lall and Wignaraja (1996) concluded that the sector on the whole was characterized by very weak technological capacity and innovative capability. The best among them were merely capable of using imported technologies relatively well. As such, the manufacturing firms are highly vulnerable to international competition.

Private Sector Development

The most important private entrepreneurial activity during the early post-independence period was within the cocoa sector. It contributed 12 per cent of the gross domestic product in the 1960s, 60–70 per cent of the total export earnings, and 30 per cent of government revenue (Huq 1989). However, the ideological slant of the government's economic policies meant that the comparative advantage that Ghana had in the cocoa sector at that time was not fully utilized. Not only did cocoa producers witness a sharp decline in their real income due to state control of producer prices,[2] they also experienced chronic shortages of required inputs.[3] Consequently, there was a drastic reduction in the volume and value of cocoa exports.[4] Arguably, this provided disincentives to local production and created distortions in inter-sector comparative efficiency.[5] The process of private capital accumulation and investment was therefore stifled.

Although ignored by the government in its economic development strategies, the informal sector has remained the mainstay of the economy, contributing over 50 per cent of gross domestic product (Abaka 1993). It is composed of the agricultural sector, which is characterized by peasant farming involving rural family units, and the local distributive sector, which is dominated by female traders.[6] Only a handful of traders have substantial independent operational capital,

---

[2] Cocoa producers received in 1980–81 only 20 per cent of what they received in 1962–63.

[3] Only 20 per cent of required inputs for the cocoa farmers were available in the country in 1977 (Huq 1989).

[4] By 1980, Ghana's cocoa exports were only one-third of its volume of exports in the early 1960s.

[5] It has been estimated that the landed import prices in 1982 were less than 10 per cent of the farm gate prices of domestically produced goods (Huq 1989).

[6] Mercantile activities have always remained outside effective state control.

while most operate as single-person trading units. The export trading subsector is, however, dominated by male traders, some of whom export local products that are usually sold by their female counterparts on the domestic market (Kuada and Sørensen 2000). Although substantial economic resources are controlled by the distributive sector as such, the atomistic composition of the sector greatly limits its capacity to influence the pattern of economic direction in the country in any authoritative manner.

Enterprise Specialization and Development

Whitley (1990) mentions two distinct features in the analysis of coordination and interdependence of enterprises within a national context. The first is inter-sector alliances (i.e., horizontal coordination) and the second is the involvement of state agencies in the coordination of economic activities around politically defined economic objectives (i.e., vertical coordination).

Unlike the Asian economies analyzed by Hamilton and Biggart (1988) as well as Whitley (1990, 1991), long-term horizontal linkages are hitherto virtually nonexistent in the Ghanaian economy. Local businesses are rather fragmentary, and there is a pronounced mistrust among Ghanaian businesspeople for non-kin business partners. There is a strong aversion to engage in joint ownership arrangements with fellow Ghanaians, even when such arrangements are judged to be of extreme importance to the growth of their enterprises.[7] This aversion is partly due to the fear of local entrepreneurs of losing managerial control over their firms and an eventual take-over by a 'smarter' partner. Business contacts between suppliers and their customers are mainly transactional rather than relational. Thus, resource-sharing arrangements found in some Asian countries through horizontal business links

[7] Our respondents at the African Project Development Facility (APDF) in Accra showed an obvious bewilderment about Ghanaian investors' unwillingness to enter into joint ownership with either local or foreign investors even when economic analysis shows evident benefits for such an arrangement.

(Whitley 1990, 1991) are lacking in Ghana (Aryeetey et al. 1984; Danida 1995).

Furthermore, Ghanaian entrepreneurs engage in several unrelated businesses at the same time, many of them not formed on the basis of the specialized skills and core competence of their owners or managers. The rationale for such unrelated diversification (even when the investment in each is relatively meager) is one of hedging against an unwelcome turn of events in each business sector and an attempt to stay outside the reach of and control by public agencies. The cultural obligation of finding jobs for relatives and friends also justifies the creation of new enterprises. An entrepreneur who would like to maintain a disciplined ('professional') management in his or her key firm may establish a couple of other secondary firms on which family members are employed; the key firm is thereby kept free from family interference.

Authority, Loyalty and Management Style

Authority systems in Ghanaian enterprises tend to be highly personal. Kuada (1994) coins the term *authoritarian-benevolence* to describe the dominant leadership style in Ghana. This conforms with conventional cultural guidelines discussed below. Due to the wide power distance in the country, senior managers perceive the conspicuous exercise of power as a source of respect and status within the immediate environment. Being a status symbol, power may be displayed for its own sake and not necessarily as a means of influencing situations and attaining specific organizational goals. Characteristics of such leadership behaviour include close supervision of subordinates, elaborate instructions on all matters and disapproval of deviations from such instructions. This is not to say that such exercise of power is always to the disadvantage of the organization in which the leader participates. For example, in matters of resource acquisition within muddled political and administrative systems, the relative power differences of the leaders representing the competing organizations or units within a given organization can determine the amount of resources they can bring home. In such situations, however, the manager may be consciously exercising his or her power to support the attainment of specified organizational goals.

Although authoritarian directives are generally administered by superiors, managers are selective in their patronage of subordinates, providing extra opportunities and privileges to those closest and subservient to their interests. Thus, the Ghanaian employee knows that it is necessary to cultivate the 'right' people, particularly his immediate superior, in order to have a successful career. Since seniority in traditional social structures commands unflinching loyalty, a subordinate tends to believe that his or her superior is likely to value personal loyalty and goodwill over and above competence. It is this reciprocity of support and benefit that sustains superior-subordinate relationships. However, unlike Asian countries such as Japan, South Korea and China (Hamilton and Biggart 1998; Whitley 1991), employee commitment in Ghana is not long term. Training investment can therefore be lost through high labour turnover among the managerial cadre, many of whom migrate to take up new jobs in foreign countries.

Recent Economic Policies

The unsuccessful experiments with state entrepreneurship, the discouragement of private capital accumulation, poor management and undisciplined implementation of economic policies combined to inflict serious economic hardship on Ghana between 1965 and 1985. The immediate decline occurred in all major sectors of the economy and was combined with high rates of inflation (reaching 120 per cent annually in the early 1980s) as well as a destabilization of the state budget.[8] At the same time, the population was growing at an annual rate of 3 per cent and the urban population at about 5 per cent, leading to a severe pressure on the supply of all goods and services and a high rate of unemployment, particularly in the urban areas (see Loxley 1988 for a detailed account).

[8] Government revenue covered less than half of the 1981–82 total expenditure (Nugent 1995).

From 1984, the Rawlings government initiated a series of economic policies under the World Bank-sponsored structural adjustment program aimed at reversing the economic decline. The key elements of the economic recovery program included liberalization of prices, rationalization and privatization of state-owned enterprises, extensive infrastructural rehabilitation projects and legal provisions aimed at improvement of the overall investment climate in the country. In the area of public sector investment, a three-year public investment program was introduced since 1986 as a means of streamlining and directing public expenditure to specified growth objectives. About 60 per cent of all public investment program funds have been allocated to infrastructural rehabilitation (roads, highways, ports, etc.), 30 per cent have been devoted mainly to the rehabilitation of the cocoa and mining sector and 10 per cent for social sector development, including health and education (Tsikata and Amuzu 1997). At the same time, efforts were made to reduce the dependence of state-owned enterprises on state subvention through divestiture and demand for improved efficiency and financial management. Public sector employees were also redeployed in large numbers while fees were introduced in the educational, health and other social sectors.

The reduced state involvement in the vertical coordination of economic activities creates a situation in which local entrepreneurs operate more independently. In more recent years, the vertical coordinating role has been increasingly played by both locally formed industry (product) associations and foreign state (development) agencies. The catalytic role of the foreign agencies as authoritative systems has encouraged cross-border interfirm links and ownership relations (such as joint ventures). The implications that these new developments carry for the business system are explored subsequently.

The Institutional Context of the Ghanaian Business System

This section examines the background and proximate institutions (using Whitley's terminology) that have impacted the characteristics of the Ghanaian business system discussed above. The background institutions discussed here are the Ghanaian family structure (which defines the expectations and obligations of individuals and influences the business decisions of local entrepreneurs) and the extent of non-kin relations and trust. This is followed by discussions of Ghana's post-independence political institutions and administrative arrangements to provide an insight into the proximate institutions and explain the nature of relationship between the business community and the state machinery. The section also discusses the cross-border inter-firm relations that have emerged within the export sector in recent years.

Familism, Individual Obligations and Business Decisions

From a sociological perspective, it is valid to state that the family is the primary social unit in relation to individuals in the Ghanaian society.[9] In this regard, all values are determined by reference to the maintenance, continuity and functioning of the family group. Within such a social framework, all purposes, actions, gains and ideals of individual members are evaluated by comparison with the fortune of the family as a whole. Individual members of the family are bound to one another by the collective moral rules and obligations of the family. The family therefore limits, influences and, in some situations, determines the individual's activities in society.

The patterns of dependence affect the dominant personality traits that sociological studies have uncovered in Ghana. Assimeng (1981), for example, observes that 'conformity and blatant eschewing of individual speculations' as well as 'unquestioning acquiescence and accommodationism' are dominant characteristics of the behaviour of young Ghanaians. This, he argues, is due to the collectivist social structure that strongly encourages the maintenance of the status quo and the avoidance of any serious disruption of the specific social order. The leadership styles found in Ghanaian firms and public

---

[9] The Ghanaian concept of family embraces everyone having the same ancestral root. The nature of the obligations to family members is, however, determined by whether the community is matriarchal or patriarchal.

institutions have apparently been influenced by this culturally motivated collective disposition.

When viewed in terms of the requirement that a society must be able to mobilize loyalty and commitments to collective entities beyond the immediate family to ensure effective coordination of economic activities (Whitley 1992b:21), the Ghanaian social structure appears to offer a weak basis for effective market-firm interaction. However, as will become evident in the management of leading exporting firms discussed below, the fulfillment of family obligations may not always impede the management of business entities. In some situations, family commitments ensure intra-organizational cohesion and improve the competitive capability of firms.

Non-kin Trust Relations and their Managerial Implications

Moving away from the immediate family confines, it can be noticed that the patterns of socialization in urban communities in Ghana and within educational institutions have emerged as a context within which strong bonds of relationship and trust are developed outside the family circles. It has also produced a new means for achieving social mobility, replacing ascribed positions that are in traditional societies (Assimeng, 1981). As a result, new subcultures are formed among the highly educated members of the society who have their roots in shared intellectual and social experiences from school days. Alumni, Old Boys Associations and Professional Bodies are among organizations that provide institutional framework for socialization among the élite groups within the Ghanaian society, occasionally cutting across ethnic divides. Top executives in Ghana have generally attended the same schools and normally participate in the same social clubs. It is therefore not unusual for them to share a common frame of reference and managerial perception. However, non-kin trusts are, as stated earlier, still weak in inter-firm relations. Ghanaian entrepreneurs are generally unwilling to enter into joint ownership arrangements with local investors in order to avoid the sharing of authority that such an arrangement can entail. Thus, with limited prospects for bank loans and other external financial arrangements, entrepreneurs are compelled to rely on their meager savings to finance business growth.

The Political System and the Administrative Machinery

Turning now to the proximate institutions, political authority in Ghana has been consistently centralized before and during the aftermath of political independence. It has either taken the form of one-party civilian monopoly as under Nkrumah during the first half of the 1960s or through military dictatorships. This fact has several implications for the formulation and implementation of major economic policies that formed the context of business development in the country. First, democratic decision-making processes at top political levels have been lacking. Since the policies of military regimes did not require the endorsement of the citizens and the governments were not held accountable for their decisions, there was no pressure on them to undertake continual judicious assessment of their decisions. Secondly, the administrative class of the country (i.e., the civil servants) and the military rulers did not share a common educational background and career aspirations. There was therefore no firm basis for the administrative and political institutions to evolve a common and committed approach to development in the country. Thirdly, each successive military government saw its period of administration as temporary, i.e., to prepare the way for a new civilian administration. Thus, apart from Rawlings' second military government (1982–92), none of the military governments considered long-term coherent economic development as a primary objective. What counts as a proximate institution in Ghana therefore has no solid political foundation nor a purposeful and consistent direction.

It is also important to note that the economic development policies and strategies initiated under the Nkrumah government necessitated the establishment of several ministries and specialized public institutions to act as coordination and control instruments for the state and to provide and supervise the infrastructural framework for state entrepreneurial activities. The rapidity with which the organizations were created, however, resulted in an acute dearth of skilled managerial staff to fill the various vacancies. Many of them were filled with less qualified people who were offered the jobs on the basis of nepotism or as a token of gratitude for political favours. The degrees of responsibility and status assumed by top of officials in the public institutions were therefore disproportionate to the qualifications and capacity of some of them, and this had evident implications for the management of the institutions.

Stated differently, while loyalty within family circles is based on accepted ascribed status and position, loyalty within the political hierarchy involves personal subordination to individual leaders or people in authority. Such loyalties are usually motivated by expectations of short-term personal gains. As Nugent (1995) informs, the attitude exhibited by most Ghanaians to their politicians has deep historical roots in the Asante state machinery, which was built on the principle that those chosen to exercise power also have the responsibility to actively further the economic prosperity of their subjects. Hence kinship relations with top politicians and civil servants have enabled a limited segment of the society to make enormous quick returns by off-loading imported goods on the black market, particularly in the 1970s and early 1980s, when import licenses were issued under the pretext of import restriction.[10] Corruption has, therefore, flourished within the public sector and has tainted the image of the state machinery.

In summary, the failure of state entrepreneurship in the 1960s and 1970s and the general high level of unemployment weakened people's confidence in the state's capacity to organize economic activities. Interaction between the state machinery and the private business sector has been strictly regulatory. Furthermore, the drastic economic decline of the period compelled public officials to engage in morally questionable

---

[10] Statements made by each new political leader to legitimate his own policies clearly indicate that corruption and economic mismanagement are officially recognized problems. Analysts of Ghana's economy wonder how the citizens have been able to tolerate such naked avarice and mismanagement by their leaders for so long. See, for example, Huq 1989; Nugent 1995.

behaviours, thereby further damaging people's respect for state authority.

Thus, despite examples of excellent individual behaviour and commitment to work, the public institutions in Ghana are generally perceived by the citizens (especially private business-people) as excessively bureaucratic and staffed by corrupt and poorly motivated officials who calculatedly impede economic and non-economic activities in the country (Huq 1989; Nugent 1995). Furthermore, in the perception of the business community, interdepartmental work within the Ghanaian administrative machinery is poorly coordinated, and firms use unduly large resources to muddle through the administrative jungle to comply with the institutional directives relating to their businesses.

Ghana's Export Sector Development: Some Empirical Evidence

As mentioned earlier, the Rawling government has discontinued the policy of overwhelming direct state ownership of enterprises and import substitutions and has endorsed the pursuance of export-led growth based on private entrepreneurship. The response of private businesspeople to state initiatives to develop the export sector has received limited empirical investigation. Available figures show that exporters are gradually responding to the changed economic climate. However, the responses are still relatively weak. According to ISSER (2000), in the period 1994 to 1999, total exports increased nominally by 70 per cent, bringing its share of gross domestic product to around 27 per cent. The export sector diversification has remained relatively low, with the three main traditional products (gold, timber and cocoa) accounting for 70 per cent of total exports in 1999, while non-traditional exports accounted for only 11.2 per cent. The number of non-traditional export products has increased from 99 in 1986 to 270 in 1999. The increase is partly due to a reclassification of products. In comparison, the number of exporters of non-traditional products has steadily increased from 373 in 1986 to 1,331 in 1988 and to 3,339 in 1996. However, the number fell to 2,597 in 1999. The average export per exporter has increased from US\$ 47,000 in 1994 to US\$ 156,000 in 1999.

In this section of the chapter we report the results of empirical studies we conducted into the internationalization of 20 Ghanaian firms of non-traditional products (Kuada and Sørensen 2000) and into the international strategic alliances of 10 Ghanaian firms.[11] Furthermore, we discuss some of the government initiatives and the manner in which they have altered the exporters' perception and relationship to the proximate institutions.

Profiles of Ghanaian Export Businesses

Judging from the results of our recent studies into the internationalization process of Ghanaian firms, two groups of people have responded positively to the new open economy and its export opportunities. The first group is composed of local entrepreneurs who started their export businesses from scratch. The second group are managers of already established manufacturing enterprises who turned to exports in order to improve their capacity utilization in the light of declining local market opportunities. Examining the first group in more details one notices that nearly all of them have previous managerial experiences either from established private enterprises before starting on their own or from managing their own firms within non-export business. The entry into the export business is therefore their second career undertaking. It is remarkable to observe that only one of 20 firms has an owner with a career background in the public sector (a former university professor). Although it was anticipated that the structural adjustment program, with its focus on a lean public sector, would motivate public employees to go private and become entrepreneurs, one is tempted to hypothesize that the public sector appears not to produce entrepreneurs to the same extent as the private

---

[11] The findings from the study of international strategic alliances are preliminary as the study is a longitudinal one.

sector. However, before any policy conclusions are drawn, it is important to note that a number of public employees have remained in their jobs while starting a private business. The job in the public sector provides access to 'free' resources, including means of communication, transport and extensive spare time, which reduce the resources required to start a new business.

Another distinct characteristic of this entrepreneurial group is that most of them have fairly high education (a first university degree or above) and are members of established professional bodies. All of them have exposure to foreign cultures (mostly Western Europe or North America) either by studying in these countries and/or working there. This evidence collaborates with recent findings reported by Lall and Wignaraja (1996) in their study of the manufacturing sector in Ghana.

Economic survival appears to be the overriding motive of most of the entrepreneurs. Nearly all of them have rounded their mid-forties before starting their businesses and did so because their salaries at the time were inadequate to cater for the immediate needs of the family let alone provide for their pension age. Thus, economic difficulties can act as a catalyst that sets a change process in a business system in motion— at times, as can be seen below, in spite of the institutional context.

Regarding the impact of the background institutions on export business, most of the entrepreneurs have shown innovative examples of accommodating their culturally imposed obligations without sacrificing their professional effectiveness. There are examples of entrepreneurs assigning recruitment responsibilities to their expatriate managers and holding themselves in the background. In this way they can defend themselves against any accusations of not employing family members. Others establish farms and other businesses that can absorb family members, thereby keeping them away from their export businesses. Where family involvement is permitted, family members employed in managerial positions are exclusively the children and wives of the owners, all of whom are shareholders in the company. By giving them a direct stake in the business and offering them opportunities for training abroad, these family members not only show commitment but also have the requisite knowledge to carry out their responsibilities in the companies.

State Coordination and Promotional Arrangements for the Export Sector

Annexure 6.1 provides a list of institutions established or revamped under the structural adjustment program to directly promote the activities of exporting firms or to facilitate the export sector development in general. Other institutions have been strengthened to regulate activities within the sector and to discourage unwarranted behaviour of firms. A few of the institutions have been established or funded by foreign aid organizations such as the United States Agency for International Development (USAID) as their contribution to the export sector development program. (For details on export promotion programs, see Tetteh 1996.)

Our studies of the internationalization process of Ghanaian firms addressed among other things the following questions with respect to the relationships between the export businesses and the institutions: To what extent are their activities geared to the needs of the firms? Are the firms aware of the various facilities that they offer? To what extent do they use them? How do the firms perceive the institutional context in general?

The results show that the Ghana Export Promotion Council appears to have made the most distinctive impact on the operations of the exporting firms. All serious exporters are registered with the Council. The Council, through its contact with leading trading organizations in potential export markets as well as such multilateral agencies as the United Nations-funded International Trade Centre, acts as the first stop for foreign wholesale-retail chains or their agencies interested in sourcing their goods from Ghana. It, therefore, provides neophyte exporters with the requisite information about foreign markets and arranges exhibition tours and trade fairs for them. The rest of the facilitating institutions are either unknown to the respondents or their activities are considered to be of no notable importance to their operations.

Apart from the Ghana Export Promotion Council, the foreign-sponsored agencies appear to be doing better than the local ones. The Trade and Investment Programme sponsored by USAID has been mentioned by 20 per cent of the respondents as making a notable contribution to the export business environment.

The role of the regulatory institutions is mixed, partly due to the new export incentive programs they have been required to administer in recent years. Most of the respondents consider the Customs, Excise and Preventive Service to be an institution that is a potential source of benefit. This is, apparently, due to the duty drawback scheme administered by Customs, Excise and Preventive Service, which reimburses exporters for import duty previously paid for the materials used in producing the export products. The underlying logic of the scheme is good. However, many exporters consider the procedure for reclaiming the duty to be unduly cumbersome and time-consuming, and only a small number of firms attempt to reclaim it.

In summary, the governmental proximate institutions related to export promotion schemes and activities have not been perceived by exporters as playing the key role in export development as originally envisioned. Part of the reason is that the institutions are poorly resourced. Part of the reason may be that exporters and businesspeople in general are used to seeing public institutions as regulatory and exploitative and are unable to believe that positive changes can be made within the institutions within such a short span of time. Stories still circulate within the business community about how difficult it is for business owners to make any sense of the administrative jungle and to comply with the institutional directives relating to their businesses. Many find it more rewarding to ignore the export institutions, even where economic incentives have been promised. Some of the companies are either simply unaware of the facilities provided by the institutions or make unrealistic demands and expect support beyond the capability of any export promotion system.

Furthermore, it can be argued that, while the activities of most institutions are geared to export promotion, i.e., downstream activities, a number of Ghanaian firms internationalize through upstream activities. Thus, the institutions may actually be offering services not immediately relevant to some of the firms. This discrepancy between needs and services offered may be a reflection of the lack of constructive dialogue between the business system and the government institutions.

Non-governmental Coordinating Institutions

Non-governmental institutions such as the Ghana National Chamber of Commerce, the Association of Ghanaian Industries together with business clubs such as the Danish-Ghanaian Business Club and social clubs such as Rotary provide avenues for formal and informal business interactions within the export sector. In addition to this, a number of trade and product associations have been established in recent years, particularly within the non-traditional export sub-sector, to organize and support interaction among firms to solve common problems. Such product associations are promoted by the Federation of Associations of Ghanaian Exporters, which also serves as an official link for the firms in their interactions with the public sector. Units funded by international organizations (such as the African Project Development Facility) have also been established in recent years to support businesses in general. Within this network of formal and semi-formal structures, it has been possible for the enterprising Ghanaian firms to get access to business information, new ideas and technology to improve their activities and to jointly work towards the amelioration of their business conditions, particularly with respect to the public institutions.

Cross-national Inter-firm Relations

The foreign business systems faced by the neophyte Ghanaian exporters can, broadly speaking, be divided into two: (1) the neighbouring African countries, and (2) the mature market economies, notably Western Europe. Within Europe, the market may in turn be divided into the general European market and specific segments comprising Ghanaian and African customers.

The official export to neighbouring countries is relatively small but the unofficial (i.e., unregistered and often head-loaded) export is unknown but believed to be fairly high. Problems such as differences in language and business traditions as well as poor infrastructure combine with limited competitive advantages to weaken exporters' interests in cross-border trade. Only the non-registered (illegal) exporters have apparently been capable of overcoming these barriers by simply ignoring them—at some risk (Sørensen and Nyanteng 2000).

The export to Europe is risky and often not very lucrative. Rarely does the Ghanaian producer and exporter have a competitive advantage vis-à-vis other African countries. Although the Ghanaian pineapple is said to be both juicy and sweeter than pineapples from the Ivory Coast, it is not easy to get this message across to the European consumers. In addition to this, low production capacity, instability in product quality, low efficiency and limited knowledge about the European markets make them targets for possible opportunistic behaviours of European importers. The infrastructural facilities are also not of a level capable of supporting high level of export activity. One pineapple exporter even felt compelled by lack of adequate and regular space on commercial aircrafts to establish his own air cargo company to support his business. In sum, rarely can Ghanaian exporters dictate the terms of exchange. Mostly, their weak position enjoins them to adapt to the foreign business systems if they want to integrate into the world economy.

Combining the data from the two studies of exports and strategic alliances respectively, the findings indicate two distinct modes of interaction by developing country based firms with European market actors.

- Serious exporters may establish long-term contractual relationship with European importers, although the actual orders may be irregular and filled under spot-market conditions. Since Ghanaian exporters have very little insight into the mechanisms of the European market, they fall prey to the opportunistic behaviour of the importers, most of whom are small and in marginal positions within the commercial sectors of their countries.

- Companies may also enter into long-term partnership relations with European companies. The latter provide them with assistance on commercial terms (e.g., in the areas of technology, equipment, management and finance) in exchange for getting access to the local markets.

Seen from a Ghanaian company's viewpoint, the first type of cross-national business relations may be labeled downstream internationalization, and the latter may be termed upstream internationalization.[12] The empirical evidence shows that leading fresh pineapple and fruit juice exporters as well as exporters of seafood targeted at European consumers consider such long-term relations with importers to be imperative to their export performance. Where the degree of perishability of the exported products is high, long-term supplier-distributor relations reduce the exporters' anxiety about the market behaviour, if the European distributors provide the exporters with reliable market information and treat them fairly.

The upstream approach to internationalization has been adopted, for example, by producers of seafood for exports. Leading entrepreneurs in this sector have realized that their technological capacity levels as well as production and management expertise fall short of the requirements for successful performance on the global market. For this reason they have all sought assistance from bilateral aid organizations to find European counterparts that can assist them in upgrading their technology and training their staff to meet European standards. The emerging relationships are expected to be long term, and the European counterparts are expected to undertake equity investments in the Ghanaian firms and/or assume the responsibility for marketing the Ghanaian products in Europe.

These cross-national business relations invariably entail interaction between two business systems, i.e., the Ghanaian business system and the business systems of the various European countries in which their partners are located. The

---

[12] The concepts of upstream and downstream internationalization are discussed in detail in Kuada and Sørensen (2000).

interacting business systems may provide opportunities in some and create constraints for the relationship in other respects. However, during the course of interaction among the business partners, they may ignore or reduce the constraints or stimulate changes, particularly in the technology-dependent, i.e., the Ghanaian business system.

Theoretical Reflections on the Ghanaian Evidence

The Ghanaian evidence presented above provides some useful insights into the strengths and weaknesses of the existing models for business systems analysis within a global context. The aim of this section of the chapter is to draw attention to some of the issues not explicitly reflected in Whitley's model presented in Figure 6.1 and to offer suggestions for its extension. The discussions here are motivated by the following three observations:

- The conception of government-business relations in the model is too simplistic.
- The model does not adequately capture and discuss the interrelation among units from cross-national business systems.
- Although the model is predicated on the understanding that reality is socially constructed, the implications of this assumption for research into business systems seem to be ignored.

As argued below, the understanding of government-business relations and cross-national inter-firm relations must be explicitly introduced into the model since they underscore the patterns of change that must be expected in the business systems of the emerging market economies. Furthermore, the concepts of perception and interaction must be given more adequate attention in the analysis of the relationships between the various actors within and across business systems.

Government-business Relations

Arguably, the degree and results of interaction between the actors within the proximate institutions and the business community will produce an intersubjective understanding (positive or negative) between businesspeople and officials within the state organs. This perception and understanding will guide their subsequent behaviour towards each other. As the Ghanaian evidence suggests, when government-business relations have been characterized by mutual suspicion and discontent over several decades, it becomes extremely difficult to repair the damage and restore mutual confidence among the actors. This partly accounts for the limited impact of government schemes to promote and facilitate export initiated in Ghana since the mid 1980s.

The government's difficulties in reaching out to the business community lie further in the inability of successive governments to establish political legitimacy and build goodwill with the people. They have therefore been unable to extend their administrative powers to the grassroots level. That is, this level of the economy has always succeeded in keeping itself out of the reach (exit option) of state control. Other segments of the economy find it attractive to do the same. Although palaver, i.e., extensive discussions of problems and issues (voice option), is a key feature of the Ghanaian culture and administration in the traditional communities, post-independence governments have declined to use this approach in their relations with the business community.

However, our interviews with heads of the export development institutions suggest that the present government is anxious to establish a constructive dialogue with the business community, while the latter remains skeptical about the sincerity and capacity of government institutions to pursue genuine partnership relations.

These observations show that good insight into the business system development in a given country requires an explicit inclusion or modeling of government-business relations. This will enable the researcher to capture the dynamics of the relationship and thus focus less on its structure and causality. It is equally essential that the modeling of the relations be open-minded in order to avoid any pre-conceived views that may prevent a researcher from capturing the uniqueness of a country's government-business relations.

To this end, we introduce a general taxonomy of modes of governance of an economy and the impact that each mode can have on the relationship between government and business. Sørensen (1994) identified five major modes, presented in Table 6.1. They range from the central planning mode at one extreme to the laissez-faire mode of governance at the other. In between them lie the other three modes, where the relationship between government institutions and business is characterized either by division of labour, dialogue or supremacy on the part of government.

Analysts of business systems, in general, acknowledge the importance of the state's role in the management of market economies. The generally accepted view is that the state, as reflected in the Public Policy Supremacy model, has overwhelming power over businesses established within its jurisdiction. While this view may be true for some Asian countries (Wade 1990), it is not universally valid. There is little doubt that the policy formulation processes of the state machinery are important to an understanding of business systems development. However, taking the Scandinavian countries as an example, the dialogue between equal and socially legitimate partners, as reflected in the partnership model (see Table 6.1), may also constitute the core of and basis for the relationship between the government and the business community, and thus the basis for a policy formulation process.

Among the modes of governance suggested in Table 6.1, the public policy supremacy mode appears to capture the relationships that existed between government and business in several African countries until a decade ago. As indicated in the Ghanaian case, the trend today is towards dialogue, i.e., the partnership mode of governance. It is therefore purposeful to devote closer attention to this latter mode of governance in order to anticipate the nature of relationships that may be present in the business systems of some emerging market economies.

The partnership model assumes that the government and the business community are not hostile to each other, that they see each other as valuable and legitimate social actors. The model also assumes some measure of democratic attitudes. In

Table 6.1

Roles and Models of Governance in an Economy

Types of governance	Centre of authority	
	Public authority (public sector)	Private autonomy (private sector)
Laissez-faire	Minimize	Maximize
Mixed economy	Division of labour between the government and the private sector based on effectiveness and efficiency.	
Partnership oriented	Dialogue between government and the private sector, taking place within a network of public and private institutions.	
Public policy or government supremacy oriented	The government represents a unified political power and through policies, the government shapes or directs the actions of private businesses.	
Central planning	Maximize	Minimize

Source: Sørensen (1994).

the partnership model, interaction is a key concept. The interaction consists of an open dialogue that takes place in and through a set of public and private institutions, organizations and firms, or institutions with representatives from both the public and the private sector. The institutions, when properly managed, are not just another layer of bureaucracy but are able to carry out essential tasks, resolve conflicts and develop new ideas through their interaction. The institutions are loosely coupled and coordinated, i.e., they have some resources of their own and some degree of autonomy to deal with their areas of responsibility. Given this arrangement, the partnership model envisages the creation of a multicentered power structure, in contrast to the unified power structure of the public policy supremacy model. New institutions are created when either the business side or the government side feels the need, i.e., faces a problem that needs its attention. If both sides perceive the same need, a joint institution may be created.

Studying government-business interaction by focusing on organizations and the institutions has some additional advantages. An institution reflects the values in society and also power structures. It therefore reveals both barriers to and capability for change in a given society. At the more specific level, the goals, the resources and the tasks of the institutions can be identified and their organizational performance assessed. Finally, their relations to and positions vis-à-vis other organizations and institutions can be mapped and analyzed.

Thus, in a partnership model, the basic analytical unit is the institution, while the focus in the public policy supremacy model is on the policy and its formation. Viewing the state from an institutional perspective places the business system (by way of the firm) and the state (by way of state agencies) on the same analytical platform, making it possible to study their actual interaction.

Applying the partnership model in research investigations entails the identification of the public and private institutions that are relevant to a specific policy area of interest, e.g., export promotion. The identified institutions are studied in terms of their modes of organization, their resources, activities, ways of operation and, in particular, their patterns of interaction.

The institutions carry out one or more of the following five activities:

- Policy formulation: The formulation and analysis of problems and the offering of solutions.
- Campaign activities: The formulation and dissemination of the views held by the institution in question.
- Discourse activities: Testing the rationale underlying policies and views.
- Negotiations: Establishment of procedures as well as discussion of issues and formulation of compromises or resolution of conflicts.

- Implementation activities: Implementations of tasks and monitoring of performance.

The five activities constitute the dialogue between the government and the business community. The activities range from the more abstract level of conceptualization and policy analysis and formulation down to carrying out the daily activities. It is essential to note, that, in the partnership model, policies are not formulated by institutions over and above the day-to-day activities. They often emerge from the daily dialogue and activities within and between the implementing institutions.

Cross-country Interaction between Business Systems

As indicated earlier, Whitley intended to develop a framework for the comparison of market economies rather than understanding the interaction between different business systems. Although comparative studies of business systems are useful in their own right, the increasing globalization of businesses makes the study of interaction of business systems of equal, if not greater importance (Ohmae 1990; Levitt 1983). The question is whether the existing framework can handle the interaction. What happens when different business systems interact? Do they get into unresolved conflicts where war is the only outcome (re: the Cold War)? Do they transfer elements from one system to another, trying to replicate home-bred successful recipes abroad? Does the business system integrate or merge into one—a new business system (although not according to the same rationale as in economics), or does the interaction create a sub-business system that can code and decode messages from their underlying national business systems?

These pertinent issues have not been fully addressed in the present chapter and doubtlessly warrant elaborate research attention.

Our investigation of the internationalization process of Ghanaian companies, however, offers some insight into alternative ways of integrating developing country-based firms into the world economy and the role the proximate institutions play in the process. We have suggested that the various internationalization approaches can be placed into two broad categories: upstream and downstream modes of internationalization. Each approach has a different set of dynamics. In the case of exports, as the major downstream mode of internationalization, the proximate institutions will still be influential through the support they accord exporters who need to adjust to the requirements of other business systems they intend to penetrate with their products and services.

In case of foreign direct investment in a given country, the proximate institutions described in Whitley's model (Figure 6.1) are also influential in designing the conditions for such investments by foreign companies. However, the influence is limited by the fact that, to be attractive for such investment, the country must, to some extent, adjust to the needs of the investors. In addition, the influence is constrained by sharp competition between incentive packages from different countries.

Finally, in case of strategic alliances[13] (the major mode of upstream internationalization), the proximate institutions are less influential. The daily interaction at company level between two business systems and the building of long-term relationships between the companies enable the business systems to construct their own realities since they, unlike a government, are not bound by any state rationale.

It has been indicated above that Ghanaian companies increasingly form alliances and partnerships with developed country firms. The common denominator of these relationships is the sharing of complimentary resources and opportunities. For growth-oriented manufacturing firms, alliances with partners in the developed countries have the objective of raising their competitive capabilities through the improvement of their financial, technological as well as human resources. Since the process involves unlearning old habits enshrined in the prevailing Ghanaian business context and replacing them with

---

[13] Strategic alliances are here considered at the company level. However, according to Dunning (1995), we are now moving towards what he terms 'alliance capitalism'.

new ones, the relationship must be of a long-term nature in order to produce the desired impact.

For industrialized country firms that participate in this arrangement, their transactions with the developing country firms will constitute downstream internationalization, i.e., selling equipment and expertise. Their decisions to participate in the relationship will depend on their assessment of how the relationships fit into their overall international business objectives and strategies. The theoretical understanding underlying this perspective is that the parties enter this relationship on their own volition and will continue to do so as long as it remains attractive and mutually beneficial.

These observations have two implications. First, the unilateral adaptation process in the conventional view of internationalization of companies is replaced by mutual adaptation and construction. Through simple partnerships, an interaction process is started, often leading to more complex modes of cooperation and hence the creation of a new business system that cuts across countries. Second, the lead role of proximate institutions in the shaping of the business system is further undermined by an increase in international interaction. Although firms are embedded in a national institutional context, they are not defined by any national criteria *per se*. In that sense, they are borderless.

This is not the case with governmental institutions. They are defined and thus demarcated by the concept of a nation-state. For them, globalization or de-nationalization means losing their rationale for existence, while firms can relatively easily redefine their geographical scope and participate in the development of new non-national bounded business systems. Thus, when firms from two business systems start interacting, they will simultaneously unlearn and learn, or together build new ways of conducting their businesses based on new norms and values.

These observations imply that the comparative approach to business systems studies requires a revision. The state should remain as an important actor, but its supremacy should be modified for two reasons: (1) The state itself is increasingly integrated into a global economy, interacting with other states through supranational arrangements. (2) The role of the individual government must be modified to accommodate cross-country business interactions. These interactions have dynamics of their own that in turn, will influence the government and the proximate institutions at large. The primary actors in a globalization process will be companies in specific business systems. They may seek support from the proximate institutions, notably the government and the financial institutions, and may have to change old values (i.e., change or modify the background institutions) in order to operate effectively within the global arena.

Thus, adding globalization to the model puts the institutional context into a more supportive role compared to its leading role in the original model. Such changes are not necessary if the way the business system is constituted is already compatible with the requirements from other business systems or the global market at large. This will be the case if the interacting companies are located in business systems that are culturally similar.

Critique and Elaboration of Whitley's Analytical Model

The Ghanaian case also highlights some other fundamental issues in the study of business systems development. It has been shown that interaction and perception are useful concepts in understanding the relationship between businesspeople and officials in the proximate institutions in a given country. As discussed earlier, Ghana is currently in the midst of an institutional change, i.e., a move away from a public policy supremacy orientation to a partnership orientation in the management of the relationship between government and business. Efforts are under way to establish appropriate institutional arrangements capable of setting a mutually acceptable agenda and rules for the dialogue. Nevertheless, many members of the business community remain skeptical about the sincerity and capacity of government institutions to pursue a genuine partnership relationship.

The skepticism of the business community relates both to the prevailing mindset of public employees as well as to actual experience from business development programs initiated by government agencies. The orientation of the public employees towards private business has been shaped, to a large extent, by the public policy supremacy orientation to government-business relations. Relatedly, the actual public programs in support of business have not been comprehensive enough to convince the business community that the government is prepared to collaborate with them.

This relates to Whitley's view that business systems are socially constructed, emerging out of the interaction among people. Although there is no consensus on the definition of the concept of social construction, it is possible to grasp its essence by saying what it is not. It is neither the physical or environmental construction of reality as assumed in empiricism, nor is it the pure mental construction of reality assumed in rationalism. It is in-between these two extremes and thus part of the general project of generating new ways of understanding social life in the social sciences (Slife and Williams 1995; Hirschman and Holbrook 1992).

As discussed by Popova and Sørensen (1996), two key concepts underlie the social construction perspective in social science. They are: (1) the mental interpretation of events and context by the individual, and (2) the social interaction between actors through overt acts and communication (language). The individual interpretation of events and context in general creates uniqueness, while social interaction creates understanding and common world views. This, by implication, means that social construction of reality takes place in individuals' performance of their everyday activities.

If the above perspective of social construction is explicitly introduced into the existing business systems framework, it will free the public and private actors from their deterministic structural web and emphasize the inter-subjective perceptions that they construct through their everyday interactions.

This brings us to the final remark about the existing model's appropriateness for the study of cross-national interactions among business partners. The social construction of reality by actors -coming from disparate sociocultural and economic settings is always problematic. When businesspeople share a common sociocultural background, their perceptions and interactions are informed by shared frames of understanding. Cross-national business interactions are usually deprived of the shared assumptions and accepted rules of behaviour that smooth the process of interaction. The participants therefore need to make deliberate efforts to create and sustain trust among themselves. For this reason, we suggest that the background institutional components in Whitley's model should be supplemented with factors such as cross-cultural trust, degree of cultural compatibility as well as actors' insight into the degree of similarity and differences between the business systems.

Conclusions

Previous studies of business systems have been concerned with the description and comparison of the unique national recipes found in each country. By placing the descriptions only at a macro level of aggregation, the dynamics of interaction (and the attendant actor perceptions) that form the undercurrent of change within and between business systems do not receive the explicit attention they deserve in the analysis. This chapter has argued that the institutional context of businesses is characterized by continuous interaction by actors within the respective business systems and their supporting institutions in the sense of daily collaborative routines. The interaction offers the actors the opportunity to continuously assess and develop perceptions of each other and, in turn, choose the appropriate behaviour as initiatives or responses to initiatives from others. The evidence from Ghana, however, illustrates the difficulty of unlearning past negative perceptions and replacing them with positive ones. The authoritative position of the state and its established proximate institutions therefore depends on the perceptions and confidence accorded it by the business community, therefore arguing in favour of explicit modeling of the government-business relations using models that grasp the dynamic processes of the interaction.

Furthermore, it has been found that business systems are not confined units as generally assumed. A relatively open economy such as the Ghanaian creates opportunities for the development of an undercurrent of interaction between firms from different business systems. This creates diversity and induces change. In addition, it further weakens the lead position of the background and proximate institutions. While the proximate institutions in particular are constrained and legitimized by the concept of the nation-state, firms are borderless, in the sense that they are able and ready to participate in the creation of new business systems across borders.

We have also argued that, in a global economy, it is important explicitly to model the implications of intensive interaction between enterprises from different business systems. This interaction may be strong enough to reverse the basic relationship between the institutional contexts and the business system, i.e., the business system is not formed by the background and proximate institutions but largely by other business systems.

The basic problem within the present concept of business systems is that it views reality as structures that, although socially constructed, are difficult to change. However, being social constructions, the actual construction process is more important than any given structure at a specific point in time. Social construction in this regard is best understood as a process of individual perception and communication among interactants leading to the development of common world views. As researchers, we may, from time to time, want to take a snap-shot of the process and label it the structure of the business system in order to take stock of the situation and/or compare different systems. This is acceptable as long as social construction is understood as an ongoing process.

Annexure 6.1

Institutional Context and Export Support Schemes in Ghana, 1995

Type of institution	Name of institution	Type of scheme	Main content of scheme
Promotional	Ghana Export Promotion Council (GEPC)	Export promotion	Ensuring the success of the national export diversification drive through an *Contd.*

Contd.

Type of institution	Name of institution	Type of scheme	Main content of scheme
Facilitating	Private Enterprise and Export Development (PEED)	Export finance	extensive scope of activities Promoting the growth of private Ghanaian exporters by providing short-term credits to exporters and providing technical assistance
Facilitating/ Promotional	African Project Development Facility (APDF)	Advisory services	Preparing feasibility studies and helping entrepreneurs to secure financing from banks and appropriate sources of capital
Regulatory	Customs, Excise and Preventive Service (CEPS)	Duty drawback	Duty drawback customs: refund of duty, etc., paid on imports that are later re-exported
Facilitating	International Executive Service Corps (IESC)	Executive services	Making available to individual firms volunteer executive industry specialists for periods ranging from 2 to 6 months
Facilitating	Trade and Investment Programme (TIP-Ghana)	Institutional support services	Influencing changes in official policies

Contd.

Contd.

Type of institution	Name of institution	Type of scheme	Main content of scheme
			that hinder exports and removing confusing rules and regulations and bottlenecks such as documentation in exporting
Facilitating	Technoserve	Production and marketing assistance	Assisting small-scale farmers and farmers' cooperatives in production, management and marketing
Promotional	Ghana Investment Promotion Centre (GIPC)	Investment promotion	Attracting foreign investors and encouraging local investors through the creation of favourable conditions
Facilitating/ Promotional	Ghana National Chamber of Commerce (GNCC)	Information and relational services	Enhancing international trade opportunities through information and contacts
Facilitating/ Promotional	Trade Promotion Unit (TPU) of Ministry of the Trade and Industry (MOTI)	Trade promotion	Formulating policy, regulating and resolving export trade problems
Facilitating	Export Finance Company (EFC)	Export finance	Extend loan facilities to finance export trade

Contd.

Contd.

Type of institution	Name of institution	Type of scheme	Main content of scheme
Facilitating	Amex International Inc. of USA (on USAID contract in Ghana)	Technical assistance	Providing technical assistance services to non-traditional export firms (e.g., market identification, market analysis and upgrade of production and management capacity)
Facilitating	Signa One	Policy guidelines	Assisting MOTI in making the policy framework export friendly
Facilitating	Medium Term Plan for Non-Traditional Exports (MTP-NTE)	Sector development services	Diversifying the export base and increasing the ratio of non-traditional exports to traditional exports
Facilitating	Private Enterprise Foundation (PEF)	Coordination	Sustaining dialogue between the government and the private sector
Facilitating	Ghana Standards Board	Quality standards	Ensuring quality standards to make exports competitive
Promotional/ Facilitating	Ghana Trade Fairs Authority	Promoting export through fairs	Organizing local and international trade fairs and exhibitions

7

Firms in the South: Interactions between National Business Systems and the Global Economy

Henrik Schaumburg-Müller

Firms in the private sector of developing countries are increasingly seen as the main drivers of development dynamics. However, local structures and global integration constitute major challenges for such an endeavour. The aim of this chapter is to contribute to the understanding of how firms in the South develop and sustain themselves under the various prevailing national and international conditions. In the search for such an understanding, it is believed that seeing firms as organizations interacting in their social and institutional environment provides a suitable point of departure.

The tradition for studying the nature of business organization embedded in its social context and the way firms operate interacting with markets and institutions challenges the view of the firm as a uniform and universal organization operating through market relations. This tradition has moved the analysis of transactions beyond the dichotomy of being organized either through markets or hierarchies. It acknowledges the interactions between economic actors in various forms and modes of rewarding (Grabher 1993).

In most developing countries, the framework for private sector development has been or is undergoing dramatic shifts as both policies and international economic relations change. Opening the economies is likely to impact significantly how production is organized in the South. The assumption is that the international dimension is becoming more important for understanding business systems in developing countries.

This situation provides challenging questions. What is the outcome of the interaction between local and international processes? What are the changes and dynamics that this inter-action creates, and what are the opportunities for the local systems to enhance their performance and effectiveness? These questions have been examined before but not so much in the perspective of combining the business system approach with studies of international business. The contributions of this chapter should be seen in this perspective.

The level of analysis of business systems can vary. Sometimes it is the country but in other studies it may be a unit (industry or area) within a country. The approach assumes a certain degree of social and cultural homogeneity. Kristensen (1996b) talks about ideal types of national firms. The most substan-tial contributions on business systems from developing coun-tries deal with dominating national systems, mostly related to larger companies, and have been confined to experiences in East Asia (Whitley 1992a, 1996a; Lim 1996). However, much of the empirical literature on business systems in the industri-alized countries in fact deals with business networks within specific subnational regions of these countries (Whitley 1992b; Whitley and Kristensen 1996). In order to broaden the scope of discussion, this chapter also draws on the debate of indus-trial districts in developing countries. In most cases the litera-ture on industrial districts, similarly to the business system tradition, examines informal ways of cooperation and trust-based relations between firms. It views the network of firms in relation to the local social and institutional context. Including the debate of industrial districts provides some advantages; it gives much more material from developing countries beyond East Asia, gives more information on small- and medium-sized companies and provides more empirical substance on how industrial districts are linked to the inter-national economy.

Although firms are embedded in their social context and interact with local markets and institutions, most firms or networks of firms develop cross-border business relationships, and companies everywhere are increasingly exposed to international competition. The institutions and barriers that protect the local area from the wider context tend to diminish rather than increase. Time will show whether the globalization scenario for the twenty-first century is true: only the firms that participate in global business and have a hard time competing will flourish and the ones that do not will be losers (Lehmann 1996). What is important here is to discuss how the many and diverse forms of international transactions affect the organization of production, control of resources and formation of the locally embedded firm.

To bridge this gap between national embeddedness and international competitive dynamics the presentation here explores how analytical concepts and tools from international business can be combined with the embeddedness approach to business organization and contribute to understanding business systems developing in the volatile conditions of developing countries. These issues are important for development studies and policies; they push the debate away from the simplified dichotomy of state versus market.

International organizations have taken a narrow perspective on prescribing policy for developing the private sector. Privatization, liberalization, opening of the economy, restructuring and other conditions for establishing an enabling environment tend to follow standard prescriptions, with little room for considering the specific local and international context of the country and its firms.

The issues addressed raise some difficult and comprehensive questions. The presentation will be exploratory and it does not aim to offer final explanations to all issues raised.

Section two explores the tradition of looking at the organization of firms and networks of firms embedded in the national or local context in relation to the situation in developing countries. The section uses the business system approach and studies of industrial districts. Section three briefly discusses how international business uses contextual and network approaches and thereby contribute to and probably complement the way of looking at firms as national embedded. Section four explores how international transactions and activities affect business organization from the perspective of developing countries. Section five summarizes the discussion and reflects on how research can be further pursued.

Understanding how Business is Organized in the South

The Embedded Firm and the South

Instead of seeing firms as nuclear units organizing and operating independently in transparent and competitive markets, implying that only one model can be used to understand firms, a tradition has now been established of examining economic organization in firms as interacting with markets and in a social and institutional context. This perspective of the embedded firm encourages more differentiated analysis and understanding of how the firm and society are linked (Granovetter 1985).

The approach of the embedded firm and the system surrounding it to understand the industrial development of private business has so far mainly been considered in relation to industrialized economies.

Development studies have demonstrated how various social structures and institutions develop differently in different societies. The embeddedness approach provides an opportunity to study firms in a similar differentiated way, taking into account the specific social and institutional context of developing countries. However, for both industrialized and developing countries, the emphasis on embeddedness does not imply that economic organization is predetermined by social values, culture, beliefs, etc. (Grabher 1993). Embeddedness signifies how economic organization interacts with social actors and institutions and thereby that economic organization also affects other social actors, markets and institutions.

The Business System Approach

The business system approach identifies distinctive and effective forms of economic organization based on the connections between dominant social institutions and ways of coordinating economic activities. The approach discusses the systems that have proved effective and stable in capitalist organized economies. It includes the relationships between firms and markets. Differences in major institutions thus generate significant variation in how firms and markets are structured and operate (Whitley 1992d, 1999).

Even the highly industrialized countries of Europe often differ in how firms are organized (Whitley and Kristensen 1996). This is associated with the different perspectives and aspirations of social actors and institutional arrangements and how firms operate in relation to each other and to markets. Such differences result in distinct business systems. Whitley identifies three constituting categories with 13 characteristics that contribute to forming a business system (Whitley 1992d):

(a) The nature of firms as economic actors

- Extent of decentralization of economic power to private interests.
- Separation of property rights owners from management of economic activities.
- Self-sufficiency of economic actors.
- Diversity of activities and resources controlled by leading firms.

(b) Market relations

- Extent of long-term, reciprocal obligations between firms.
- Significance of intermediary organizations in coordinating flows and strategies.
- Dependence of market relations upon personal ties.

(c) Authoritative coordination and control systems

- Impersonality of authority relations.
- Distance of superiors from subordinates and tasks.

- Centralization of coordination and control.
- Integration and interdependence of activities and resources.
- Specialization of tasks, roles, skills and authority.
- Employer–employee commitment and the nature of the employment system.

This list should not be considered exhaustive. The characteristics are not independent of each other but will usually occur in certain combinations. Whitley (1992d) identifies five different types of business systems.

1. In the first type, the isolation and self-sufficiency of firms are high either because they are in situations of considerable insecurity, lack of trust and a lack of stable institutional procedures governing arm-length relations. Isolation and self-reliance tend to encourage personal relationships and a preference for high flexibility in production and marketing operations.
2. In a second system there may be institutional differentiation and pluralism, such as the Anglo-Saxon societies, which have stronger institutions ordering impersonal relations that then tend to develop partitioned systems management and firm organization. Financial institutions facilitate the separation of owners and managers. This can be termed the pluralistic business system model.
3. A third system is constituted by economies that have closer relations between financial institutions, state agencies and industrial companies. Whitley calls it a collaborative system.
4. The fourth system is one in which the state coordinates the economy and plays an active role in development but private firms retain considerable autonomy. However, top management has to maintain good relations with the state élite. This is called the coordinated business system.
5. In the fifth system the state dominates the economies and the political executives and bureaucratic elite play the leading role in coordinating investment strategies and resource allocation. This is the state-dependent business system.

There are few contributions indicating how various national or subnational business systems can be placed within these five types. Whitley places the Anglo-Saxon societies in the second type; the systems in other industrialized countries could be of the collaborative or cooperative nature. The questions of how these types can adopt developing country systems and whether they are adequate must be left to further empirical studies. It may turn out that new combinations of characteristics can be identified, resulting in other types of systems than those mentioned above. Whitley considers South Korea to be a collaborative type in which financial institutions and the state together with the business community are closely interlinked in a relatively centralized and authoritarian system.

One can only make some tentative hypotheses of how other developing countries fit into the typology. Few developing countries may have a differentiated and pluralistic system. Some developing countries can probably be accommodated in some of the other types described above. Similar to South Korea, rapidly industrializing countries may be categorized within the collaborative system. Countries in which the state also plays a leading role in industrialization but independent financial institutions are not developed could have a state-dependent system, especially for countries in which the state itself owns manufacturing companies. Privatization policies may change the position. Egypt could be such a case but together with many other least developed countries Egypt could also be in the self-sufficient category when the state pulls back and trust between the main actors is low. Where the interest of the state is more indirect, the coordinated business system might be relevant. Using a number of systems that each has a set of characteristics is a practical way to study business systems empirically. Going beyond the level of characteristics to explain what constitute embeddedness, Kristensen (1996b) provides an underlying theoretical framework on how firms are constituted differently in various countries. Based on four interacting elements in the construct of the national firm he draws the following Figure 7.1 (Kristensen 1996b:20).

It is the processes of social interaction that form firms, not a deterministic economic process. The social division of

Figure 7.1
The National Construction of the Firm

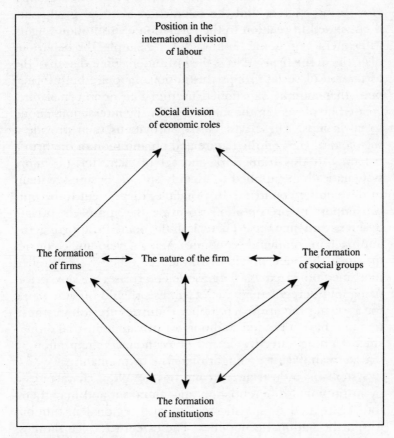

Source: Whitley and Kristensen (eds.). 1996b:20. *The Changing European Firm: Limits to Convergence.* London: Routledge.

economic roles varies in different countries and is considered to correspond to economists' concept of the social division of labour (Kristensen 1996a). Two interdependent spheres constitute the social division of economic roles: the formation of firms and the formation of social groups. The formation of firms is determined by the interactive strategies between firms within the country. The formation of social groups covers the division of economic roles between capitalists, managers and labourers and the relationships between these three groups. How firms operate and the interaction of social groups are then viewed in relation to the formation of institutions, again with interaction going both ways. For example, the behaviour of actors in the firms reflects the institutional foundation of the formation of social groups. Institutions here are both formal ones that may be sanctioned by the state or informal ones created by players in the markets or by the interaction among social groups. These basic social formations then provide a sociological view on the nature and organization of the firm.

How can this framework and set of characteristics more systematically be applied to identify specific business systems in developing countries? In principle, there seem to be only two important preconditions to using the approach: private business and markets. There is little point in applying the approach in command economies. Many developing countries in which the state previously owned or otherwise controlled most medium-sized and large-scale enterprises are now privatizing and deregulating. Such countries should provide scope for applying the approach. Other countries are still in transition and have a limited tradition for private industrial ownership. Finding effective forms of economic organization in private manufacturing might therefore be premature.

Systems in industrialized countries are often characterized by institutional differentiation and pluralism and may therefore be related to specific regions and regional institutions within the national economies. The extent to which business system studies should use the whole country or subnational region as the unit of analysis depends on the homogeneity of culture and institutions within the country. However, some of the basic contributions in the literature operate with the characteristics of the typical national firm in a cross-national comparative perspective (Whitley and Kristensen 1996). Southeast Asia's industrializing countries often have a sharp division between the Chinese business communities and another part of the private sector dominated by nationals. As institutions, markets and policies can reflect this division, applying two interlinked business systems might be appropriate. India, another advanced industrialized developing country, has very large nationwide conglomerates, almost like South Korea's *chaebols*, and then another layer of more regional and industry-specific but still large-scale companies. Other developing countries have self-sustained large-scale companies with few relations to the small-scale sector, which has numerous individual firms. As different business communities can be observed, research needs to keep in mind whether a single distinct national or subnational system can be identified or different systems operate side by side.

The business systems studied in East Asia represent three very distinct industrial systems: the *kaishas* of Japan, the *chaebols* in South Korea and the Chinese family business system as it operates today in Taiwan (Whitley 1992a). The last two cases are in developing countries that have advanced very rapidly in the industrialization process, and the systems identified dominate the national economies. Elaborate institutional systems have been created, and state policies have supported industrialization. Shared social values and cultural homogeneity have also contributed to the formation of distinct national systems. The same set of characteristics cannot necessarily be expected to be present in other developing countries, especially in those where manufacturing is not a dominant sector.

The distinction between industrialized and non-industrialized countries today is loose, and developing countries have a wide range of degrees of industrialization. Nevertheless, some characteristics are still likely to play a more important role for some of these countries in explaining how private business is organized and managed.

First, the private manufacturing sector may be rudimentary or only recently developed, sometimes still based on craft business traditions. First-generation entrepreneurs may still dominate even large private business firms. This often provides importance to basic cultural networks such as the family, clan, caste and ethnic groups not only within the firms but also in relations between firms and in relations with the state and its bureaucracy. If domestic private business has a weak social base, both the state and foreign companies often play more important roles in directly owning and managing production.

Second, the role of government is different in developing countries. It is both present and absent in another manner than in western societies. It is present in the sense that the state either controls production directly in selected sectors or intervenes and regulates production, investment, the supply of credit and other aspects of private business. It is absent in the sense that the formal institutional and legal framework is often lacking or insufficient for business operations. This makes both entry to and exit from private business difficult.

The third characteristic, related to the above, is that when public-sector regulation is characterized by discriminatory incentives or restrictions, the result tends to be rent-seeking activities. In such an environment actors may operate with the main purpose of exploiting rent-seeking opportunities. This is not only to be regarded as opportunistic behaviour; it often affects the social structure and interaction between social groups, not least between politicians, bureaucrats, managers and owners. Corruption will often play an important role in decision-making.

Fourth, transparency and access to information are limited both in relation to the private business sector and the intervening government sector. The communication infrastructure is less developed, and economic actors therefore operate under greater uncertainty.

Although the social groups in developing countries are the same in principle as in industrialized countries, at least two groups of economic actors in many developing countries play a qualitatively as well as quantitatively different role for private-sector development: intermediaries and multinational corporations. They both significantly influence the characteristics of business systems. The role of multinational corporations is discussed later.

Intermediaries and rent-seekers often play economically dominant roles in developing countries (Oman 1994; Grabher 1993). As mentioned above, their actions can be promoted by discriminatory policies that create institutional regimes allowing inefficiency and rent-seeking in markets and other forms of transaction. Such actors can be important partners in developing country systems, as they control economic resources and markets. The question, however, is how the efficiency of such a system can be assessed. Development studies have contributed to explain the emergence and function of intermediaries. Explanations often pointed at the state and its intervention. However, the state and its intervention are also seen as contributing to the creation of effective business systems. More research is needed on how the state intervenes in combination with the formation of social groups and the kind of institutions and the enforcement of policies that this interaction produces.

This discussion leads back to the basic elements in the model for the construct of the firm. Here the nature of the firm is the centerpiece in the interaction of the model. But difficulty arises in societies in which firms are not the main concern in the social construct and the basic institutions are not formed with the purpose of promoting the formation of private companies. The social construct has taken place without industrial organization. Processes in agriculture and trade have dominated the formation of social groups and economic organization of production in many poorer and less industrialized countries. Studies of business systems in developing countries often need to examine the formation of social groups and institutions outside manufacturing to understand the background for economic organization and the nature of the firm in the industrial sector.

In a broader perspective, another question is how the effectiveness of the systems of market-oriented capitalist firms should be assessed in the context of a developing economy? Is it economically efficient if the prices used, all are institutionally dependent? Or is it qualities within the system that enable firms to be learning entities and to produce synergy in respond to changing circumstances that matters?

Industrial Districts and Flexible Production

All business system literature from industrialized countries deals extensively with subnational industrial districts or clusters organized as production systems by firms within a specific locality (Whitley 1992b; Whitley and Kristensen 1996). There is a similar tradition of studying industrial districts in developing countries. This literature is much richer than the one trying to identify and characterize business systems at a national level of developing countries (United Nations 1994).

A main emphasis within both traditions is an understanding of economic organization that goes beyond the standardized definition of a firm and Williamson's previously mentioned transaction dichotomy of markets versus hierarchies. Multiple paths are accepted for inter-firm relations, the interdependence between firms and markets and the role played by local institutions for the understanding of effective forms of economic organization. Analyses of industrial districts or clusters in recent literature also have a common understanding of firms and inter-firm relations as linked to the social, cultural and political environment (Nadvi and Schmitz 1994).

There are several forms of firms geographically concentrated in developing countries, including industrial districts, export zones and science and technology parks. Porter (1990) views industrial clusters as relationships of mostly vertically connected firms within a broadly defined industry that create national comparative advantages. In the Porter terminology, the geographical limitation of the cluster may be the country as a whole. The important aspects are the dynamics and the synergy created by the clustered firms that interact and create competence and competitiveness.

All these forms of industrial organization can be important for developing countries but may not be equally interesting for the study of firms and industrial organization in a social context. The focus is on the arrangements of cooperation by which the firms are interlinked and organized to become effective production systems. An important characteristic is that the firms interact with each other beyond the transaction forms based on markets or hierarchies.

This is close to the concept of the industrial district as defined by van Dijk (1994): 'a group of independent industrial firms which have developed strong relations among themselves, which have fostered innovation and contributed to higher (collective) efficiency'.

Synthesis work on industrial districts and clusters in developing countries finds that there is broadly based experience in organizing production (Nadvi 1994; Nadvi and Schmitz 1994; Späth 1994; United Nations 1994; van Dijk et al. 1997; Schmitz and Nadvi 1999). Although the industrial district model found in industrialized countries may not be similarly applied (Späth 1994), there is evidence from many developing countries and across major industries of production being organized by firms interacting and establishing a division of labour between them in either geographically or sectorally defined areas. The extent to which the characteristics of industrialized countries can be found varies from case to case. Networks of cooperating firms in developing countries are not a recent phenomenon; some industrial districts in Brazil and India, for example, date back to the early industrialization of the two countries. The tradition of cooperation between firms to compensate for large-scale investments and Taylorist organization has been present in developing countries. Certain common features such as a concentration of smaller, owner-managed firms in the networks, however, seem to prevail (Nadvi and Schmitz 1994). As mentioned, the evidence is from all developing country regions, but there are fewer references from Africa, possibly because Africa has less experience with manufacturing and entrepreneurial development than other regions. However, recent research has also shown how networks and entrepreneurial cooperation flourish among informal and small-scale enterprises in Africa (van Dijk et al. 1997).

The synthesis work provides some important preliminary conclusions. The firms in the industrial district rarely constitute a homogeneous group but tend to be distinguished by internal hierarchies. In vertically organized networks, subcontracting by relatively large firms is often the main rationale of the network relations. The role of social formation is inadequately researched. Although underlying shared social and cultural values strengthen network formation in many cases, important examples contradict this rule. The importance of local associations of entrepreneurs only arises as the inter-firm cooperation matures. Labour relations are also inadequately studied, but network cooperation does not seem to ensure better wages and working conditions. Government action and initiatives can play an important role in supporting networks but are not responsible for creating them.

For industrialized countries, the distinction of the low-road versus the high-road industrial district model has played an important role. The low road signifies the use of simple technology and unskilled labour with limited growth potential; the high-road model comprises skilled labour using new technology to experience learning processes and dynamics. A similar separation in two models is not found as a general pattern for industrial districts in developing countries (Nadvi and Schmitz 1994). The matrix of characteristics is more complicated, and dynamic development for networks can occur, for example, with unskilled labour applying modern technology.

The experience from developing countries also seems to suggest that the industrial networks are more susceptible to exogenous factors and events that may threaten their competitiveness and survival. These exogenous factors usually involve technology or market changes. Networks are therefore rarely stable but change significantly over time. If not—as some of the African cases suggest—they may not be growing and play a dynamic role in the industrial development (Rasmussen 1991).

The literature on industrial districts in developing countries is therefore especially preoccupied with the problem of restructuring industrial organization. The business system approach emphasizes economic organization within the social and institutional context and demonstrates how these systems form relatively stable relations (Whitley 1996a), whereas studies of industrial districts focus more on reorganization and how change and renewal take place, leading to industrial transformation (Humphrey 1995). This difference in the two approaches does not rule out both viewing firms as being embedded in their social context and finding the forms of cooperation among actors to be crucial for understanding how systems operate.

The pressure to reorganize industries and become competitive under dramatic changes in industrial policies has led to a preoccupation with the introduction of new ways of managing and organizing production. Such initiatives do not usually rely on new internally developed models but more often on 'imported' models. However, the ones found in the industrial districts may not simply be a replica of European or Japanese models but are often adapted to local circumstances (Humphrey 1995).

In the organization of production networks among independent firms, the concept of trust has come to play an increasingly important role in understanding how the cooperation is not only able to function but also creates its technologically dynamic role (Pyke and Sengenberger 1992). In the social reality of many developing countries, trust may be difficult to imagine beyond family and kinship bonds. However, there are examples from developing countries of cooperation based on trust in villagers' organizing agricultural production and horizontal sharing of labour among craftspeople. However, collective work efforts can also be found where the organization is based only on power and exploitation. What is interesting in the complicated picture of social relations in developing countries is that, theoretically and empirically, trust can be established and developed among otherwise unrelated actors. Development of trust therefore neither has to be based on common social norms and culture nor has it to rely on a common reconstruction of history among actors (Lorenz 1993). This possibility seems to be particularly interesting for societies in which exploitation and mistrust have otherwise ruled social relations, such as in the organization of agricultural production and other spheres of social life.

Contributions from International Business

Shared Perspectives

The discipline of international business is concerned with how firms organize their international transactions. An important element of explaining firms' international transactions is that the firm has some specific advantages it can exploit in competition with other producers when exporting or locating production abroad or it can gain such advantages through external transactions. Both cases challenge the assumptions of perfect competition, transparent markets and identical competing firms. The business system approach and international business are therefore similar with respect to recognizing that the organization of both markets and production cannot be explained by perfect markets and the survival of the 'best' firms with identical technologies. In recent discussions of identifying firm-specific advantages, attention has increasingly been focused on the organization and management of firms rather than on more narrowly defined technology advantages.

Local firms have strategies aimed at offsetting the advantages of foreign production. One set of strategies includes the potential to exploit the division of labour within networks of local firms using flexible production systems. If successful, however, such local networks may easily develop specific advantages themselves and start exploiting these on international markets, especially when they are located in small economies.

In order to explain how firms develop competitive advantages, international business studies operate with frameworks viewing these advantages as the relations between the firm and its environment. Porter's diamond (Porter 1990) is a well-known example of such a framework. Although it does not link the firm to the basic social formation, the diamond nevertheless accommodates relations to formal institutions and the main categories of economic actors in the society. The tradition of comparative corporate governance studies has a similar perspective in explaining management strategies and examining the institutional framework (Lehman 1996).

International business studies have increasingly been occupied with transnational alliances and international or global production networks (Dicken 1992). Developments in infrastructure and communication have diminished the importance of proximity. They have also made it possible to break up the value chain into smaller elements and to achieve much more flexibility in the location of productive processes. Understanding international production and globalization also builds on rejecting the Taylorist understanding of the firm (Oman 1994).

International business as a discipline has also been active in understanding international business relationships that extend the network-based kind of non-market cooperation between culturally and geographically distant firms. Studies confirm that such network cooperation maintains many of the national network characteristics and transactions. Cultural differences can be overcome by creating an appropriate atmosphere in the exchange relationships (Forsgren and Johanson 1992). Power is also an important factor in international networks in which both small and large firms participate.

Multinational corporations operating internationally in alliances, networks or alone are still national firms. It is a misconception to think that multinational corporations are necessarily stateless because they pursue a global or any other form of transnational strategy (Hu 1992). Very few multinational corporations are not in some way rooted in a nation-state system.

However, there are also major differences between the studies of business systems and international business. Different questions are asked. The business system approach makes comparative studies of how firms operate effectively in various markets and institutional contexts; international business tries to understand how firms organize their resources and operate effectively in different countries and institutional systems.

Commodity Chains and Truncated Production Systems

As shown above, international business extensively uses such terms as networks, cooperation and alliances. Here these terms signify transnational transactions as opposed to transactions in national or subnational networks. Multinational corporations are linked into networks and alliances in various ways. In some important sectors such as the automobile industry, they often rely on alliances or joint ventures. However, understanding how firms in developing countries become integrated in international networks requires examining commodity chains, which explain how international production and trade are organized (Gereffi 1996a). The literature distinguishes between producer-driven and buyer-driven commodity chains; the former signifies that a transnational manufacturer organizes production, and in the latter case production is established by a buyer such as large retailers, designers or trading companies. The producer-driven chains are found within technology-intensive industries such as automobiles and electronics, whereas the supplier-driven chains are concentrated on labour-intensive consumer goods such as leather goods, toys, kitchen appliances, and especially textiles and garments (Christerson and Appelbaum 1995).

Both forms of chains are important for developing countries, as they link local firms as subsidiaries or subsuppliers to corporations embedded in other countries. The outcome for local firms depends both on the national context and on the strategies of the nationally based multinational corporation. Different outcomes are possible within individual industries depending on the nationality of the leading multinational company. The constellation of this double-embeddedness is crucial for the possible upgrading and restructuring of firms in the host-country business system. Both within electronics and garments, experience has shown how firms in East Asian countries have learned and been upgraded to produce higher value-added components or products in various ways (Gereffi 1996a).

Local institutional and policy arrangements that enable the internationalization of industrial production have often been influenced from the outside for the sake of securing macro-economic balance and maximizing short-term international production efficiency. Even in the macro-economic perspective, such strategies may be shortsighted. They lack dynamics and depend on institutional trade policy arrangements with little control from the home country. Trade policies in garments in the United States and Europe have caused such production organization to flourish in developing countries searching for export earnings (Mortimore and Zamora 1996). This kind of export-oriented industrialization is usually deprived of dynamic perspectives and can in this respect be compared with the consumer-based import substitution industrialization (Storper 1995). When the country loses its comparative labour cost advantage, the production disappears. No firms are established that can organize and develop effective and sustainable production.

The Local and the Wider Context

Industrial Districts in International Competition

Although studies of industrial districts concentrate on local inter-firm relations and the institutional conditions, the literature illustrates how the firms are interlinked in a wider context (Nadvi and Schmitz 1994).

Industrial districts are rarely closed self-contained systems. Those located in open economies are especially exposed to external competition and will often have external economic and technological links that may influence the internal organization of production and the social relations. The most apparent link is that both export and import increase with the growth of production in a district. Some firms may expand and become large-scale worldwide exporters, with the other firms in the cluster linked in vertical systems, as has been the case with the Sinos Valley's footwear industry in Brazil described by Schmitz (1995). The case from Brazil is similar to the experience of the export-oriented footwear industry in northern Italy. The Mexican cluster in the same industry, being more oriented towards the domestic market, has been less dynamic and not able to adapt similarly to competitive changes (Rabellotti 1995).

In other cases, industrial districts are created from the very beginning to produce for export markets and obtain specific import and other forms of concessions. Trade links may not interfere much with how production is organized and the firms managed. The firms can be thoroughly based in the local social and institutional context, but on the basis of their survey, Nadvi and Schmitz (1994) indicate the important role traders play in the development of industrial clusters. Export traders are often active agents for the transfer of new technologies, design, etc. from the outside into the cluster. Sources of competitiveness in export markets are important for dynamic growth in the industrial networks.

External links go beyond trade relations. Other forms of impact include ownership relations, production agreements and subcontracting, technology transfers and adopting principles on the organization of production and on management.

How these various international business relationships influence the organization of production varies according to the commitment in the relationship, the industry and the available resources in the district. Two important external influences are the introduction of flexible production systems and the links between industrial district firms and international commodity chains.

Adopting flexible production techniques and management principles inspired by the Japanese model is one pronounced way in which small firms in industrial districts have tried to organize their production and maintain competitiveness. With the decreased importance of the Ford–Taylor production model, alternative flexible production systems have gained importance in many industries. In industrial districts, flexible specialization means a distinct division of labour and close cooperation between firms, which make it possible to exploit specialization but also quickly change production (van Dijk 1994). The encounters have been many where local firms and industries try to adopt flexible management and production principles based on the Japanese model and organize firms based on this. The studies of such encounters are well documented for both industrialized and developing economies (Humphrey 1995). Flexible organization of production is often seen as an alternative to the internationalization of production processes as a means of maintaining competitiveness without relocating production. The geographic proximity reduces transaction costs; the informal links and control mechanisms work better; and—not least—it saves time and maintains close contact with the final market, which allows for quick changes of products.

The application of flexible production models are based on the notion that ideas and systems are transferable and can flow from firms organizing production in one context to firms in another context. Flexible production models are explicitly a transplant of foreign organizational and management structures introduced to domestic firms and business networks. Introduction of flexible production and management systems can therefore be regarded as a way of internationalizing the organization of production. These changes take place to strengthen international competitiveness and to adapt to the requirements of global markets.

The Japanese flexible production model may be transferred and implemented by local managers and not as a development within the social and institutional framework of the firm or the industrial district. However, the outcome depends on local actors and therefore varies according to the commitment, interest and resources present in firms. Studies of the diffusion of the new management techniques in developing countries show examples in which the local management introduced the techniques but the principles were not easily implemented at the production system level, where the benefits of synergy and cooperation between firms become effective (Kaplinsky 1995). Three constraints specific to developing countries are mentioned: shortcomings in education and training, lack of inter-firm relations and poor infrastructure. Introduction of flexible production systems is no inherent guarantee for competitive success but requires network learning and appropriate institutional arrangements (Galhardi 1994).

The difficulty in adopting flexible production systems is not only caused by the introduction of new production techniques. Flexible production has as much to do with the management and organization of production within and between firms. It therefore affects the established ways of work, relations between managers and employees and the behaviour of the managers of cooperating firms. It requires change in the institutional rules governing the organization of production and can therefore meet resistance (Kaplinsky 1995). The essence here is, however, that this kind of strategy designed to maintain effective production cuts into the established systems and is based on outside models that change basic characteristics in the organization of production (Kenney and Florida 1994).

The new production techniques have been introduced when local managers see it as a way to maintain competitiveness, but often they are required from outside by multinational corporation managers or as a demand to a subcontractor (or subcontractor system) from a foreign buyer.

The apparel and garment industry is an example of an industry in which two modes of production organization continue to exist: the geographically concentrated networks of flexible production located in industrialized countries and the international commodity chains including low-wage countries. Firms have made efforts to apply flexible and just-in-time production as an alternative to moving production to low-wage economies. Increasingly, however, international production takes the form of network production in a commodity chain with value-added functions at various locations. Firms in, for example, the United States design and make orders to firms in South Korea, Taiwan or Hong Kong which organize production in low-wage East Asian or Latin American countries such as China, Thailand and the Dominican Republic. Such transnational subcontracting networks can, however, be organized within a rather uniform management context. Many United States firms utilizing these global networks have been based on ethnic links by Asian entrepreneurs in the United States (Christerson and Appelbaum 1995). Many of the transaction cost-saving characteristics of the local networks are maintained in the global and also flexible production network through such personal relations. The question is whether similar links can be established without the ethnic element or without being organized entirely within the hierarchy of a single firm?

The possibilities for relocating production, which increase significantly by breaking up the value-added chain, can also result in truncated production. In such a form of industrial organization firms have limited embeddedness in the local social or institutional structure, and there is hardly any perspective for learning and upgrading. Many export zones in developing countries are well-documented cases of such situations. Besides export zones, however, the result can be truncated industrial production in almost any export industry in which multinational corporations can establish footloose production processes with little investment. The organization of such production—whether firms are subsidiaries or subcontractors in commodity chains—is found in important manufacturing industries such as textiles, garments and other consumer and assembly production. It represents a system with little local embeddedness interacting mainly with foreign markets and firms. Besides using unskilled and often unorganized labour, the firms have little linkage otherwise to the local economy. Those who control the organization of production are embedded in a different social context.

An interesting question is whether business systems and global commodity chains should be seen as competing or complementary forms of economic organization. They are both concerned with systems of economic organization. Whitley (1996a) finds the two approaches complementary: the former focuses on specific configurations of firms and markets established in distinctive institutional contexts, whereas the commodity chain analysis deals with coordinating economic activities across national boundaries. Gereffi (1996b) maintains, however, that the commodity chains tend to diminish the influence of national institutions and business systems. The way firms organize production is increasingly determined by their position in a global commodity chain and not by their national origin.

Business Systems and Internationalization

The model in Figure 7.1 determines the national dimension of the business system by 'the location in the international division of labour' (Kristensen 1996b:20). The model does not really develop the factors that determine the location. However, the position today of an economy in the international division of labour is both volatile and difficult to define. The position changes with the shifts in comparative advantages and the competitiveness of the national firms compared with those of other economies. Many developing countries with a high growth rate cannot any longer be placed as natural resource exporters or in the low-cost labour category. The location of production shifts quickly between countries. High-income economies produce, trade and consume the same range of goods and services, and the scope for an international division of labour therefore becomes narrow. National comparative advantages are replaced by firm-specific advantages with fierce competition among companies of various countries. How do these developments affect the business system model?

Kristensen (1996b:33) points to the importance of these international forces for the evolution of the country-based business system: 'The dynamics going on within all these formations, when challenges from international competition and global technology arise, are more than complicated'. The following sections take up some issues of interaction between the national context and the international environment.

Being based in a national social context formed over time, business systems are expected to represent stable formations (Whitley 1992c). They are not changed easily by other changes in a society, including the openness of the economy to the outside world. International developments that might interfere and change the national business system can result from the development of international institutions or from national policies and internationalization. Whitley has studied such impacts in revisiting the three East Asian business systems (Whitley 1996b). Although business in Japan and South Korea and the Chinese family business system have continued to internationalize, the fundamental structure and the way of operating are the same as earlier. For example, although South Korean *chaebols* have increasingly been making foreign direct investment abroad, the operation and organization of these can just be seen as an extension of the *chaebol* system operating in the domestic economy and does not change the fundamentals of the *chaebols*. The other two Asian systems are similar in this respect. Whitley's conclusion is that the systems fundamentally are unchanged despite otherwise turbulent developments inside and outside the national environment.

The analysis of the much more diversified business systems in Southeast Asian countries concludes that changes in response to regional economic dynamics take place faster there than in Northeast Asia given that the established systems are less entrenched than they are in Japan and Korea (Lim 1996). The reason may be the government, which in these two countries has been very active in controlling the industrialization process. In such Southeast Asian countries as Thailand and Malaysia, the role of the government and ties between the bureaucracy and the business community have been different. Although the Chinese business community in both countries—as in most other of the region's countries—play a very important role in the private sector, the relations between actors are not so strongly institutionalized as in Japan and South Korea.

Japan and South Korea have also been effectively more closed economies, although they followed the export industrialization strategy and later became large foreign direct investors. Foreign multinationals have not invested directly to any great extent in these two countries. Multinational corporations play a more decisive role in many other developing countries, perhaps not in the overall industrial picture but often in leading manufacturing industries such as the automobile industry in Mexico. In relation to Whitley's observations, the question can be turned around; how does the organization of production in Japanese and South Korean subsidiaries affect the business system in the host countries? Can multinational corporations dominate how production is organized in the manufacturing sector in host countries and constitute an implant to the national business system? Will local actors and institutions only play a more marginal role?

The recent economic crisis in Asia has fundamentally shaken the believe that the business systems of the region were stable and could produce continuous growth. The crisis demonstrated how the global financial system had deeply penetrated into local business, flooding local firms with cheap but short-term and mobile credit in foreign currency (Lim 1997). The inadequacy of local business practices was, however, exposed. Dependence of personal ties had replaced sound economic analysis and risk evaluation. More fundamentally, the crisis has revealed how basic relationships between the main actors in the systems have been affected by widespread corruptive behaviour. Corruption between firm owners, managers, bureaucrats and politicians organized in different ways, although benefiting selected firms, has reached exorbitant proportions in several Asian countries and has produced a shaky future for the private sector (Khan 1998). The influence of external institutions on the crises has been widely discussed, but while some national systems may fairly easily be reconstituted others will require fundamental reform of basic institutions.

Relations between a parent company from one business system and an affiliated firm located in another can have other outcomes than the one reflected by the East Asian cases, in which the subsidiaries are dominated by firm organization of the home country. Especially in mergers and acquisitions, a subsidiary may be able to maintain its particular organization and continue to be embedded in the local context. Subsidiaries need not become extensions of controlling mother organizations. The case of a joint venture appears to be similarly open. However, in more general terms the outcome seems to be a strategic corporate issue and to depend on the ability of the management of the subsidiary to understand and operate in a cross-cultural environment.

Kristensen (1994) portrays the encounter of a multinational enterprise and a locally embedded and flexible specialized firm. The case illustrates the situation of what happens when the multinational firm takes over a local company rooted in local relations and institutions. In this case, the local management system represents the flexible and locally based production system, while the multinational parent company by its way of controlling economic efficiency does not impose or suppose to have a superior management system. A Danish firm is being taken over by a British multinational corporation and is able to maintain its systems of organizing production and management while living up to the expectations of the British owners. At the same time, the Danish firm is able to outmaneuver its immediate German superiors within the corporation. Kristensen speculates whether the successful outcome from the viewpoint of the Danish firm and its British owners would also materialize if the takeover had been by a firm embedded in the German business system.

Firms based in different business systems can also cooperate in third countries and establish firms in which the organization of production contains elements from both home countries' systems and is adapted to the host country environment (Ernst 1994c).

Each of the three constituting categories of a business system—the nature of firms as economic actors, market relations and authoritative coordination and control systems—can be assessed in relation to the internationalization processes.

Firms in the private sector have gained increased economic power, as developing countries have been opening their economies and privatized state enterprises. Compared with a situation with import substitution, this reduces the self-sufficiency of the economy as a whole and often also for the individual firm, which gets a broader scope for external sourcing as an alternative to internal production. Likewise, the open economy provides incentives for firms to export. Opening the economy also means that foreign direct investment takes place and foreign firms control resources and activities of national firms. The relations between the company managers of local activities and owners change with foreign ownership. Internationalization processes therefore seem able to change the nature of firms as economic actors affected by factors outside the national institutional framework.

Characteristics under the category of market relations are also likely to change when the economy opens to new markets and new actors. In many industries, firms are confronted with new competing imports in their domestic markets, and other industries are directed toward export markets. In both cases firms have to adapt to new competitive conditions and form new strategies accordingly. Impersonal market relations and intermediaries may replace personal business relationships— but not necessarily. However, cultivating external business relations and operating on international markets requires communication and cross-cultural management skills. Relations change with internationalization and require new skills and insights for firms.

It may be difficult to say much in general on how the various characteristics under the category of authoritative coordination and control systems may change as a result of being exposed to the internationalization processes. Management practices in Japan, South Korea and the Chinese business system were maintained for a long time despite internationalization. The cited case of Kristensen (1994) also demonstrated the survival of the domestic system despite the exposure to foreign owners and to other ways of organizing production. However, these discussions also show that dominant foreign ownership and the introduction of new management systems can influence the relations between employer and employees, between owners and managers and other coordination and control functions. In Bangladesh, the recent development of a whole new garment export industry controlled from the outside has created an entirely new labour force of female wage labourers formerly residing in a completely different social environment in the rural areas of the country.

The question is when these changes result in more fundamental change of a business system at the national level or when foreign actors and institutions contribute to the formation of a business system without being part of the social context in the country. Such a discussion goes beyond the characteristics and must include the constituting elements in the formation of national business systems as discussed by Kristensen (1996b).

One aspect to consider is that external forces do not affect the organization of production equally in all national firms. In most cases relatively few industries in developing countries are closely linked to the international economy. These industries are often textile and garments, electronics, automobiles or other labour-intensive consumer goods.

Another question is whether business systems in developing countries are more exposed to changes from external forces than the systems in industrialized countries. First, the characteristics of production in industrialized countries can change. Few will claim that the characteristics of industrial organization in the United Kingdom have not changed in the two decades since Thatcherism was introduced. Adoption of Japanese management systems has been one factor contributing to change in production organization. Second, shifts in many developing countries can be initiated by internal policy as well as institutional changes or by external internationalization factors. This can happen when the national business system is less developed and matured, especially with respect to the basic institutions necessary to operate and finance private business.

Turning back to the model for constructing national firms and organizing production (see Figure 7.1), it appears to be the formation of firms that is exposed to external forces. Affiliates of multinational corporations, joint ventures, licensing and international subcontracting all potentially contribute to the formation and management of local firms. The encounter may turn out such that local social and institutional forces dominate the organization of production, but the opposite is also possible. Second, external actors and institutions may also influence the formation of national institutions—often in the formal and legal rules. External relations and actors are, however, less likely to influence the formation of national social groups and the informal institutions between national actors. Stable relations and informal institutions between domestic firms can even reinforce themselves in international competition (Kristensen 1994).

There may be limits to embeddedness. Granovetter's claim that markets and organizations are embedded has been criticized for possibly going too far, '[losing] a grip on the phenomenological distinctiveness of, say, commodified exchanges in markets and also of bureaucratic impersonality in imperfectly coordinated organizations' (Ingham 1996). In the international economy, it appears strange to claim that the world market for many consumer goods should be understood as embedded in a specific national context. The same can increasingly be said about the international capital market. Globalization has especially weakened national financial institutions. An important institution in the formation of a national business system thereby becomes integrated in the global financial market (Oman 1994). The actors on these markets may still be embedded in a national context, but this does not mean that the organization and operation of the markets is still embedded or dominated by any single national institutional system. Whether the same is true for large multidivisional transnational firms with loose structures of global corporate governance is more difficult to say.

Conclusions and Perspectives

Conclusions

This chapter has discussed how the business system approach in more general terms can be applied to the development of private sector business in developing countries and examined how an international perspective contributes to explaining the formation and operation of business in a world of global economic activities.

The strength of using the business system approach on developing countries is that it moves the debate of industrialization in developing countries away from the stereotype in which industrialization is seen as a universal process with fixed policy recommendations. The approach focuses attention on the specific social and institutional formations and thereby follows present trends in other areas of development studies. However, the business system characteristics and types need to be developed further before the approach can become a handy tool for studies in developing countries. Business systems in developing countries must be studied using a framework that considers the international aspects: external actors, markets and institutions. To accommodate some of the aspects needed, Figure 7.2 provides a simplified framework for some of these interactions.

This figure cannot be directly compared with Figure 7.1 on the national business system construct. In Figure 7.2, the circle representing the national business system is assumed to be based on the basic formations stipulated in Figure 7.1 but is then extended to indicate that external interaction may contribute to the formation of firms and industrial organization in developing countries.

Perspectives

Pursuing the use of the business system approach on developing countries brings forth many challenging issues that need to be studied further. As already mentioned, the basic concepts and tools have to be discussed in relation to the circumstances in developing countries. The most appropriate way to do this is likely to be in connection with specific empirical studies.

The following challenging research perspectives can be suggested:

- The question of convergence of broader cultural values and social systems in the North and the South, which constitute the foundation of institutions and social formations for national business systems.

Figure 7.2
Developing Country Business Systems in a Global Context

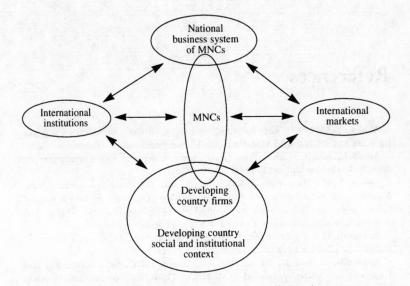

- Is there an Asian and Latin America bias in what has been said about business systems and industrial districts, whereas it may prove much more challenging to use the models for studies in Africa?
- How should we approach the question of whether the models are developed in relation to effective business systems? What is the meaning of effective, and can we imagine business systems that survive without being effective? How do we approach this normative issue, which can prove to be very important for development studies?

References

Abaka, E.K. 1993. 'The Informal Sector in Ghana: An Overview', paper presented at the National Workshop, 16–17 November. Accra, Ghana.

Amsden, A. 1989. *Asia's Next Giant: South Korea and Late Industrialization*. New York: Oxford University Press.

————. 1993. 'The Japanese Model of Late Industrialization in other East Asian Nations', paper presented to the workshop on 'Japan as Techno-Economic Superpower: Implications for the United States'. Santa Fe, New Mexico: Los Alamos National Laboratory, Centre for National Security Studies.

Antonelli, C. (ed.). 1989. *New Information Technology and Industrial Change—The Italian Case*. Dordrecht: Kluwer Academic Publishers.

Antonelli, C. and **D. Foray.** 1991. 'Technological Clubs: Cooperation and Competition', paper presented at the 7th ThinkNet Commission Meeting: 'Scenarios Toward a NetWorld Order'. Paris.

Aryeetey, E. et al. 1994. 'Supply and Demand for Finance of Small Enterprises in Ghana', *World Bank Discussion Papers 251*. Washington, D.C.: World Bank.

Assimeng, M. 1981. *Social Structure of Ghana*. Accra, Ghana: Ghana Publishing Corporation.

Balassa, B. 1981. *The Newly Industrialising Countries in the World' Economy*. New York: Pergamon.

Bark, T. 1991. 'Anti-Dumping Restrictions against Korean Exports: Major Focus on Consumer Electronics Products', manuscript. Seoul: Korea Institute for International Economic Policy.

Battacharya, A. and **M. Pangestu.** 1993. *The Lessons of East Asia; Indonesia: Development, Transformation and Public Policy*. Washington, D.C.: World Bank.

Beetham, D. 1991. *The Legitimation of Power*. London: Macmillan.

Bell, M. and **Keith Pavitt.** 1993. 'Technological Accumulation and Industrial Growth: Contrasts between Developed and Developing Countries', *Industrial and Corporate Change*, Vol. 2, No. 2.

Benjamin, S.J. 1993. 'Urban productivity from the grassroots', *Third World Planning Review*, Vol. 15, No. 2.

Benjamin, S.J. and **N.M. Bengani.** 1998. 'The Civic Politics of Industrial Districts in Delhi', in **P. Cadène** and **M. Holmström** (eds.), *Decentralized Production in India: Industrial Districts, Flexible Specialization, and Employment*. New Delhi: Sage.

Berger, S. and **R. Dore** (eds.). 1996. *National Diversity and Global Capitalism*. Ithaca, New York: Cornell University Press.

Bieber, D. et al. 1991. 'Autonomie and Beherrschung in Abnehmer-Zuliefererbeziehungen', in H.G. Mendius et al. (eds.), *Zulieferer im Netz*. Koeln (Cologne): Bund Verlag.

Blakely, E.J. 1994. *Planning Local Economic Development—Theory and Practice*, Second Edition. Thousand Oaks: Sage.

Bloom, M. 1992. *Technological Change in the Korean Electronics Industry*. Paris: Development Centre Studies, OECD.

Bongardt, A. 1991. 'Global Competition by Innovation—The Case for R&D Cooperation in the Vertical Chain', mimeo. Brussels: European Research Institute.

Bowie, A. 1994. 'The Dynamics of Business-Government Relations in Industrialising Malaysia', in A. MacIntyre (ed.), *Business and Government in Industrialising Asia*. St. Leonards, NSW: Allen and Unwin.

Breman, J. 1985. 'A Dualistic Labour System?' in R. Bromley (ed.), *Planning for Small Enterprises in Third World Cities*. Oxford: Pergamon. Original version published in *Economic and Political Weekly*, 27 November and 4 and 11 December 1976.

Bunce, V. and **M. Csanadi.** 1993. 'Uncertainty in the Transition: Post Communism in Hungary', *East European Politics and Societies*, Vol. 7.

Cadène, Philippe and **M. Holmström** (eds.). 1998. *Decentralized Production in India: Industrial Districts, Flexible Specialization, and Employment*. New Delhi: Sage.

Carlsson, Bo and **R. Stankiewicz.** 1991. 'On the Nature, Function and Composition of Technological Systems', *Journal of Evolutionary Economics*, Vol. 1, No. 2.

Caulkin, S. 1994. 'This Year's Moral', *Observer*, 16 October 1994.

Chandler, A.D. 1977. *Visible Hand—The Managerial Revolution in American Business*. Cambridge, Mass.: Belknap Press.

———. 1990. *Scale and Scope*. Cambridge, Mass.: Belknap Press.

Christensen, Jens F. 1996 'Innovative Assets and Inter-Asset Linkages—A Resource-Based Approach to Innovation', *Economics of Innovation and New Technology*, Vol. 4.

Christerson, Brad and **Richard P. Appelbaum.** 1995. 'Global and Local Subcontracting: Space, Ethnicity, and the Organization of Apparel Production', *World Development*, Vol. 23, No. 8.

Ciborra, C. 1991. 'Alliances as Learning Experiments—Cooperation, Competition and Change in Hightech Industries', in L. Mytelka (ed.), *Strategic Partnerships—States, Firmas and International Competition*. London: Pinter.

Coase, R. 1937. 'The Nature of the Firm', *Economica*, N.S. 4.

Computergram. 3 February 1994.

Crossley, N. 1996. *Intersubjectivity: The Fabric of Social Becoming*. London: Sage.

Csanadi, M. 1997. 'The Legacy of Party-States for the Transformation', *Communist Economies and Economic Transformation*, Vol. 9.

Cumings, B. 1997. *Korea's Place in the Sun*. New York: Norton.

Daems, H. 1983. 'The Determinants of the Hierarchical Organisation of Industry', in Arthur Francis, Jeremy Turk and Paul Willman (eds.), *Power, Efficiency and Institutions*. London: Heinemann.

Dahlman, C., B. Ross-Larson and **L. Westphal.** 1987. 'Managing Technological Development: Lessons from the Newly Industrialising Countries', *World Development*, Vol. 15, No. 6.

Danida. 1995. 'Capital Fund for SMEs in Ghana', study prepared for Danida. Aalborg: Aalborg University.

Das, K. 1996. 'Collective Dynamism and Firm Strategy: The Flooring Tile Cluster in Gujarat, India'. Working Paper 76. Ahmedabad: Gujarat Institute of Development Research.

Dataquest, 1987. 'History of SemiConductor Industry—South Korea', *Annual Report 1987*. San Jose, CA.

————. *Annual Report 1993*. San Jose, CA.

————. *Annual Report 1996*. San Jose, CA.

Dicken, P. 1992. *Global Shift: Transforming the World Economy*. London: Paul Chapman Publishing Ltd.

DiMaggio, P.J. and **W.W. Powell.** 1983. 'The Iron Cage Revisited: Institutional Isomorphism and Collective Rationality in Organizational Fields', *American Sociological Review*, No. 48.

Doleschal, R. 1991. 'Daten und Trends der bundesdeutschen Automobil-Zuliefererindustrie', in H.G. Mendius et al. (eds.), *Zulieferer im Netz*. Koeln (Cologne): Bund Verlag.

Doner, R.F. 1991. *Driving a Bargain. Automobile Industrialization and Japanese Firms in Southeast Asia*. Berkeley: University of California Press.

Dosi, G. et al. (eds.). 1988. *Technical Change and Economic Theory*. London: Pinter Publishers.

Dunning, J.H. 1995. 'Reappraising the Elective Paradigm in the Age of Capitalism', *Journal of International Business*, Third Quarter.

Economist. 10 May 1997.

Electronic New. 12 June 1993.

Ernst, D. 1983. *The Global Race in Microelectronics*, with a foreword by David Noble. Frankfurt and New York: MIT.

————. 1987. 'U.S.-Japanese Competition and the Worldwide Restructuring of the Electronics Industry—A European View', in J. Henderson and M. Castells (eds.), *Global Restructuring and Territorial Development*. London: Sage.

————. 1990. 'Programmable Automation in the Semiconductor Industry—Reflections on Recent Diffusion Patterns', report prepared for the OECD Development Centre. Paris: OECD.

————. 1992. 'Networks, Market Structure and Technology Diffusion—A Conceptual Framework and Some Empirical Evidence', report prepared for the OECD Secretariat. Paris OECD.

————. 1994a. 'Carriers of Regionalization? The East Asian Production Networks of Japanese Electronics Firms'. Working Paper 73. The Berkeley Roundtable on the International Economy. Berkeley: University of California at Berkeley.

————. 1994b. 'Network Transactions, Market Structure and Technological Diffusion—Implications for South–South Cooperation', in L. Mytelka (ed.), *South–South Cooperation in a Global Perspective*. Development Centre Documents. Paris: OECD.

————. 1994c. 'The Limits to the Japanese Model: The East Asian Production Networks of Japanese Electronic Firms', *NORD-SÜD aktuell*, 4. Quartel.

————. 1996a, 'Globalization, Convergence and Diversity: The Asian Production Networks of Japanese Electronics Firms', forthcoming in: M. Borrus,

D. Ernst and S. Haggard (eds.), *Rivalry or Riches: International Production Networks in Asia*, Ithaca, New York: Cornell University Press.

Ernst, D. 1996b. 'From Partial to Systemic Globalization. International Production Networks in the Electronics Industry', report prepared for the Sloan Foundation project on the Globalization in the Data Storage Industry, Graduate School of International Relations and Pacific Studies, University of California at San Diego, jointly published as *The Data Storage Industry Globalization Project Report 97–02*, Graduate School of International Relations and Pacific Studies, University of California at San Diego, and *BRIE Working Paper # 98*, the Berkeley Roundtable on the International Economy (BRIE), University of California at Berkeley, April 1997.

————. 1997a. 'Partners in the China Circle? The Asian Production Networks of Japanese Electronics Firms', in Barry Naughton (ed.), *The China Circle*. Washington, D.C.: The Brookings Institution Press.

————. 1997b, 'What Permits David to Grow in the Shadow of Goliath? The Taiwanese Model in the Computer Industry', a study prepared for the U.S.-Japan Friendship Commission, the Institute for Information Industry (III), Taiwan and The Berkeley Roundtable on the International Economy (BRIE), University of California at Berkeley. Also published as International Business Economics Research Paper Series 1997-3, Centre for International Studies, Aalborg University, March. Forthcoming in: Borrus, M., D. Ernst and S. Haggard (eds.), *Rivalry or Riches: International Production Networks in Asia*, Ithaca, New York: Cornell University Press.

Ernst, D. and **D. O'Connor.** 1992. *Competing in the Electronics Industry. The Experience of Newly Industrialising Economies*. Paris: Development Centre Studies, OECD.

Ernst, D., L. Mytelka and **T. Ganiatsos.** 1998a. 'Export Performance and Technological Capabilities—A Conceptual Framework', in D. Ernst, T. Ganiatsos and L. Mytelka (eds.), *Technological Capabilities and Export Success in Asia*. London: Routledge Press.

Ernst, D., T. Ganiatsos and **L. Mytelka** (eds.). 1998b. *Technological Capabilities and Export Success—Lessons from East Asia*. London: Routledge Press.

Ernst, Dieter and **J. Ravenhill.** 1997. 'Globalization, Convergence, and the Transformation of International Production Networks in Electronics in East Asia', paper prepared for the XVII World Congress of the International Political Science Association (IPSA), Seoul, 17–21 August.

Ernst, D. and **B-Å. Lundvall.** 1997. 'Information Technology in The Learning Economy—Challenges for Developing Countries', paper prepared for international conference on 'Evolutionary Economics and Spatial Income Inequality', Oslo, May. Published as DRUID Working Paper # 97-12, Aalborg University, Denmark: Department of Business Studies.

Evans, P. 1995. *Embedded Autonomy. States and Industrial Transformation*. Princeton: Princeton University Press.

Far Eastern Economic Review. 19 November 1992.

————. 21 December 1995.

————. 2 May 1996.

————. 13 June 1996.

————. 30 January 1997.

————. 19 February 1998.

Fields, Karl J. 1995. *Enterprise and the State in Korea and Taiwan*. Ithaca, New York: Cornell University Press.

Financial Times. 9 January 1997.

Foray, D. and **B.A. Lundvall.** 1996. 'The Knowledge-Based Economy: From the Economics of Knowledge to the Learning Economy', editors' Introduction to: *Employment and Growth in the Knowledge-Based Economy.* Paris: OECD.

Forsgren, M. and **J. Johanson** (eds.). 1992. *Managing Networks in International Business.* Philadelphia: Gordon and Breach.

Foss, N.J. 1996. 'Capabilities and the Theory of the Firm', DRUID Working Paper # 96–8, June. Copenhagen: Department of Industrial Economics and Strategy, Copenhagen Business School.

Friedman, D. 1988. *The Misunderstood Miracle.* Ithaca, New York: Cornell University Press.

Fruin, M. 1992. *The Japanese Enterprise System—Competitive Strategies and Cooperative Structures.* London: Clarendon Press.

Galhardi, R.M.A.A. 1994. 'Flexible Specialization, Technology and Employment: Networks in Developing Countries', paper for the workshop on 'Industrialization, Organisation, Innovation and Institutions in the South', Vienna.

Gee, S. and **W-J. Kuo.** 1994. 'Taiwan's Export Success and Technological Capabilities: The Case of Textiles and Electronics', in D. Ernst, T. Ganiatsos and L. Mytelka (eds.), *Technological Capabilities and Export Success—Lessons from East Asia.* Cambridge: Cambridge University Press.

———. 1998. Chapter on Taiwan, in D. Ernst, T. Ganiatsos and L. Mytelka (eds.), *Technological Capabilities and Export Success in Asia.* London: Routledge.

Gereffi, G. 1994. 'The Organization of Buyer-Driven Global Commodity Chains: How US Retailers Shape Overseas Production Networks', in G. Gereffi and M. Korzeniewicz (eds.), *Commodity Chains and Global Capitalism.* Westport: Praeger.

———. 1996a. 'Commodity Chains and Regional Divisions of Labor in East Asia', *Journal of Asian Business*, Vol. 12, No. 1.

———. 1996b. 'Global Commodity Chains: New Forms of Coordination and Control Among Nations and Firms in International Industries', *Competition and Change*, Vol. 4.

Gereffi, G. and **M. Korzeniewicz** (eds.). 1994. *Commodity Chains and Global Capitalism.* London/Westport, Conn: Greenwood Press/Praeger.

Gerlach, M.L. 1992. *Alliance Capitalism—The Social Organization of Japanese Business.* Berkeley: University of California Press.

Gomez, E.T. 1995. *Political Business. Corporate Involvement of Malaysian Political Parties.* Townsville: James Cook University of North Queensland.

———. 1997. 'Political Business in Malaysia', Occasional Paper, No. 8, Copenhagen: Copenhagen Business School, DICM.

———. 1998. '"Political Business" in Malaysia: Cronyism, change and crisis', paper presented to a workshop on 'East Asian Development Models in Crisis' held at Manchester Business School, 9th June.

Gomez, E.T. and **K.S. Jomo.** 1997. *Malaysia's Political Economy. Politics. Patronage and Profits.* Cambridge: Cambridge University Press.

Gorter, P. 1996. *Small Industrialists, Big Ambitions.* New Delhi: Oxford University Press.

Grabher, G. 1993. 'Rediscovering the Social in the Economics of Inter-firm Relations' in Gernot Grabher (ed.), *The Embedded Firm; On the Socioeconomics of Industrial Networks.* London: Routledge.

Graham, E.M. 1994. 'Financial Liberalization and the Environment for U.S. Investment—A Private U.S. Perspective', in *Korea's Economy 1994*, Vol. 10. Washington, D.C.: Korea Economic Institute of America.

Granovetter, M. 1985. 'Economic Action and Social Structure: The Problem of Embeddedness', *American Journal of Sociology*, Vol. 91, No. 3. Also in: M. Granovetter and R. Swedberg (eds.). 1992. *The Sociology of Economic Life*. Oxford: Westview Press.

Granovetter, M. and R. Swedberg (eds.). 1992. *The Sociology of Economic Life*. Oxford: Westview Press.

Granstrand, O., L. Håkanson and S. Soelander (eds.). 1992. *Technology Management and International Business: Internationalisation of R&D and Technology*. New York: Wiley.

Green, R.H. 1987. *Ghana: Stabilization and Adjustment Programmes and Policies*. World Institute for Development Economics Research.

Hamilton, G.G. and N.W. Biggart. 1988. 'Market, Culture and Authority: A Comparative Analysis of Management and Organization in the Far East', *American Journal of Sociology*, Vol. 94, supplement. Also published in M. Granovetter and R. Swedberg (eds.). 1992. *The Sociology of Economic Life*, Oxford: Westview Press.

Hamilton, G.G., W. Zeile, and W.J. Kim. 1990. 'The Network Structures of East Asian Economies', in S. Clegg and G. Redding (eds.), *Capitalism in Contrasting Cultures*. Berlin: de Gruyter.

Heuzé, G. 1992. 'Introduction' to G. Heuzé (ed.), *Travailler en Inde/The Context of Work in India*. Paris: Collection Purusārtha, Éditions de l'École des Hautes Études en Sciences Sociales.

Hill, R.C. and Y.J. Lee. 1994. 'Japanese Multinationals and East Asian Development', in L. Sklair (ed.), *Capitalism and Development*. London: Routledge.

Hirschman, E.C. and M.B. Holbrook. 1992. *Postmodern Consumer Research: The Study of Consumption as Text*. Thousand Oaks: Sage.

Hofstede, G. 1982. *Cultural Pitfalls for Dutch Expatriates in Indonesia*. Deventer/Jakarta: TG International Management Consultants.

Hofsteede, W.M.F. 1971. *The Decision Making Process in Four West Javanese Villages*. Nijmegen: Offsetdrukkerij faculteit der Wiskunde en Natuurwetenschappen.

Hollingsworth, R. and R. Boyer. 1997. 'Coordination of Economic Actors and Social Systems of Production', in J.R. Hollingsworth and R. Boyer (eds.), *Comparing Capitalisms: The Embeddedness of Institutions*. Cambridge: Cambridge University Press.

Holmström, M. 1976. *South Indian Factory Workers: Their Life and their World*. Cambridge etc.: Cambridge University Press; and New Delhi: Allied Publishers, 1978.

———. 1984. *Industry and Inequality: The Social Anthropology of Indian Labour*. Cambridge/Hyderabad: Cambridge University Press/Orient Longman.

———. 1993. 'Flexible specialization in India?', *Economic & Political Weekly*, Vol. 28, No. 35.

———. 1994. 'Bangalore as an Industrial District: Flexible Specialization in a Labour-Surplus Economy?', revised version of a report to the Overseas Development Administration ('A New Direction for Indian Industry? Bangalore as an Industrial District', 1993). Pondy Papers in Social Sciences, No. 14. French Institute of Pondicherry and School of Development Studies discussion paper, University of East Anglia.

Holmström, M. 1997. 'A Cure for Loneliness? Networks, trust, and shared services in Bangalore', *Economic & Political Weekly*, Vol. 32, No. 35.

————. 1998a. 'Bangalore as an Industrial District: Flexible Specialization in a Labour Surplus Economy?', in P. Cadène and M. Holmström (eds.), *Decentralized Production in India: Industrial Districts, Flexible Specialization, and Employment*. New Delhi: Sage.

————. 1998b. 'Industrial Districts and Flexible Specialization: The Outlook for Smaller Firms in India', in P. Cadène & M. Holmström (eds.), *Decentralized Production in India: Industrial Districts, Flexible Specialization, and Employment*. New Delhi: Sage.

Hopkins, T.K. and **I. Wallerstein.** 1986. 'Commodity Chains in the World-Economy'. *Review*, Vol. 10.

Hu, Y-S. 1992. 'Global or Stateless Corporations are National Firms with International Operations', *California Management Review*, winter.

Hulst, W. 1991. 'Indonesië Staat of Valt met Chinezen: Soeharto zint op economische dwangmaatregelen', *Financieel Economisch Magazine*, No. 23.

Humphrey, J. 1995. 'Introduction (to Industrial Organization and Manufacturing Competitiveness in Developing Countries)', *World Development*, Vol. 23, No. 1.

Huq, M.M. 1989. *The Economy of Ghana: The First 25 Years since Independence*. London: Macmillan.

Hutchful, E. 1995. *Structural Adjustment in Ghana, 1983–94*. Copenhagen: Centre for Development Research.

Hyden, G. 1994. 'The Role of Social Capital in African Development—Illustrations from Tanzania'. Occasional Paper No. 12. Roskilde: International Development Studies, Roskilde University.

Imai, K.I. and **Y. Baba.** 1991. 'Systemic Innovation and Cross-Border Networks. Transcending Markets and Hierarchies to Create a New Techno-Economic System', in *Technology and Productivity: The Challenge for Economic Policy*, Paris: OECD.

Ingham, G. 1996. 'Some Recent Changes in the Relationship between Economics and Sociology', *Cambridge Journal of Economics*, Vol. 20.

ISSER. 2000. *The State of the Ghanaian Economy in 1996*. Legon: University of Ghana.

Jacobs, J. 1992. *Systems of Survival: A Dialogue on the Moral Foundations of Commerce and Politics*. London: Hodder & Stoughton.

Jakarta Post. 30 October 1994.

Janelli, R.L. and **D. Yim.** 1993. *Making Capitalism. The Social and Cultural Construction of a South Korean Conglomerate*. Stanford, CA: Stanford University Press.

Jesudason, J.V. 1989. *Ethnicity and the Economy: The State, Chinese Business and Multinationals in Malaysia*. Singapore: Oxford University Press.

————. 1997. 'Chinese Business and Ethnic Equilibrium in Malaysia', *Development and Change*, Vol. 28.

Jomo, K.S. (ed.). 1994a. *Japan and Malaysian Development: In the Shadow of the Rising Sun*. London: Routledge.

————. 1994b. 'The Proton Saga: Malaysian Car, Mitsubishi gain', in Jomo K.S. (ed.), *Japan and Malaysian Development: In the Shadow of the Rising Sun*, London: Routledge.

Jomo, K.S. and **Ch. Edwards.** 1993. 'Malaysian Industrialisation in Historical Perspective', in Jomo K.S. and Ch. Edwards, *Industrialising Malaysian. Policy, Performance, Prospects*. London: Routledge.

Jordaan, R. 1985. 'Folk Medicine in Madura (Indonesia)', Ph.D. thesis. Leiden: Leiden University Press.

Joshi, H. 1980. 'The Informal Urban Economy and its Boundaries', *Economic & Political Weekly*, 29 March 1980.

Jun, Y-W. and **S-G. Kim.** 1990. *Structure and Strategy in the Korean Electronics Industry*, report prepared for the OECD Development Centre. Paris: OECD.

Kam, Wong Poh. 1991. *Technological Development through Subcontracting Linkages.* Tokyo: Asia Productivity Organization (APO).

Kaplinsky, R. 1994. *Easternization: Spread of Japanese Management Techniques to Developing Countries.* London: Frank Cass & Co.

———. 1995. 'Technique and System: The Spread of Japanese Management Techniques to Developing Countries', *World Development*, Vol. 23, No. 1.

Kartodirdjo, S. 1972. 'Agrarian Radicalism in Java: Its Setting and Development', in Holt (ed.), *Culture and Politics in Indonesia*. London: Cornell University Press.

Keesing, R.M. 1985. *Cultural Anthropology: A Contemporary Perspective*. New York: Holt, Rinehart.

Kenney, M. and **R. Florida.** 1994. 'Japanese Maquiladoras: Production Organization and Global Commodity Chains', *World Development*, Vol. 22, No. 1.

Kim, E.M. 1997. *Big Business, Strong State: Collusion and conflict in South Korean Development, 1960–1990.* Albany: State University of New York Press.

Kim, H.S. 1991. ' Ideology of Science and Technology and the Korean Society', in Korean Industrial Research Society (ed.), *Korean Society and its Dominant Ideologies*. Seoul.

———. 1993. 'Technological Innovation and Industrial Relations', paper presented at a 'Korean Industrial Relations Society' Conference, Seoul.

Kim, Linsu. 1993. 'The Structure and Workings of the National Innovation System in Korea', paper presented at the conference on 'Redefining Korean Competitiveness in an Age of Globalization'. Center for Korean Studies, University of California at Berkeley.

Kim, S.G. (ed.). 1995. *Review of Science and Technology Policy for Industrial Competitiveness in Korea*. Seoul: Science and Technology Policy Institute (STEPI).

Kim, S.R. 1996. 'The Korean System of Innovation and the Growth Dynamics of the Semiconductor Industry: Politics and Governance', manuscript, SPRU, University of Sussex.

Kim, I.Y. and **S.Y. Chung.** 1991. 'R&D Cooperation Between Large Manufacturing Companies and Suppliers', mimeo, Science and Technology Policy Institute, Korea Advanced Institute of Science and Technology, Seoul.

Kim, I.Y. and **C.Y. Kim.** 1991. 'Comparison of Korean to Western R&D—Project Selection Factors for New Product Development', mimeo, Science and Technology Policy Institute, Korea Advanced Institute of Science and Technology, Seoul.

Kim, H.K. and **S-H. Lee.** 1994. 'Commodity Chains and the Korean Auto Industry', in G. Gereffi and M. Korzeniewicz (eds.), *Commodity Chains and Global Capitalism*. London: Greenwood Press.

Kimman, E.J.J.M. 1981. *Indonesian Publishing: Economic Organizations in a Langganan Society*, Baarn: Hollandia.

Knorringa, P. 1991. *Small Enterprises in the Indian Footwear Industry: A Case Study of the Agra Cluster. Research Report to the Ministry of Development Cooperation.* Amsterdam: University of Amsterdam.

Knorringa, P. 1994. 'Lack of Interaction between Traders and Producers in the Agra Footwear Cluster', in P.O. Pedersen, A. Sverrisson and M.P. van Dijk (eds.), *Flexible Specialization: The Dynamics of Small-scale Industries in the South*. London: Intermediate Technology Publications.

————. 1998. 'Barriers to Flexible Specialization in Agra's Footwear Industry', in P. Cadène and M. Holmström (eds.), *Decentralized Production in India: Industrial Districts, Flexible Specialization, and Employment*. New Delhi: Sage.

Khan, M.H. 1998. 'Patron-Client Networks and the Economic Effects of Corruption in Asia', *The European Journal of Development Research*, Vol. 10, No. 1.

Kogut, B. 1985. 'Designing Global Strategies: Comparative and Competitive Value-added Chains', *Sloan Management Review*, Summer.

————. 1991. 'Designing Global Strategies: Comparative and Competitive Value-added Chains'. UNCTC.

Kogut, B. and **E. Zander.** 1993. 'Knowledge of the Firm and the Evolutionary Theory of the Multinational Corporation', *Journal of International Business Studies*, Vol. 24, No. 4.

Kohama, H. and **S. Urata.** 1993. 'Protection and Promotion of Japan's Electronics Industry', in Inoue, Ryuichiro et al. (eds.), *Industrial policy in East Asia*. Tokyo: JETRO.

Koo, H. 1993. 'Strong State and Contentious Society', in H. Koo (ed.), *State and Society in Contemporary Korea*. Ithaca: Cornell University Press.

Kristensen, P.H. 1992. 'Strategies against structure: Institutions and economic organisation in Denmark', in R. Whitley (ed.), *European Business Systems. Firms and Markets in their National Contexts*. London: Sage.

————. 1994. 'Strategies in a Volatile World', *Economy and Society*, Vol. 23, No. 3.

————. 1996a. 'On the Constitutions of Economic Actors in Denmark: Interacting Skill Containers and Project Coordinators', in R. Whitley and P.H. Kristensen (eds.), *The Changing European Firm*. London: Routledge.

————. 1996b. 'Variations in the Nature of the Firm in Europe', in R. Whitley and P.H. Kristensen (eds.), *The Changing European Firm; Limits to Convergence*. London: Routledge.

————. 1997. 'National Systems of Governance and Managerial Strategies in the Evolution of Work Systems: Britain, Germany and Denmark Compared', in R. Whitley and P.H. Kristensen (eds.), *Governance at Work: The Social Regulation of Economic Relations*. Oxford: Oxford University Press.

Krugman, P. 1994. 'The Myth's of Asia's Miracle', *Foreign Affairs*, Vol. 73, No. 6.

KSIA (Korean Semiconductor Industry Association). 1993. *Strategy for the Development of the Korean Semiconductor Industry*. Seoul: KSIA.

Kuada, J. 1980. 'The Industrial Sector in Ghana's Economic Development Process: Problems and Prospects', *Journal of Management Studies*, Ghana, Vol. 12, No. 1.

————. 1994. *Managerial Behaviour in Ghana and Kenya. A Cultural Perspective*. Aalborg, Denmark: Aalborg University Press.

Kuada, J. and **O.J. Sørensen.** 2000. *Internationalisation of Companies from Developing Countries*. Birmingham, New York: The Haworth Press.

Lachaier, P. 1992. '"Employeurs-employés" et "employés-employeurs" dans les firmes lignagères industrielles du secteur de la mécanique de Puna', in G. Heuzé (ed.), *Travailler en Inde/The context of work in India*. Collection Purusãrtha. Paris: Éditions de l'École des Hautes Études en Sciences Sociales.

Lall, S. and **Ganeshan Wignaraja.** 1996. 'Skills and Capabilities: Ghana's Industrial Competitiveness'. *Development Studies Working Papers No. 92.* Oxford: University of Oxford.

Lane, C. 1996. 'The Social Constitution of Supplier Relations in Britain and Germany: An Institutionalist Analysis', in R. Whitley and P.H. Kristensen (eds.), *The Changing European Firm.* London: Routledge.

Lane, C., and **R. Bachmann.** 1996. 'The Social Construction of Trust: Supplier Relations in Britain and Germany', *Organization Studies,* Vol. 17, No. 3.

Lazerson, M.H. 1988. 'Organisational Growth of Small Firms: An Outcome of Markets and Hierarchies', *American Sociological Review,* 53.

Lazonick, W. 1991. *Business Organization and the Myth of the Market Economy.* Cambridge: Cambridge University Press.

Lazonick, W. and **J. West.** 1998. 'Organizational Integration and Competitive Advantage', in G. Dosi, D. Teece and J. Chytry (eds.), *Technology, Organization and Competitiveness.* Oxford: Oxford University Press.

Leach, E.R. 1960. 'Introduction' to E.R. Leach (ed.), *Aspects of Caste in South India, Ceylon and North-West Pakistan.* Cambridge: Cambridge University Press.

Lee, J-J. 1992. 'The Status and Issue of Management Dynamism and Four Case Studies in the Republic of Korea', in *Management Dynamism. A Study of Selected Companies in Asia.* Tokyo: Asian Productivity Organization (APO).

Lehmann, J-P. 1996. 'Corporate Governance in East Asia & Western Europe: Competition, Confrontation & Cooperation', paper for the Second International Forum on Asian Perspectives. Paris: Asian Development Bank and OECD Development Centre.

Levitt, T. 1983. 'The Globalization of Markets', *Harvard Business Review,* May–June.

Lim, L. 1996. 'The Evolution of Southeast Asian Business Systems', *Journal of Asian Business,* Vol. 12, No. 1.

———. 1997. 'The Southeast Asian Currency Crisis and its Aftermath', *Journal of Asian Business,* Vol. 13, No. 4.

Llerena, P. and **E. Zuscovitch.** 1996. 'Innovation, Diversity and Organization from an Evolutionary Perspective—Introduction and Overview', *Economics of Innovation and New Technology,* Vol. 4, No. 2.

Lorenz, E.H. 1993. 'Flexible Production Systems and the Social Construction of Trust', *Politics & Society,* Vol. 21, No. 3.

Loxley, J. 1988. *Ghana: Economic Crisis and the Long Road to Recovery.* Ottawa: The North-South Institute.

Lubis, T.M. 1993. *In Search of Human Rights: Legal-Political Dillemma's of Indonesia's New Order 1966–1990.* Jakarta: PT Gamedia Pustaka Utama.

Lundvall, B-A. 1988. 'Innovation as an Interactive Process: From User-Producer Interaction to the National System of Innovation', in Dosi et al. (eds.), *Technical Change and Economic Theory.* London: Pinter.

———. (ed.). 1992. *National Systems of Innovation: Towards a Theory of Innovation and Interactive Learning.* London: Pinter.

Machado, K.G. 1989/90 'Japanese Transnational Corporations in Malaysia's State Sponsored Heveay Industrialization Drive: The HICOM Automobile and Steel Projects'. *Pacific Affairs* 62.

———. 1994. 'Proton and Malaysia's Motor Vehicle Industry', in Jomo K.S. (ed.), *Japan and Malaysian Development: In the Shadow of the Rising Sun.* London: Routledge.

Machado, K.G. 1997. 'Growing Complexity of the East Asian Division of Labour: Implications for Regionalism and ASEAN Industrial Development'. IKMAS Working Papers, No. 89, 1997.

MacIntyre, A. 1994. 'Business, Government and Development: Northeast and Southeast Asian comparisons', in A. MacIntyre (ed.), *Business and Government in Industrialising Asia*. St Leonards, NSW: Allen and Unwin.

Mahathir, M. 1991. *Malaysia: The Way Forward*. Kuala Lumpur: Working Paper to the Malaysian Business Council, mimeo.

Malaysian Industry. April 1996.

————. May 1996.

Malerba, F. and **L. Orsenigo.** 1996. 'The Dynamics and Evolution of Industries', *Industrial and Corporate Change*, Vol. 5, No. 1.

Maskell, P. 1996a. 'Learning in the Village Economy of Denmark: The Role of Institutions and Policy in Sustaining Competitiveness', *DRUID Working Paper # 96–6*. Copenhagen: Department of Industrial Economics and Strategy, Copenhagen Business School.

————. 1996b, 'The Process and Consequences of Ubiquification', paper prepared for the DRUID workshop, January 1997, Department of Industrial Economics and Strategy, Copenhagen Business School.

Mathew, P.M. 1995. *Productivity and Economic Transformation: Towards a Flexible Specialization Model for Rural Industries*. Tokyo: Asian Productivity Organization.

Mathew, P.M. and **J. Joseph.** 1994a. 'Can Flexible Specialization be the Alternative? An Exploratory Study on the Cane & Bamboo Industry', Occasional Paper 15, mimeo. Vennala, Cochin: Institute of Small Enterprises & Development.

————. 1994b. 'Towards an Alternative Approach to the Development of Traditional Industries: A Study on Cane and Bamboo Industry', SIDBI/ISED Joint Project. Cochin: Institute of Small Enterprises and Development.

Mauss, M. 1954 (originally 1925). *The Gift: Forms and Functions of Exchange in Archaic Societies*. London: Cohen and West.

McIntyre, Andrew. 1992. *Business and Politics in Indonesia*. Sydney: Allen and Unwin.

Meillassoux, C. 1973. 'Are there Castes in India?', *Economy and Society*, Vol. 89, No. 2.

Misra, B.B. 1961. *The Indian Middle Classes*. London: Oxford University Press.

Moon, C. 1994. 'Changing Patterns of Business-Government Relations in South Korea' in A. MacIntyre (ed.), *Business and Government in Industrialising Asia*. St. Leonards, NSW: Allen and Unwin.

Mortimore, M. and **R. Zamora.** 1996. 'The International Competitiveness of the Costa Rican Clothing Industry', draft paper. Santiago: ECLAC/UNCTAD Joint Unit.

Mulder, N. 1978. *Mysticism & Everyday Life in Contemporary Java*. Singapore: Singapore University Press.

————. 1989. *Individual and Society in Java: A Cultural Analysis*. Yogyakarta: Gadjah Mada University Press.

Muskens, M.P.M. 1970. *Indonesië, een Strijd om Nationale Identiteit: nationalisten/islamieten/katholieken*. Bussum: Uitgeverij Paul Brand.

Nadvi, K. 1994. 'Industrial District Experiences in Developing Countries', in *Technological Dynamism in Industrial Districts: An Alternative Approach to Industrialisation in Developing Countries?* New York: UNCTAD/United Nations.

Nadvi, K. and **H. Schmitz.** 1994. 'Industrial Clusters in Less Developed Countries: Review of Experiences and Research Agenda'. Institute of Development Studies Discussion Paper No. 339.

Nasution, A. 1993. 'Reforms of the Financial Sector in Indonesia, 1983–1991', *The Indonesian Quarterly*, Vol. 21, No. 3.

Nishida, J.M. and **S.G. Redding.** 1992. 'Firm Development and Diversification Strategies as Products of Economic Cultures: The Japanese and Hong Kong Textile Industries', in R. Whitley (ed.), *European Business Systems: Firms and Markets in their National Contexts.* London: Sage.

Nelson, R. and **S.G. Winter.** 1982. *An Evolutionary Theory of Economic Change.* Cambridge and Mass.: Bellknap Press.

Nugent, P. 1995. *Big Men, Small Boys and Politics in Ghana:* London: Printer.

OECD. 1992. *Technology and the Economy. The Key Relationships.* Paris: OECD.

Ohmae, K. 1990. *The Borderless World: Power and Strategy in the Interlinked Economy.* New York: Harper & Row.

———. 1991. *The Borderless World: Power and Strategy in the Interlinked Economy.* New York: Harper & Row.

Okyu, Kwon. 1994. 'Financial Liberalization and Environment for U.S. Investment', in *Korea's Economy 1994.* Washington, D.C.: Korea Economic Institute of America.

Oman, C. 1994. 'The Policy Challenges of Globalisation and Regionalisation', *OECD Development Centre Policy Brief*, No. 11. Paris: OECD.

Orru, M., N.W. Biggart and **G. Hamilton.** 1997. *The Economic Organisation of East Asian Capitalism.* Thousand Oaks: Sage.

Pangestu, M. 1993. 'The Role of the State & Economic Development in Indonesia', *The Indonesian Quarterly*, Vol. 21, No. 3.

Penrose, E.T. 1959. *The Theory of the Growth of the Firm.* Oxford: Oxford University Press.

Piore, M.J. and **C.F. Sabel.** 1984. *The Second Industrial Divide: Possibilities for Prosperity.* New York: Basic Books.

Pocock, D.F. 1962. 'Notes on Jajmāni Relationships', *Contributions to Indian Sociology*, Vol. 6.

Polanyi, K. 1957. 'The Economy as Instituted Process', in K. Polanyi et al. (eds.), *Trade and Markets in the Early Empires.* New York: Free Press.

———. 1959. 'Anthropology and Economic Theory', in M.H. Fried (ed.), *Readings in Anthropology*, Vol. 2. New York: Thomas Y. Crowell Company.

Politiken. 17 December 1997.

———. 21 December 1997.

Popova, J.F. and **O.J. Sørensen.** 1996. 'Marketing as Social Construction: Alternative Views on the Interface between the Enterprise and the Environment'. Paper presented at the Workshop on Business Systems in the South, 22–24 January. Copenhagen: Copenhagen Business School.

Porter, M. 1980. *Competitive Strategy.* New York: Free Press.

———. 1990. *The Competitive Advantages of Nations.* London: Macmillan Press.

Price Waterhouse. 1993. *Doing Business in Indonesia,* information guide. Jakarta: Price Waterhouse.

Pyke, F. and W. Sengenberger (eds.). 1992. *Industrial Districts and Local Economic Regeneration.* Geneva: International Labour Office.

Rabellotti, R. 1995. 'Is There an "Industrial District Model"? Footwear Districts in Italy and Mexico Compared', *World Development,* Vol. 23, No. 1.

Räsänen, K. and R. Whipp. 1992. 'National Business Recipes: A Sector Perspective', in R. Whitley (ed.). 1992. *European Business Systems. Firms and Markets in their National Contexts.* London: Sage.

Rasiah, R. 1996a. 'Between Authoritarianism and Ecclecticism: Proton's Labour Strategies in Malaysia', mimeo. Kuala Lumpur: IKMAS, UKM.

————. 1996b. 'Rent Management in Malaysias PROTON', in M. Kahn and K.S. Jomo (eds.), *Rents and Development.* Cambridge: Cambridge Press.

————. 1997. 'A System Approach to Understanding Malaysia's Industrialization'. *Occasional Paper,* No. 21. Copenhagen: Copenhagen Business School, DICM.

Rasmussen, J. 1991. 'The Local Entrepreneurial Millieu: Linkages and Specialization among Small Town Enterprises in Zimbabwe', *Research Report,* No. 79. Copenhagen: Department of Geography, Roskilde University, Centre for Development Research.

Redding, G. 1990. *The Spirit of Chinese Capitalism.* Berlin: De Gruyter.

Robison, R. 1986. *Indonesia: The Rise of Capital.* Sidney: Allen & Unwin.

Sabel, C.F. 1982. *Work and Politics: The Division of Labor in Industry.* Cambridge: Cambridge University Press.

Sabel, C.F. et al. 1991. 'Kooperative Produktion. Neue Formen der Zusammenarbeit zwischen Endfertigern und Zulieferern', in H.G. Mendius et al. (eds.), *Zulieferer im Netz.* Koeln (Cologne): Bund Verlag.

Sahlins, M. 1972. 'On the Sociology of Primitive Exchange', in M. Sahlins, *Stone Age Economics.* London: Tavistock Publications.

Sako, Mari. 1992. *Prices, Quality and Trust.* Cambridge: Cambridge University Press.

Sato, Y. 1993. 'The Salim Group in Indonesia: The Development and Behavior of the Largest Conglomerate in Southeast Asia', *The Developing Economies,* Vol. 41, No. 4.

Schmitz, H. 1995. 'Small Shoemakers and Fordist Giants. Tale of a Supercluster', *World Development,* Vol. 23, No. 1.

Schmitz, H. and B. Musyck. 1994. 'Industrial Districts in Europe: Policy Lessons for Developing Countries'. *World Development,* Vol. 22, No. 6.

Schmitz, H. and K. Nadvi. 1999. 'Clustering and Industrialization: Introduction', *World Development,* Vol. 27, No. 9.

Schultz, C.J. and A. Pecotich. 1997. 'Marketing and Development in the Transition Economies of Southeast Asia: Policy Explication, Assessment and Implications', *Journal of Public Policy & Marketing,* Vol. 16, No. 1.

Schwarz, Adam. 1994. 'Empire of the Son', *Far Eastern Economic Review,* Vol. 14.

Shiba, T. and M. Shimotami. 1997. *Beyond the Firm: Business groups in international and historical perspective.* Oxford: Oxford University Press.

Silverberg, J. (ed.). 1968. *Social Mobility in the Caste System in India.* The Hague: Mouton.

Slife, B.D. and **R.N. Williams.** 1995. *What's behind Research?: Discovering Hidden Assumptions in the Behavioral Sciences.* Thousand Oaks: Sage.

Smitka, Michael. 1991. *Competitive Ties: Subcontracting in the Japanese Automotive Industry.* New York: Columbia University Press.

Sørensen, O.J. 1994. 'Government-Business Relations. Towards a Partnership Model', *Working Paper Series,* No. 9. Aalborg: International Business Economics, Centre for International Studies, Aalborg University.

Sørensen, O.J. and **V.K. Nyanteng.** 2000 'Ghana's Exports to Neighbouring Countries', *The Journal of Management Studies,* Vol. 15, No. 2.

Späth, B. 1994. 'Implications of Industrial Districts for Upgrading Small Firms in Developing Countries: A Synthesis of the Discussion', in *Technological Dynamism in Industrial Districts: An Alternative Approach to Industrialisation in Developing Countries?* New York: UNCTAD/United Nations.

Stokes, E. 1959. *The English Utilitarians and India.* Oxford: Clarendon Press.

Storper, M. 1995. 'Territorial Development in the Global Learning Economy: The Challenge to Developing Countries', *Review of International Political Economy,* Vol. 2, No. 3, Summer.

Storper, M. and **A.J. Scott.** 1992. *Pathways to Industrialization and Regional Development.* London and New York: Routledge.

Sun, The, 4 May 1996.

Swedberg, R. 1997. 'New Economic Sociology: What has been Accomplished, What is ahead?' *Acta Sociologica,* Vol. 40, No. 2.

Tam, S. 1990. 'Centrifugal versus Centripedal Growth Processes: Contrasting Ideal Types for Conceptualising the Developmental Patterns of Chinese and Japanese Firms', in S. Clegg and G. Redding (eds.), *Capitalism in Contrasting Cultures.* Berlin: De Gruyter.

Teece, D., G. Pisano and **A. Shuen.** 1995. 'Firm Capabilities, Resources, and the Concept of Strategy', forthcoming in, *Strategic Management Journal.*

Tetteh, D.O. 1996. 'Institutional Support for Non-Traditional Exports in Ghana'. MBA thesis. Legon: School of Administration, University of Ghana.

Tewari, M. 1995. 'When the Marginal becomes Mainstream: Understanding the Sources and Organization of Small-firm Growth in Ludhiana's Industrial Regime', Ph.D. dissertation. Department of Urban Studies and Planning, Massachusetts Institute of Technology.

———. 1998. 'The State and the Shaping of the Conditions of Accumulation in Ludhiana's Industrial Regime: An Historical Interpretation', in P. Cadène and M. Holmström (eds.), *Decentralized Production in India: Industrial Districts, Flexible Specialization, and Employment.* New Delhi: Sage.

Torii, T. 1991. 'Changing the Manufacturing Sector, Reorganizing Automobile Assemblers, and Developing the Auto Component Industry under the New Economic Policy', *The Developing Economies,* Vol. 29, No. 4.

Torp, J.E. 1997. 'International Acquisitions and Industrial Districts', Occasional Paper No. 20, Department of Intercultural Communication and Management, Copenhagen Business School.

Trevelyan, C.E. 1838. *On the Education of the People of India.* London.

Tsikata, G.K. and **G.K. Amuzu.** 1997. 'Fiscal Development', in V.K. Nyanteng (ed.), *Policies and Options for Ghanaian Economic Development.* Ghana: The Institute of Statistical, Social and Economic Research.

United Nations. 1994. *Technological Dynamism in Industrial Districts: An Alternative Approach to Industrialisation in Developing Countries?* New York: UNCTAD/ United Nations.

van Dijk and **Meine Pieter.** 1994. 'The Interrelations between Industrial Districts and Technological Capabilities Development: Concepts and Issues', in United Nations, *Technological Dynamism in Industrial Districts: An Alternative to Industrialization in Developing Countries?* New York: UNCTAD/United Nations.

van Dijk, Meine Pieter and **Roberta Rabellotti** (eds.). 1997. *Enterprise Clusters and Networks in Developing Countries.* London: Frank Cass. 1997.

Wad, P. 1996a. *Enterprise Unions: From Backward to Vanguard Unionism?* DICM Working Paper No. 7. Copenhagen: Copenhagen Business School/DICM.

―――. 1996b. 'The Malaysian Policy of Enterprise Unionism and its Socio-Economic Impact'. Research Seminar Paper, mimeo. Copenhagen: Copenhagen Business School/DICM.

―――. 1997. 'Business Systems and Industrial Relations in Malaysia: The Restructuring of the Automobile Industry'. Occasional Paper No. 14. Copenhagen: Copenhagen Business School/DICM.

Wade, R. 1990. *Governing the Market. Economic Theory and the Role of Government in East Asian Industrialization.* Princeton: Princeton University Press.

Weiss, L. 1995. 'Governed Interdependence: Rethinking the Government-Business Relationship in East Asia', *The Pacific Review,* Vol. 8, No. 4.

Westney, E. 1996. 'The Japanese Business System: Key Features and Prospects for Changes', *Journal of Asian Business,* Vol. 12.

Whitley, R. 1987. 'Taking Firms Seriously as Economic Actors: Towards a Sociology of Firm Behaviour', *Organization Studies,* Vol. 8, No. 2.

―――. 1990. 'Eastern Asian Enterprise Structures and the Comparative Analysis of Forms of Business Organization'. *Organization Studies,* Vol. 11, No. 1.

―――. 1991. 'The Social Construction of Business Systems in East Asia'. *Organisation Studies,* Vol. 12, No. 1.

―――. 1992a. *Business Systems in East Asia: Firms, Markets and Societies.* London: Sage.

―――. (ed.). 1992b. *European Business Systems. Firms and Markets in their National Contexts.* London: Sage.

―――. 1992c. 'The Social Construction of Organizations and Markets: The Comparative Analysis of Business Recipes', in M. Reed and M. Huses (eds.), *Rethinking Organization.* London: Sage.

―――. 1992d. 'Varieties of Effective Forms of Economic Organisation: Firms and Markets in Comparative Perspective'. Working Paper, No. 221, Manchester Business School.

―――. 1994a. 'Dominant forms of Economic Organisation in Market Economies', *Organization Studies,* Vol. 15, No. 2.

―――. 1994b. 'The Internationalization of Firms and Markets: Its Significance and Institutional Structuring', *Organization,* Vol. 1, No. 1.

―――. 1996a. 'Business Systems and Global Commodity Chains: Competing or Complementary Forms of Economic Organisation?', *Competition and Change,* Vol. 1.

―――. 1996b. 'Continuity and Change in East Asian Capitalism: The Limited Effects of Internationalisation and Domestic Change on the Business Systems of

Japan, Korea and Taiwan', mimeo. Discussion Draft Paper. Manchester: Manchester Business School, University of Manchester.

Whitley, R. 1996c. 'The Social Construction of Economic Actors: Institutions and Types of Firm in Europe and Other Market Economies', in R. Whitley and P.H. Kristensen (eds.), *The Changing European Firm. Limits to Convergence.* London: Routledge.

————. 1997. 'The Social Regulation of Work Systems: Institutions, Interest Groups and Varieties of Work Organisation in Capitalist Societies', in R. Whitley and P.H. Kristensen (eds.), *Governance at Work: The Social Regulation of Economic Relations in Europe.* Oxford: Oxford University Press.

————. 1998. 'Contrasting Capitalisms: The Institutional Structuring of Business Systems'. Paper presented to a conference on 'Institutions and Development', Gjerrild, 5–7 March 1998.

————. 1999. *Divergent Capitalisms: The Social Structuring and Change of Business Systems.* Oxford: Oxford University Press.

Whitley, R. and **L. Czaban.** 1998. 'Institutional Transformation and Enterprise Change in an Emergent Capitalist Economy: The Case of Hungary', *Organization Studies*, Vol. 19, No. 2.

Whitley, R. and **P.H. Kristensen** (eds.). 1996. *The Changing European Firm; Limits to Convergence.* London: Routledge.

————. (eds.). 1997. *Governance at Work: The Social Regulation of Economic Relations.* Oxford: Oxford University Press.

Williamson, O.E. 1975. *Markets and Hierarchies: Analysis and Antitrust Implications.* New York: Free Press.

Wiser, W.H. 1936. *The Hindu Jajmāni System.* Lucknow: Lucknow Publishing House. Reprinted 1958.

Womark, J.P. et al. 1990. *The Machine that Changed the World.* New York: RA.

Woo, J-E. 1991. *Race to the Swift.* New York: Columbia University Press.

World Bank. 1993. *The East Asian Miracle: Economic Growth and Public Policy.* Washington, D.C.: World Bank.

Zeile, W. 1996. 'Industrial Policy and Organisational Efficiency: The Korean Chaebol Examined', in G. Hamilton (ed.), *Asian Business Networks.* Berlin: de Gruyter.

About the Editors and Contributors

The Editors

Gurli Jakobsen is an Associate Professor at the Department of Intercultural Communication and Management, Copenhagen Business School, Denmark. With a background in Sociology (M.Sc.) and Business Administration (Ph.D.), her field of research has been small enterprise development and cooperative organizing. She has published internationally on learning processes and business development in cooperative type enterprises in Latin America. Dr Jakobsen's present research focuses on the role of 'learning milleus' for emergent entrepreneurship in smaller enterprises.

Jens Erik Torp is an Associate Professor at the Department of Intercultural Communication and Management at the Copenhagen Business School. With a background in Economics (M.Sc.) and Business Administration (Ph.D.) he is at present doing research on the interface between international economic drivers and locally rooted business development in Southern Africa. He has also studied business development in Europe and the US, highlighting the cultural dimensions of mergers and acquisitions.

The Contributors

Dieter Ernst is Visiting Professor at the Department of Industrial Economics and Strategies, Copenhagen Business School, Denmark.

Mark Holmström is Senior Lecturer in Social Anthropology, School of Development Studies, University of East Anglia, United Kingdom.

John Kuada is Associate Professor in International Management at Aalborg University. He received his B.Sc. and MBA degrees from the University of Ghana and Ph.D. from the Copenhagen School of Business. He has taught marketing and management in several African and European universities and has been consultant to government organizations and private companies on management-related issues. His research interests are in intercultural management, cross-national inter-firm relations as well as international marketing. He has published two books and contributed several book chapters on issues relating to international marketing and management in developing countries. His articles have also appeared in such journals as *Journal of Euromarketing* and *Journal of Management Studies*.

Martijn F.L. Rademakers is a Strategist at DWM Strategy Works and has a formal hospitality agreement with the Business and Society Management Department, Erasmus University, Rotterdam, the Netherlands. Earlier, he was Research Associate, Erasmus University Rotterdam; Researcher, LPPM, Jakarta; and Research Assistant, Policy and Organization Sciences Department, Tilburg University. Currently, he is involved in research projects on (semi)-governmental supply chains and inter-corporate governance. He has published on family businesses in Indonesia, business associations, and inter-firm cooperation in the agribusiness.

Henrik Schaumburg-Müller is an economist and Associate Professor at the Department of Intercultural Communication and Management at the Copenhagen Business School. His university career has mainly centered on research and teaching within the disciplines of development studies and international business. His recent research focuses on 'Business in development' and studies how private firms in developing countries emerge, develop and sustain themselves within various institutional frameworks. The geographical focus is on

Asia. His recent fieldwork in Malaysia and Thailand has contributed to two research themes on Danish exporting SMEs and their import agents in Malaysia and Thailand and the governed business system in Malaysia and Thailand. This research draws on the broad field of economic organization. He has for many years combined his academic work with practical experience as a consultant for international aid agencies with assignments in developing countries. His work on planning, implementation and evaluation of aid activities has given a thorough insight to countries in Asia, Africa and Latin America. It has also stimulated his academic work on aid related issues like aid to private sector development and on evaluation of foreign aid. His teaching concentrates on the Master Programme 'Development Studies and Intercultural Business Strategy'.

Olav Jull Sørensen has been a Professor of International Business since 1991. He studied marketing in Denmark and at the University of Wisconsin. Since 1974, he has been affiliated with Aalborg University. He has been the initiator and coordinator of the M.Sc. programme in international business. As a Senior Lecturer of the School of Administration, University of Ghana from 1976–78 his research naturally became development oriented and today he is the coordinator of a research programme the aim of which is to study the integration of the Ghanaian companies in the world economy. At present, he is the President of the International Society for Marketing and Development.

Jos R. van Valkengoed is an Auditor of the GE Corporate Audit Staff based in Fairfield, USA. Prior to this, he worked for GE Capital at different locations in Europe and Asia. He was Researcher at the Indonesian management institute LPPM, Jakarta; and Research Assistant at the Policy and Organization Sciences Department of Tilburg University, the Netherlands.

Peter Wad is senior research fellow at the Department of Intercultural Communication, Copenhagen Business School. He has conducted research on Malaysian labour market issues for many years and especially investigated industrial relations and trade union issues. Recently he undertook a study of the national auto manufacturers in Malaysia and South Korea within a broader research project on business in development. He has published widely, begin a co-editor of several publications and a guest editor of thematic issues of various journals, including an issue on Malaysia in the *Copenhagen Journal of Asian Studies*.

Richard Whitley is Professor of Organizational Sociology at Manchester Business School, University of Manchester. Recently he was Visiting Professor at the Institute of Innovation Research, Hitotsubashi University, Tokyo and Fellow in Residence at the Netherlands Institute for Advanced Study. His recent books include *Divergent Capitalisms: The Social Structuring and Change of Business Systems* (Oxford University Press, 1999) and the *Intellectual and Social Organization of the Sciences* (Oxford University Press, second edition 2000). Between 1993 and 1997 he was Co-Director of the European Science Foundation's Programme on European Management and Organizations in Transition and is currently directing an ESRC project on Japanese and Korean expatriate managers in the UK in the ESRC's Programme on Transnational Communities.

Subject Index

Author Index